SOCIAL RESEARCH
MATTERS

Sociology of Children and Families series

Series editors: **Esther Dermott** and **Debbie Watson**,
University of Bristol, UK

The Sociology of Children and Families monograph series brings together the latest international research on children, childhood and families and pushes forward theory in the sociology of childhood and family life. Books in the series cover major global issues affecting children and families.

Forthcoming in the series:

Designing Parental Leave Policy:
The Norway Model and the Changing Face of Fatherhood
Elin Kvande and **Berit Brandth**, March 2020

A Child's Day:
Children's Time Use in the UK from 1975–2015
Killian Mullan, July 2020

Sharing Care:
Equal and Primary Caregiver Fathers and Early Years Parenting
Paul Hodkinson and **Rachel Brooks**, November 2021

Out now in the series:

Nanny Families:
Practices of Care by Nannies, Au Pairs, Parents and Children in Sweden
Sara Eldén and **Terese Anving**, July 2019

Find out more at
bristoluniversitypress.co.uk

SOCIAL RESEARCH MATTERS

A life in family sociology

Julia Brannen

BRISTOL
UNIVERSITY
PRESS

First published in Great Britain in 2021 by

Bristol University Press
University of Bristol
1-9 Old Park Hill
Bristol
BS2 8BB
UK
t: +44 (0)117 954 5940
e: bup-info@bristol.ac.uk

Details of international sales and distribution partners are available at bristoluniversitypress.co.uk

© Bristol University Press 2021

British Library Cataloguing in Publication Data
A catalogue record for this book is available from the British Library

ISBN 978-1-5292-0857-3 paperback
ISBN 978-1-5292-0856-6 hardcover
ISBN 978-1-5292-0859-7 ePub
ISBN 978-1-5292-0858-0 ePdf

Cover design: blu inc, Bristol
Front cover image: Judith Thomland/Alamy Stock photo

Contents

Acknowledgements

As this book argues, the pursuit of much funded research relies on communities of practitioners. This means that its success depends in large part upon the people in the research team. In the book I pay tribute to the senior colleagues with whom I have had the privilege to work; they acted as mentors and sponsors early in my research career. Here I wish to thank a number of other colleagues who warrant special mention. Ann Phoenix joined Thomas Coram Research Unit shortly after me in 1983 to work on the same programme of work but on a different project. I am grateful to Ann for her generosity and insightful comments on my early writing. Ann Mooney also joined the unit in the early 1980s to work on the Daycare project. Ann is the finest field worker with whom I have worked and a pleasure to collaborate with, as we did on several subsequent projects. Pamela Storey is a researcher with whom I worked closely for several years and whose many talents I admire greatly. Another key figure in the lives of all those who have spent time in the unit is Charlie Owen. Charlie helped us with data analysis and was vital in our coming to terms with the information technology age, a stalwart figure in the trade union and someone who treated everyone the same, whatever their status.

The success of research teams has a great deal to do with those who lead them and their members. Over the past ten years I have had the pleasure to collaborate on a succession of projects with two outstanding researchers, Rebecca O'Connell, an inspirational project manager, and Abigail Knight. I also wish to thank the many colleagues with whom I have worked in other UK universities, the Nordic countries, Eastern Europe, Portugal and Ireland. In addition, I wish to thank the Department of Sociology in the University of Bergen, Ann Nilsen in particular, where I was a visiting professor for more than ten years. I am especially grateful to all those family, friends and colleagues who have encouraged me to go on working and have made me feel valued. I am grateful for Graham Crow for his helpful comments on this manuscript and special thanks are due to Peter Brannen for his editorial skills.

Beginnings and Biography

> In memory the academic autobiographer's years stretch back like the wagons on those endless freight trains, observed from some hill as they carry containers across the American landscape. Seen in retrospect, the succession of trucks is less interesting than the changing territory through which they pass. (Hobsbawm, 2003: 301)

It is the principal job of a sociologist to understand and explain social phenomena. This requires setting the object of study in context. The story I will tell in these pages is not intended to be a tale of individual endeavour but an examination of the times, concerns and conditions in which the work of one sociologist develops and how a career reliant on research that is externally funded is forged. The focus on my research career, almost all of which has been spent in a university, is intended as a vehicle for understanding the conditions under which, over more than 40 years, I came to study particular topics; how these topics arrived on research agendas; and how the research was crafted and knowledge was built. The research I will discuss concerns the family and working lives of mothers and fathers, and also the lives of children, both across the life course and over historical time.

When I accepted my publisher's suggestion that I write this book, my aim was to give some sense of what it is to be a contract or funded researcher and to do this by revisiting and reviewing research projects with which I have been involved. This has been logistically difficult within one volume because of the number of projects and the length of time covered and so I have been selective. I soon discovered that my interest lay less in going over old ground and more in material from recent research. On the one hand, a present-time orientation is intrinsic to the job of a funded researcher who is required to meet deadlines and to come up with new ideas for future projects and seek new funding. On the other hand, empirical research is about 'doing' – the continuous practice of the craft of research. A dusty pile of research reports and publications and a lengthening CV are only part of the research enterprise. Thus while the foci of some of the chapters have their origins in past studies, I have often drawn for illustrative material from recent work.

Social Research Matters has two main themes that will be interwoven throughout the text. A central theme is how social research matters in relation to historical context. Ideas for social science research germinate at particular moments in time. The ways in which studies are framed and the conditions under which they get funded relate to the economic, social, policy and political contexts of the period. How researchers come to work in particular fields of study and on particular projects is dependent also on the state of social science at the time, the demand for particular expertise and the vagaries of the job market. Biographical contingencies also play a part as researchers are attracted to specific topics at particular life-course phases. A second theme of the book focuses on the practice of social research; research is a craft that is learned with and from others as well as through reading methodological texts and training. As I will argue, although the expertise of the researcher is crucial to all phases of the research process, much of the success of funded research is dependent on collaboration and the creation of conditions that are conducive to team-based research.

I embark on this endeavour with some trepidation and a lot of questions. Will I be able to recall my experiences of being a researcher after so many years? What among the memories that I summon up will I choose to draw from? How will current orientations be shaped by hindsight? How will the past influence my view of the present? Now in my seventies and writing this book in 2018/19, I am conscious of having been part of the different regimes and fashions – in politics, universities and social science – that have come and gone in my lifetime. As Carol Smart (2007) suggests, we create memories but we also censor them, omitting those that discomfort our sense of who we are in the present. Will I construe the past through rose-tinted spectacles? Alistair Thomson observes 'Memories are "significant pasts" that we compose to make a more comfortable sense of life over time, and in which past and present identities are brought more in line' (cited in Kynaston, 2017: 38). Memory is also a process that begins when experience itself has passed. We know this instinctively following the death of close loved ones: it is at these moments that memories become 'sites' to be visited rather than inhabited landscapes. Like monuments, we visit these sites and in the process we recreate them as we now would like to remember them so that 'the ruins' of memory are subject to restoration (Antze, 1996).

I am aware that in seeking to bring some coherence to the book it is easy to fall prey to the dangers of presenting my research career as a coherent narrative. In truth, trajectories in research, as they are in a person's life, lack a clear plot and are shaped by the twists and turns of fortune and what it means to be human (Andrews, 2013). The stories that we tell ourselves about our lives are based on shifting ground (Andrews, 2013). This involves 'the continuous oscillating of the different orders of past, present and future' (Brockmeier, 2000: 59, cited in Andrews, 2013). As Kierkegaard (1843) wrote:

> life must be understood backwards. But ... it must be lived forwards. And if one thinks over that proposition it becomes more and more evident that life can never be really understood in time simply because at no particular moment can I find the necessary resting place from which to understand it – backwards. (Cited in Andrews, 2013: 214–15)

In past reflections about the directions of my research I have suggested that time was a central organising theme. In a published professorial lecture given at the Institute of Education in 2002 I noted that:

> Broadly, my own research can be described as the study of family lives though, at different times, I may have described it differently. Like most sociologists I have studied lives lived in contemporary time. As I look back, I am struck by the particularity of the historical periods in which I undertook the research – which was not at all obvious to me then in the way it is now. I have also become conscious that time has been a central theme in my research. The transition to new life course phases has been a persistent interest: the study of men and women contemplating and engaging in separation and divorce, mothers returning to work after childbirth, young people entering adolescence, children starting secondary school, the experience of grandparenthood. Similarly, I have been interested in the use of time: the distribution of time and labour in marriage and parenthood, the way money and other resources are shared between men and women – frequently inequitably – in marriage and in

the household. Later, I became interested in the way parents and young people oriented themselves to time. Only in the last two decades have I begun to look at lives through the spectacles of history and to understand the importance of historical context in shaping people's lives and perspectives. This latter experience has heightened my consciousness of belonging to the post-war generation and has made me see the dangers of drawing comparisons between younger generations and my own. (Brannen, 2002b: 3)[1]

Indeed, I suppose I have always been acutely aware that events play an important part in shaping a life. But only now does it strike me as significant that I belong to a generation of sociologists who came to the subject via social anthropology in the early 1960s, a time when sociology was not yet well established in British universities. I also belong to the generation recruited to the new Women's Liberation Movement in 1970, or Second Wave Feminism as it was later termed. Similarly, I was a member of the first cohort to study research methodology when Surrey University set up a Master's course in social research in the mid-1970s, the first in the country. All three 'firsts' have played a role in influencing me to take up social science research as an occupation and they have served to chart the following 40 or so years of my life as a social researcher – the fields in which I sought to do research and my interest in the way research is done.

Writing and reflection require us to set boundaries concerning what to include and exclude, and how much a text can bear. As a member of the Women's Movement I learned that 'the personal is always political'. As I came to make sense of my own and other women's lives as mothers and members of the labour market, it became evident that the public and the private could not be disaggregated. While autobiography is not the aim of the book, I am sensitive to the dangers and temptations of this genre; I think I have always eschewed too much overt self reflexivity in my work preferring to focus my energies on imagining the other – the lives of those I have studied. Nevertheless, because the impetus to take up a particular occupation often springs from our own life course, and because our own lives are part of the wider social world, as a sociologist I need to make some reference to the personal and to give some sense of the paths I have taken and my own family background. This is a difficult task. As Virginia Woolf wrote in her unfinished 'Sketch of the past' in the late 1930s, 'I see myself as a fish in a stream; deflected; held in place; but cannot describe the stream.'

The rest of this chapter takes the form of a brief biographical memoir. As a sociologist of the family (the title of the professorship that was bestowed upon me in 1998 at the Institute of Education, University of London), I will briefly describe my social origins and the times in which my own life began and unfolded. While biographies are unique, the age cohorts to which we belong and the periods in which we develop put a collective mark on our trajectories. Later parts of my biography involve the places in which social science research was carried out and, in the next chapter, I reflect upon the research environment and the conditions that shaped it.

Social class has been at the heart of much sociological analysis: where we come from is a central part of who we are. My mother and father had very different social class origins. It is unlikely they would ever have met had it not been war time. My mother, Cecily Morgan, was born in 1913 and of middle class origin. She grew up in Highgate, north London, a prosperous area even then. Her father worked in a bank, rising to the status of bank manager in my mother's teenage years. My mother and her two sisters attended one of the first girls' grammar schools in the country, founded by a pioneer in girls' education in which academic achievement was highly prized. My mother was always proud of passing the 'matric' (in 1931) – an examination (equivalent to 'A' levels) taken at 18. She often said she wished she had been born later and been able to go to university. Instead she did a short hand and typing course at Pitman's College and became a private secretary.

My father, Henry Morgan, had a much harder life. He grew up in Cork, Ireland, during the War of Independence and the subsequent civil war 1921–22. Cork is still seen as 'the rebel county' because of its ability to produce dissenters. An Irish colleague and friend, Professor Pat O'Connor (2013: 22), describes its citizens as 'people who in Irish terms are "great craic", with a nice line in parochial arrogance and ego-mania, who believe that Cork is the centre of the universe and who dismiss any evidence that does not fit with that perception'. Migration, to Britain and America, has been commonplace among Irish people over the centuries. My own grandfather travelled back and forth between Ireland and England in search of work in the first part of his working life. In the 1920s, he was interned in Cork's gaol for two years without trial during the Irish war of independence, a critical period of my father's childhood. After his internment, my grandfather and grandmother left Ireland with their youngest child for London, where my grandfather worked for the rest of his working life on the railways, serving as secretary of his branch of the National Union of Railwaymen in London. The family returned at intervals to visit my father and my father's sister who had been left in the care of 'maiden aunts'.

Unusually for the time in Ireland, my father went to secondary school (secondary schools were fee paying and run by religious orders). This was made possible by the charity of the Catholic Church that also helped my grandmother during my grandfather's internment. When he was 16 my father passed his Intermediate Certificate (the Irish equivalent of GCSEs) after which he left Ireland for London. It seems that he soon acquired an apprenticeship, though he never described it as such, in the rapidly developing radio and electronics industry that was growing up around London. At the same time as working he also helped to support his younger brother through teacher training college in England. The electronics industry was to play an important part in the Second World War and my father was seconded to the Air Ministry at an early stage of the war and spent most of his subsequent career working for the British government in what became the Ministry of Defence. He did not, however, qualify professionally as an aeronautics engineer until he was in his forties and only then by dint of much study after a day at work.

My parents met and married during the war. Both were involved in wartime activity. My mother joined the WAAF (Women's Auxiliary Air Force) in 1942 and after training was sent to Bomber Command in High Wycombe HQ at Naphill, Buckinghamshire, to work in the secretarial section – 'not thought tough enough for training in the Transport section, which I would have preferred', she wrote in her memoir. Like many others at the time her wartime marriage followed a chance, relatively 'brief encounter'. As a young WAAF she met my father, who had been assigned to the Aeronautical Inspection Directorate that was responsible for radar systems, an important instrument in winning the war. No sooner had they met than they were married. As my mother, an inveterate letter writer, suggests in her memoir (written when she was in her eighties in the 1990s):

> the dangers and uncertainties of the times meant that almost everyone ... felt their lives were so flimsy, if I can put it that way. Bombs raining down all over the country – in fact life was very cheap and most lived for the moment and took their pleasures without reservations most of the time.... The devastation in London and elsewhere was horrific – underground stations crowded every night and the difficulties of making one's way along the platform and to the exits will remain long in my memory.

I was born in 1944 in an early 18th-century house on a large country estate on the borders of Hertfordshire and Buckinghamshire (now a famous business school) that was the wartime retreat of London's Charing Cross hospital. When I was three my parents and myself moved to north London not far from Highgate where my mother grew up but further down the hill towards Kentish Town, an area of 19th-century industrialisation and deprivation (Tindall, 2010). I can remember the bombsites in our neighbourhood as well as the 'prefab' housing which sprang up after the war. As a member of the first 'baby boomer' cohort, much of my life has been lived in what Hobsbawm (1994) called a 'Golden Age': a period of 'growth and transformation' sandwiched between an Age of Catastrophe (two world wars and the economic depression of the interwar years) and a period of uncertainty and crisis in capitalism dating from the 1970s (Hobsbawm, 1994: 6, 10). The immediate post-war period was a time of considerable change but also hardship; rationing was still in existence and most people had little money. Today, the period of the 1945–51 Labour government is nostalgically remembered for the implementation of the welfare state, in particular the setting up of the National Health Service in 1948. As John Bew (2016) points out in his biography of Clement Attlee, the Beveridge Report sold in huge numbers when it was published in the middle of the Second World War, suggesting that public opinion was favourable towards its programme of reform, a programme that was to usher in the welfare state after Labour's election in 1945.

Yet contemporaneous evidence after the war suggests little public confidence about possible improvements in people's way of life (see Kynaston, 2007); by 1945 'Orwell's earlier optimism about a newly radicalised people had completely vanished' (Kynaston, 2007: 45). In the same way that few in the media foresaw the results of the 2016 referendum concerning Britain's membership of the European Union or the huge support for Jeremy Corbyn in the 2017 general election, so it seems the results of the general election in 1945 that brought to power a Labour government came as a surprise, at least to the press. 'This is not an election that is going to shake Tory England,' declared the *Manchester Guardian* (now *The Guardian*) the day before polling (Kynaston, 2007: 70).

The north London Edwardian block of flats where we lived was owned by a private landlord. The residents were a mix of social classes, nationalities and ethnicities. I remember our flat as rather dark and gloomy but spacious. In the post-war period, even if people had money to spare there were few consumer goods to spend it on. Families made do with what they had or could get hold of. Despite the post-war hardship, I recollect my childhood as full of things to do. Mainly I think this was because our parents left us to our own devices. Certainly my sister, Sheelagh (born after the move to London), and I spent a lot of time playing with friends. Our flat's big advantage was not only its size but its garden; this meant that other children in the flats that lacked gardens came to play with us – playing in the street was not allowed by our parents. Also, there was no television to entertain us. Parliament Hill Fields and Hampstead Heath were on our doorstep and we were soon free to explore them. With friends we put on concerts and plays in our homes. Some of the fathers helped with staging and some of the mothers baked or assisted with costumes. Another project was digging for treasure on a small hillock created by war damage at the bottom of our garden where we discovered a pewter Japanese dish that sits on my hall table to this day. One summer we built a group of huts in the garden, called 'cabbies', an idea inspired by our family's first holiday in Ireland with Irish cousins.[2]

Aged "nearly six", as I kept reminding my parents, I was sent to the local Roman Catholic convent school. My mother was a 'Protestant' and my father, who grew up in Ireland, was Catholic. However, he rarely went to church. If he did he stood at the back alongside other Irish men, while my sister and I were despatched to sit near the front. Our school took from a very broad range of backgrounds and social classes. It also included 'non-Catholics' as the nuns called them (other Christians, Jews and a few Muslims). The majority of the children were from the borough and financially supported by the London County Council. The school also took some fee-paying children and a handful of boarders, including refugees. A few were from Spain, Poland, African and Caribbean countries and Persia (as it was then known), two of whom became close friends. The school was non-selective: unlike the local state primary schools, the children who attended our primary school did not take the Eleven Plus (the examination necessary to go to a grammar school). Indeed many of the children who joined the school aged 11 had failed the 11-plus. The school was not academically oriented. Most girls left school with no or few 'O' levels while only a handful stayed on. Only seven in my year went into the sixth form of whom three went to university, one to art school, one to a college of music and the two others into another form of training.

I was the first in my family to go to university. In 1962, only 2.5 per cent of women went to university compared with 5.6 per cent of young men.[3] The subject I registered for when I applied to university was not my choice. My father believed that it was better to be one of those who 'do', quoting the aphorism 'those who can't, teach'. So he encouraged me in a direction that he thought would keep me away from teaching. Together with the headmistress, a nun, they alighted upon economics as my subject of study, a subject of which I was totally ignorant. The choice of university was also serendipitous suggested by a teacher of French who I came across at a local further education evening class that I attended to help me in my 'A'-level course.

I arrived at the University of Manchester in October 1962. It was to be a turning point in my life on several counts. It was the first time I had been north of Watford and the beginning of a long affair with the north of England. At the time I was quite unprepared for what I encountered: the imposing Victorian buildings blackened by coal burning and pollution, and the shocking poverty of Moss Side, the site of the university, where local children ran barefoot. As a Londoner I was enchanted by the friendliness of the Lancashire people. However, as a 'southerner' I was considered 'different', the only one in my year in the hall of residence.

Manchester University's Faculty of Economics and Social Administration was located in an imposing building in Dover Street where Frederick Engels had once lived. In the first year we were required to take four subjects – economics, social anthropology, and government – and as a fourth, I chose mathematics for economists. I found the economics course not only boring but totally divorced from real-world issues. Unsurprisingly, having had to re-sit the first year examination in economics, I did not pursue it. I focused on social anthropology and sociology, the latter a new discipline that was developing within the department. I did not however distinguish myself in my first degree.

Nonetheless the tradition of the Manchester Department of Social Anthropology sowed seeds that came to fruition later in my life. The department had been established by a leading figure in social anthropology, Max Gluckman, who had previously headed the Rhodes Livingstone Institute in Southern Africa. A strong advocate of empirically grounded, team-based research, Gluckman created a leading department of postgraduate training that attracted a large number of left-leaning staff (Mills, 2008). He also stood out from other anthropologists of his day in his belief in interdisciplinary collaboration (Mills, 2008).

In 1960s Britain sociology developed rapidly under the umbrella of British social anthropology. Many students of social anthropology went on to found the new departments of sociology which, as Halsey (2004) suggests, ran ahead of the general expansion in higher education that followed the 1963 Robbins Report. Manchester was an important launch pad for many sociologists; a number of British Sociological Association presidents and holders of major chairs spent time at the Manchester Department of social anthropology – John Barnes, J.C. Mitchell, and Peter Worsley among them. Peter Worsley was appointed as the first professor of sociology in the university in 1964–5, the last year of my time at Manchester, and set about establishing an undergraduate course in sociology. Significant figures in the field of family studies were also students at the Manchester school among them David Morgan and Elizabeth Bott. As an undergraduate I was fortunate to have as a tutor in my last year Ronnie Frankenberg. An anthropologist under Gluckman, Ronnie was unlike his colleagues in having carried out his fieldwork in Wales rather than in Africa (Frankenberg, 1957). He was an inspirational figure. I like to think that if he and Peter Worsley had featured in my undergraduate studies earlier I might have been a better student. But hindsight is a fine thing. Yet, my undergraduate experience left its mark upon me when, several years later, I undertook a Master's and an apprenticeship in social research.

Manchester University provided its students with a vibrant social, cultural and political life. I don't think it occurred to us that we were there simply to study and get a degree. The university had a thriving Students' Union and many societies in which we were active. I was quite unprepared for my university days to end. In my last weeks at university, I have a distinct memory of standing on Oxford Road looking across at the Students' Union and thinking that I was not going to return to Manchester in the coming term. Many girls I knew had signed up to do a further course, many in teacher training. There was also an assumption among most of us that what lay ahead, after a brief spell in a job such as teaching, was marriage, followed by motherhood. Other possibilities were not discussed. In the1950s the average age of first marriage for girls was low and continued to fall until the 1960s (Shoen and Canudas-Romo 2005), while the average age at first birth was lower at the end of the 1960s than at any point since 1938.[4] As a sixties young woman, I conformed to type. Only in that brief moment standing in Oxford Road do I remember feeling a sense of uncertainty and impending loss.

The next period of my life was marked by considerable geographical mobility in the north of England. I met Peter Brannen, my future husband, at Manchester University. He too studied social anthropology but was a year ahead of me. He benefited from being part of a small group of undergraduates taught by Max Gluckman and Bill Epstein. Peter's working-class family was spread around the north-east of England. In the middle of Peter's finals his father suffered a major stroke from which he never recovered. As the oldest son of four children Peter took it for granted that he had to find a job straight after completing his degree. He was one of a handful of university graduates recruited in the national 'milk round' by an American advertising agency, and the only one with a working-class background. After a year in London, Peter decided that the world of advertising was not for him. He applied for a job as a social science researcher at Newcastle upon Tyne's Rutherford College of Technology (later to become Northumbria University) to carry out a Social Science Research Council project on the shipbuilding industry in Wallsend on Tyne. A number of research studentships were also advertised in social sciences at Rutherford and I was successful in applying for one. Together Peter and I moved to Newcastle in September 1965 and were married the following January.

Newcastle upon Tyne was a totally foreign country to me, even more 'different' than Manchester, especially as we lived in its impoverished West End. I chose as my field of postgraduate research to study the changing economic and social role of women in a west Durham mining village, Chopwell. The village was known as 'Little Moscow' because of an old association with the Communist Party. In the 1926 General Strike the Union Jack on the council offices was replaced with the Soviet flag while several of its streets had been renamed, among them Lenin Terrace and Marx Terrace. The pit finally closed in 1966, the year I did the study. Male unemployment was already high and many women were travelling outside the village to work. Over an exceptionally cold winter I conducted single-handedly a survey of 10 per cent of the village's households (1,500 were on the electoral roll). My studentship was for one year only and by then I was pregnant. I applied to transfer my study to Newcastle University but the academic who interviewed me and would have been my supervisor, Norman Dennis (one of the authors of the well-known monograph *Coal is our life*), thought a young pregnant southerner too much of a liability. Sadly, I never completed the study of Chopwell. However, its focus prefigured the research I did for my Master's dissertation written ten years later in 1976 – on mothers' return to work after their children started school. After our first son, Alex, was born in 1967 I then applied to do a Master's in social statistics at Newcastle University but was told, again by a male academic, that I might have difficulty keeping up with the men on the course (apparently there were no women)!

In 1967 the project Peter was working on was moved to the Department of Sociology, University of Durham headed by Professor John Rex. This meant that we too moved, this time to a furnished rented cottage outside Chester-le-Street a few miles from where Peter's parents and siblings lived on a council estate in Durham City. My foray into the field of social research was shelved for several years. While my lovely mother-in-law was willing to do some childcare, she already had major caring responsibilities for her severely disabled husband and an elderly aunt. Nonetheless she looked after Alex three afternoons a week while I worked part-time as a teacher in a local secondary modern school, an experience that put me off teaching for a long time!

As a researcher Peter had a fixed-term contract that ended when the research grant came to an end. So we moved again in 1969, this time to West Yorkshire – to Shipley just outside Bradford – another part of the country that was new to me. Again, Peter directed a research project on a major British industry that, in its nationalised form, was soon to disappear: this time it was steel. The study centred on an organisational and political experiment – the introduction of 'worker directors' to the board of the British Steel Corporation, a form of industrial democracy. (P. Brannen et al, 1975; P. Brannen, 1983). He and his research team covered the different regions of Britain where steel was made. Peter spent long periods in Corby in Northamptonshire organising workplace surveys and carrying out observation of the meetings of the board of the British Steel Corporation. With a husband away a lot of the time, I was confined to the home and, following the birth of our second son, Emil, caring for two small children.

In the summer of 1968 the women sewing machinists at Ford's Dagenham plant went on strike demanding the right to be graded as skilled. This led some women trade unionists to set up of the National Joint Action Campaign for Women's Equal Rights that ultimately led to the passing of Equal Pay Act in 1975, although the Ford's women sewing machinists had to wait until 1984 to receive equal pay following a further strike. This was a time of convergence between the civil rights movement and the movement for women's liberation; women were recognising the necessity to free themselves from both personal and public inequalities (Rowbotham, 1997). The first national conference of the Women's Liberation Movement took place in Oxford in late February 1969.

The three years we spent in Bradford were also a turning point for me. In the winter of 1970, within a year of our moving to West Yorkshire, a Women's Liberation group was established in Bradford (Lockyer, 2013). I was one of its first members. It was the time of the Heath Conservative government (1970–74). In the winter of 1970 the electricity supply workers went on strike resulting in major cuts to supply. I vividly recall bathing the baby by candlelight. Our

Women's Lib group met in a room above a pub in the middle of Bradford until the landlady forced us to move elsewhere because of our "outrageous discussions" that she clearly listened in to! One of several of our campaigns focused on the 'consciousness raising' of some local women factory workers. This involved leafleting the women as they arrived for their early morning shifts. However, we made little impression, not least because few of the women could read English – something we, as multiculturally sensitive left feminists, had failed to take into account! One particularly memorable campaign concerned our protest in 1971 against the abolition of free school milk in primary and nursery schools that was proposed by Margaret Thatcher, who was then Secretary of State for Education and was visiting Bradford. I vividly recall how, with her typical panache, Thatcher ignored our protest and assumed we were on Bradford's Town Hall steps to greet her. My four-year-old son, Alex, complained loudly about being taken on the demonstration that followed, while his brother, Emil, featured in a *Guardian* report: a 'crying baby in the Bradford's Town Hall gallery' who 'disrupted' the meeting of Bradford City Council that was discussing the cuts to school milk.

My time in Bradford Women's Lib brought me into contact with a range of interesting women, many of whom had not been to university, and also a prominent feminist sociologist, Professor Sheila Allen. It also introduced me to far left politics, including the International Socialists who were intent on recruiting members from our Women's Lib group, though I declined to join. It was an exciting and optimistic time. As Sheila Rowbotham (1997: 348) wrote: 'The new movement combined a sense of being unique and of coming out of nowhere with a desire for roots. Ideas seemed to be rushing through the air to be grabbed; it was as if the whole world was bursting at the seams and everything was about to change.'

Our next move again followed Peter's career as a contract researcher. In the summer of 1972 we moved to the south of England when Peter took a post as a Medical Research Council senior research fellow heading a study of the social dimensions of the management of dementia. He was attached to the new Southampton Medical School but based in Winchester. We moved to the small Hampshire town of Romsey situated near Winchester and Southampton, purchasing in an auction half of a lofty Victorian house that needed a lot of home improvements. I was still a housewife with one child not yet in school and no money or job opportunities had any childcare existed. I had time on my hands. The town was highly conservative and did not offer fertile ground for the Women's Liberation Movement. So I joined the

Labour Party. However, I soon discovered that the local branch was virtually defunct and so I set about rejuvenating it by despatching its alleged chairman and offering our home as a regular meeting place. Inspired by the Women's Movement I was determined to avoid the structures and formal procedures of the party, much to the initial consternation of the constituency party officers. However, they were soon placated when it became clear that the branch was amassing a large pool of local support to fight the two general elections that took place in 1974. Because I was increasingly frustrated with my housewife status I also joined a trade union and became a member of the non-employed category of the Association of Scientific, Technical and Managerial Staff (ASTMS).

The next turning point set me back on to a path in social research. In 1974 I saw an advertisement for the first Master's course in social research methods at the Department of Sociology at the University of Surrey, Guildford. It offered places on a full-time or part-time basis. I applied for a part-time place but was (again) unsuccessful. After an interview I was told by a male lecturer that, as a housewife, I was not a priority and could re-apply the following the year. In fury I wrote to the Chair of the British Sociological Association, Professor Margaret Stacey, who replied that she too had once suffered similar treatment. Sadly she offered me no advice as to how I might combat discrimination. So I re-applied the following year successfully and, in October 1975, embarked on a two-year part-time MSc in social research. Timing was this time in my favour, with government funding provided for those seeking to acquire new skills including 'women returners'. Under the Labour government in 1975 the Department of Employment's Manpower Commission had set up a Training Opportunities Scheme (TOPS). I was one of the 27,000 women (44 per cent of TOPS trainees) who benefited from the scheme and had to pay £150 a year only in university fees. Without that funding I doubt that I would have returned to higher education. However, the logistics were difficult, especially transport. By then Peter had been head hunted for a research post in the civil service and was working in London. As local transport was poor, this necessitated his using the family car every day to get the station some 10 miles away or staying overnight with friends in London. So, at some inconvenience, he had to forego the use of the car on the one day a week when I drove to the University of Surrey in Guildford. With two children by then at school, after-school care was generously provided by a local friend and neighbour for the two years of the course.

The course provided a very thorough grounding in the methodology of conducting empirical social research. I once counted that we carried out around thirty assignments of different kinds over the two years, including a 20,000 word dissertation. The team of lecturers who taught the course were young, enthusiastic and very supportive. I was fortunate in being taught by leading researchers and academics, including Sara Arber and Nigel Gilbert. That many of the same staff remained in Surrey University's Department of Sociology for the rest of their academic careers is testimony to their collective success in creating an excellent teaching and research environment.

For the topic of my dissertation, I chose to examine the experiences of mothers who returned to the labour market after their children started school. The choice was an obvious one, given my unfinished research on women's changing role in a Durham mining village, and also because it mirrored my own recent transition from being full-time mother to part-time student. In the mid-1970s mothers' return to work at this life-course phase, typically to part-time work (Martin and Roberts 1984), became increasingly the norm: 'Where work had once taken place between school and motherhood, now motherhood occurred in an interval between school and work' (Vincent, 1991: 183).

At the end of the course in 1977, I set about finding my first proper research job in social science research. My entry into the labour market came at a time when there were still opportunities to secure research posts without a doctorate. However, it was not a good time for research funding. The Social Science Research Council (SSRC), set up in 1965,[5] was suffering from the effects of the intervention of Margaret Thatcher, who will be forever remembered by social scientists for her declaration that 'there is no such thing as society'. As a consequence of funding cuts, SSRC centres were closed and funding for postgraduate funding severely curtailed. Following the 1982 Rothschild Report (HMSO 1982), it was agreed that the SSRC should change its name to the Economic and Social Research Council (ESRC) (Gaber and Gaber, 2005).[6]

Nonetheless, timing was in my favour. An MSc in social research and experience in empirical research were rare. Indeed, not all academics in the social sciences had PhDs at that time. I took up my first research post in January 1978 at the age of nearly 34. Unlike most mothers at the time, I was in now in full-time work. In the late 1970s, the Women and Employment Survey funded by the Department of Employment found that only 17 per cent of mothers with two children, whose youngest child was aged 5–10, were in full-time work (Martin and Roberts, 1984).

My new job meant having to uproot ourselves once again at considerable financial cost. To reconcile family life and paid work we moved to London near my new workplace, the Marriage Research Centre which was based at the Middlesex Hospital in Park Royal, West London. Its director, Dr Jack Dominian,[7] was the head of the department of psychiatry in the hospital. In my new post I was tasked with addressing what seemed like a hugely ambitious research question – to investigate the causes of marital breakdown. Not only was the assignment daunting, as a feminist I was also highly sceptical about its underlying assumption, namely that marital breakdown should necessarily be avoided. The centre's director was a prominent Roman Catholic committed to saving marriages in his therapeutic practice and writing. However, because the centre was devoted to research, he did not seek to impose his views upon us and was careful to distance himself from the centre's research in his frequent media appearances on religious television programmes.

The post afforded unique opportunities for me to learn about and observe clinical practice in both marital therapy and psychiatry. A further advantage was that I was given plenty of freedom to fashion a more manageable research project of my own. While I welcomed this opportunity I feared that if left too much to my own devices I might lose my way. So I took care to forge links outside the centre, in particular regularly participating in the British Sociological Association's London Medical Sociology Group that met regularly at the London School of Economics.

Strongly influenced by feminist politics and the increasing spotlight on gender by feminist social scientists, I set about bringing a gender perspective to the study whose focus became an examination of the help-seeking behaviour of couples who were referred to various agencies for problems related to their marriages (Brannen and Collard, 1982). Because the research environment was isolated and undemanding I was determined not to stay there too long. After two and a half years I left to take up another research post. But Jack Dominian was keen for me to see the research through to publication and paid me to complete the book I was writing. In this I was generously supported by an older colleague who had worked in the centre for some time, Jean Collard. Every week Jean would work up part of the analysis and send me the results by post (she was confined to her home in Swansea after an accident). Even though I had by that time moved to a new post, every Saturday for six months I returned to my old office in the Marriage Research Centre in Park Royal and shut myself away. Given there were no computers or social media or other electronic communication, there was nothing to distract me. It was a productive period and I still marvel at my self-discipline. I also worked in spare moments at home in between running the household and working in a new full-time research job. When Jean and I had finished the book (Brannen and Collard, 1982) one of my sons remarked that he had never noticed me writing it. It was one of the greatest compliments he ever paid me!

The new post was a research assistantship at Bedford College, University of London, in a Medical Research Council funded unit under the directorship of Professor George Brown. The project design was a prospective community study concerned to identify the causes of depression among working-class women. My main reason for taking this job was to learn more about the craft of research, to experience a larger team environment and to work under people with more experience than myself. While I learned a great deal from this study and will never forget the many hours I spent listening to the sad stories of the women I interviewed, I had many reservations about the work. In particular, the analytic approach was mechanistic; little account was taken of how women made sense of their own psychological distress. In addition, it seemed to me there were ethical and methodological questions concerning the impact of the interviews upon both the interviewees and the interviewers. At the same time I became increasingly fascinated by the ways in which research participants used the research encounter as an opportunity to embark on lengthy life stories and to use the interviews for their own ends (see Chapters 7 and 8).

After my relative autonomy at the Marriage Research Centre, I was unprepared for the lowly status of my new position and the prevailing workplace culture in the unit. As one of six female research assistants, I soon discovered that my job was confined to fieldwork and to complex transcription and numerical coding of the interviews. As to contributing to any papers that might be published from the study, it was soon clear that I would have to wait many years and that I would have little scope to contribute to the analysis. In any case the post would not have lasted long enough for that to happen. In addition, the director and I had some disagreements. The culture was not only exceptionally hierarchical it was ungenerous. When I asked quite reasonably to take a week's annual leave I was denied it. I had committed the cardinal error of mentioning that I wanted to complete the final chapter of the book I had been writing in my previous job. Perhaps the fact I was writing a book was seen as competitive or above my station. In the event, I wrote the final chapter in the mornings, and worked on the project for which I was employed in the afternoons and evenings. Most of the interviewing involved evening work. I left the job within two years. Because I was unable to take much of the annual leave due to me I asked for recompense; it is indicative of the workplace culture that I had to bring in the trade union to negotiate compensation for the time owing to me.

On 1 June 1982 I took up a new job at the Thomas Coram Research Unit (TCRU), Institute of Education, University of London. To my astonishment I discovered that a senior colleague at Bedford College had been reprimanded by my former director for having given me a reference. In addition, George Brown resigned from the Advisory Group of TCRU in protest at my appointment. Fortunately, Professor Barbara Tizard, TCRU's director, had known George for a long time and did not hold it against me. I was employed as a research officer on a six-year programme of research funded by the Department of Health and Social Security (my contract was initially for three years) called the Daycare project. It was a longitudinal study that set out to investigate the experiences of mothers before and after maternity leave and the development of their young children in different types of childcare. My immediate boss was Peter Moss, one of two directors of the programme. My job was to oversee the team of researchers who carried out the fieldwork. The structure and culture of the unit were quite different from the environment of my previous job. From the beginning Peter welcomed my contribution to every aspect of the work.

At the end of 1988 I completed my time on the Daycare study. For the first part of 1989 I was commissioned to work on a methodological paper for the Department of Health and Social Security and, with Barbara Tizard's support, spent the other part of my time transforming several chapters of data analysis that I had written for a book from the Daycare study, *Managing mothers* (Brannen and Moss, 1991), into a PhD under the supervision of Professor Ann Oakley, TCRU's deputy director. At the same time, with Ann as co-investigator, funding was gained from the Department of Health for a new three-year study of young people's health in the context of their family lives. The project began in the summer of 1989. In the course of this study, in 1991, I was fortunate to secure the University Grants Committee funded Senior Research Fellowship in TCRU. This was one of very few permanent research positions in the country that, at that time, did not require me to teach or to cover my own time from the research grants that it was my job to find funding for and direct. In 1994, with the encouragement of Professor Basil Bernstein, Pro-Director of Research at the Institute of Education, who had taken me under his wing after he acted as Internal Examiner for my PhD, I successfully applied for a readership. Four years later in 1998, I was awarded a personal chair in the sociology of the family in the Institute of Education.

Since my first research job in 1978, I have worked continuously for over 40 years in externally funded social science research with no gaps apart from three short periods of study leave. Looking back and comparing my experience with many younger researchers today I realise how fortunate I have been. From 1978 until 1991 I was on soft money, moving from one research contract to another. However the 'culture of impermanence' in social science research (a term coined by Basil Bernstein, who did much to advance the status and conditions of research staff in the Institute of Education), continues to bedevil researchers' careers, creating ever greater precariousness, an issue I go on to discuss in the next chapter. Because of the gaps in my education and employment career necessitated by motherhood and childcare, my research trajectory is not a standard one, especially compared with many of the careers of today's researchers and teaching staff. As to an academic career, that was not my aspiration; it just happened. (I suspect my rise up the ladder of the Academy would not have taken place without the encouragement of my mentors – see Chapter 2). Indeed the Zeitgeist of the times (1980–97) was to bring about change in the social order, whether this concerned women's position in society, combating racism or a commitment to the Peace Movement. While we hoped our research would contribute to these goals, we were very clear that it should not be tied to any short-term political or policy aim of the governments of the time. Importantly, we sought to do research that was methodologically robust and theoretically informed. Moreover, the idea that the *primary* goal of research was to make immediate societal or economic 'impact', as in the emphasis of today's universities and the ESRC, was not something that many of us would then have agreed with.[8] As Hammersley's (2000a)) distinction between scientific and practical research suggests, our work was intended to contribute to the cumulating body of knowledge created by the research community according to whose criteria we sought to be judged. Its relevance for a particular organisation, group or policy was not expected to be necessarily immediate or direct.

In terms of disseminating our research, some of us (at TCRU) were more interested in, and confident about, writing up research than others. In so far as we were prepared to talk about our research on TV or radio, we soon learned that live performances were preferable for ensuring that the work was not misrepresented. We also shared a desire to do justice to the data and to our research participants. For much of my early research career I did this in the only way that I knew at the time – writing books, usually in collaboration with colleagues. Chapters 3 to 8 cover some of my published work and its context from the 1980s to the present.

2

The Research Environment

This chapter focuses on my experiences of the conditions under which externally funded research is done by looking at a particular research workplace, the work practices that predominated, and the significance of research teams and mentors. I do this from the vantage point of hindsight as I look back over 40 years of research and to an environment in which research was akin to 'learning a craft'. In many respects my life as a researcher is unusual. I have been in externally funded social science research throughout my working life and, for much of the time, in the same institution and in the same research unit. The place where I have worked is not typical. It is indeed in many respects atypical. Unlike most academic and research workplaces, in the first decades of its life it was devoted solely to the conduct of externally funded research. It also offered many of its contract researchers a degree of continuity and progression not experienced by contract researchers in other academic settings in which social science research is carried out. It therefore represents a critical case not only of a relatively 'good' research workplace – in the sense of offering the possibility to sustain a research career – but also one from which to judge the effects of wider changes in research and academic environments that have taken place over its duration.

First, however, I should say something briefly about the general structures for social science research in order to set my experience in context. There are various models for conducting social science research which in effect form a continuum. At one end are individual or personal academic projects where an individual reviews, analyses, thinks and writes about some issue in their area without external support. Near to this are externally funded projects or fellowships that involve an individual academic with limited or partial funding for administrative support and field-based activities. Historically, however, most externally funded social science research has been carried out in university departments where a lecturer or professor applies for the funding, directs the research and oversees contracted research staff who do most of the data collection and analysis.

At the other end of the continuum, some universities have units or centres devoted exclusively or primarily to research while research institutes also exist outside universities – funded as charities, or by the market, or within government. Research centres also vary in structure and length of funding. Centres funded by the Economic and Social Research Council are for fixed terms; others draw on a range of funders for particular projects and activities, for example, the Centre for Research on Families and Relationships at Edinburgh University or the Morgan Centre for Research into Everyday Lives at Manchester University. However, other models also exist: those funded by the Medical Research Council and, in the 1970s and 1980s, the Department of Health and Social Security (DHSS and latterly the Department of Health) funded large research units on rolling or renewable contracts. The Department of Health units have long since disappeared and many independently funded units, for example, the Policy Studies Institute (PSI) have either ceased to exist or been absorbed into a more traditional university model. Today most research centres in universities are supported by services that are centrally organised, thereby reducing the funding that is within the control of research centres themselves. Research projects tend to be of shorter duration than they used to be. Academics and researchers at all levels typically allocate small proportions of their time to projects in order to reduce the size of the project budgets and increase their chances in the bidding process. So-called 'value for money' is now a key criterion on which research bids are written, judged and funded. But it was not always so.

When I started out in the late 1970s as a contract or funded researcher, research was an activity valued and sought after by universities. But most of the actual work was done by research assistants, many of whom were women who were on fixed-term contracts, often working part-time, a fact that further contributed to their low position on pay grades. The occupation was precarious and researchers whose central task was research were marginal to the Academy. Indeed, as the ESRC's Demographic Review of the Social Sciences (Mills et al, 2006) suggested in 2006, little change had occurred despite an increase in social science research over the ten years before the review and a considerable growth in numbers completing PhDs. Professors in social science research posts were a rarity, 'less than one per HEI [Higher Education Institution], leaving the majority of staff without such role models and viewing research-only posts as low status' (Mills et al, 2006: 92).

Today researchers in academia whose central task is research continue to suffer the continuing insecurity of the occupation. Between 1994/5 and 2003/4 the proportion of staff on fixed-term research contracts in the social sciences increased from 23 per cent to 27.5 per cent (Mills et al, 2006), despite the commitment by universities to reduce the use of insecure contracts. Funded researchers are still often part-time and on lower pay grades than lecturing staff. The lack of sustainable structures to develop their careers provides poor conditions for early career researchers to plan their lives in a society in which the cost of housing and moving house have become prohibitive. Many have to juggle research with piecemeal teaching or tutoring if they can get it. The competition for teaching posts to which some researchers aspire is fierce. In an article written in 1966 about social science research in the US, Julius Roth wrote that the 'hired hand's' status in a research organisation is seldom discussed in print nor its impact upon the data collected. The model of Roth's 'hired hand', typically female hands, still prevails.

The research workplace

There appear to be few references in the literature to the significance of the research workplace and its environs, even in texts devoted to the topic of researcher careers (Twamley et al, 2015). Yet the research workplace, by which I mean the organisational structures and cultures (which includes formal employment conditions) in which the researcher and the research project are embedded, is critical to the conduct of research (Roth, 1966), its quality and its ethical practice.

There are dangers in making claims about the past and, of course, others may view it differently. It may well be that, from the vantage point of the present, I see the past through rose-tinted spectacles, presenting the present as necessarily worse for today's researchers, especially for my younger colleagues. The early years I spent in research still stand out clearly in my mind. They were formative in the sense of Mannheim's term 'generation'. On the one hand, generations comprise collectivities 'who share the same year of birth, and are endowed, to that extent, with a common location in the historical dimension of the social process' (Mannheim, 1952 [1928] [23]: 290). On the other hand, generations generate cultures, subjectivities and action in response to the shared historical and social conditions they encounter. The conditions under which I 'grew' as a researcher and forged an identity as part of a cohort of young researchers have particular features, as I will discuss. The research environment to which those of my generation were exposed at the time appears relatively benign by today's standards. Albeit research posts were lower status and temporary, there were enough jobs for the relatively few candidates with research experience and training in research methodology.

Over the course of a career in research, I have been employed in three research centres or units (all in London) which have been devoted solely to carrying out externally funded research in the social sciences. The conditions for the research staff varied considerably. In the late 1970s my first experience offered me considerable autonomy and opportunity (described in Chapter 1). I had a three-year contract in the Marriage Research Centre based in the Central Middlesex hospital (the study was funded by the charity, the Esmée Fairbairn Trust) although there was no occupational pension scheme. However, when I left towards the end of the contract the director paid me on an hourly basis to complete the writing up of the study in my own time.

My second experience of research in the early 1980s was in a unit that was part of Bedford College in the University of London: the project was funded by the Medical Research Council (MRC). Its structure and culture were modelled on other medical research units in which the heads of projects had to be tenured 'academics' and were generally men with charge over relatively large teams of junior research assistants, mainly women. In this case we were a group of six young women deputed to carry out extensive fieldwork and coding of large amounts of qualitative data. As I suggested in the previous chapter, this particular unit was not a model workplace! Although my time at both Bedford College and the Marriage Research Centre did influence my formation, they occupied a small proportion of my life in research and, for the rest of the book, I draw on my life and work over the course of 37 years in my next workplace.

In 1982 I joined the Thomas Coram Research Unit (TCRU) which was attached to the Institute of Education, a postgraduate institute of the University of London. From the start I found the employment conditions and workplace culture greatly superior to those at Bedford College. TCRU provided a large and intellectually vibrant environment in which to work where staff felt entitled to make their voices heard. My post as a research officer involved responsibilities for other research staff and I was given considerable intellectual autonomy. I was no longer treated, as in my previous job, simply as a hired hand, that is, someone whose job was solely to collect and code data. My line manager was facilitative and supportive. The conditions of service, as set out in the human resource document of the Institute of Education, were far superior to those I had experienced elsewhere, due in part to influential figures in the Institute of Education who took up the cause of the contract researchers, in particular Professor Basil Bernstein, the Pro Director of Research, who worked hard to promote their interests. In 1977 a national breakthrough took place in the Association of University Teachers (AUT) that previously had not considered research to be a 'proper job': it implemented a code of practice for research staff and held its first national meeting of research staff in June 1979 at which the Institute of Education's active trade union was well represented.

Another advantage of the unit was that it was founded on a history of and belief in multi-disciplinarity, although I was the first person in the unit to call herself a sociologist. TCRU was established in 1973 by Professor Jack Tizard, a professor of child development, who had spent 16 years of his career in an MRC unit at the Institute of Psychiatry. The unit's original mission was to make a difference to children's lives, particularly those in institutional and other forms of care. Jack was totally committed to research and to multi-disciplinarity, as Professor Barbara Tizard, who succeeded Jack as the unit's director after Jack's untimely death in 1979, wrote in a pamphlet about the unit (Tizard, 2003). Jack also believed that one-off projects were not likely to be effective in accumulating expertise in a particular field of research and that research was more likely to flourish in settings that created some staff continuity and an intellectual critical mass. The unit was officially given its present name and moved to Coram Fields in 1973. It quickly established a distinct identity and, as I discovered when I asked around about its reputation before I joined, was a place where people could find intelligent and intelligible responses to significant social questions.

An important aspect of the unit was its material and social infrastructure. It was not only organisationally distinctive, it was geographically distant from the Institute of Education, its university host, located in Bedford Way some half a mile away. The unit was in receipt of a discrete funding stream provided by the DHSS with which Jack Tizard had established a strong relationship. In the early years of the unit the DHSS funded Jack's post, and those of several researchers and secretaries. Following a formal visit by Douglas Black (the DHSS Chief Scientist) and his team in 1975 to decide the contractual terms of the unit, it was agreed that when the initial contracts expired in 1978 the unit should be given a six-year rolling contract to be reviewed every four years (Tizard, 2003). In 1978, because of the unit's success, the University Grants Council made an award to the Institute of Education for three tenured posts to be established in the unit, the director, deputy director and senior research fellow. By 1979 there were 42 research staff and 17 projects (Tizard, 2003).

Jack Tizard's own research straddled what came to be a strong ideological divide in the social science community between basic and applied research. He believed that 'it is through a proper consideration of practical issues that social science is most likely to make theoretical advances during the present century' (Tizard, 2003: 26) and this view came to be part of the legacy that he laid down for the unit. In Jack's view the unit's research programme needed to be strategic; he rejected the emerging 'customer–contractor' model that policy makers were seeking to set up at the time in order that researchers would respond quickly to their concerns. Jack regarded this model as confining research to short-term horizons and leading to quick and simple answers (Tizard, 2003: 26). When I joined the unit, some of the unit's research was of immediate policy relevance but much was well in advance of policy makers' concerns. For example, in the case of the study to which I was recruited, the Daycare study (Brannen and Moss, 1991), the issue of mothers' employment when children were very young was not on the UK's policy agenda. Few mothers were then returning to paid employment following the birth of their children despite the introduction of maternity leave in 1975. Given the lack of any public policy commitment to providing childcare and the stringent conditions of eligibility governing the UK's maternity leave provision, this lack of policy priority was unsurprising. Nonetheless the study was funded by the DHSS – fortuitously, given the rise in maternal employment that took place in the following few years.

In my early period in the unit, there was a wide variety of activities in which researchers from different projects came together and were expected to play a full part: weekly seminars, methodological discussions, business meetings and interest groups. For several years we produced some of our own publications. While these activities developed our research, intellectual and organisational skills, the unit was also a broader occupational community. Meetings were run on democratic principles. Barbara Tizard also instituted a unit yoga class. At Christmas time, we engaged collectively in a celebratory unit meal prepared by all the unit's staff and eaten in the children's nursery below. The unit's horizontal physical space also helped shape the way it functioned. We were all on the same floor of a self-contained building, accessed by a fire escape, overlooking Coram Fields.

This physical distance from the Institute of Education and the unit's exclusive commitment to research served to create a community of researchers and a strong culture of research practice. Most people came to the unit every day of the working week. Shortly after my arrival, I decided to spend a day working from home and was surprised, on the first occasion, to receive a phone call from Barbara Tizard. Fortunately, I was able to reassure her that I was at my desk! The working day in the unit was punctuated by official tea breaks that everyone observed under the stern supervision of a formidable elderly lady called Lily Rocourt, who not only served refreshments but also 'mothered and grumbled at all the staff' (Tizard, 2003: 15). Lily lived nearby and served coffee in the morning and tea in the afternoon and then washed up. She would ring a bell and summon the staff to signal it was time for a coffee or a tea break. We then congregated in the sunny open reception area that overlooked the playground of the nursery below and beyond to Coram Fields, that was uniquely designated as a place for children in the sense that no adult was admitted without the company of a child. These breaks not only provided refreshment and sociability but also served to strengthen the intellectual and occupational culture of the unit and integration across projects and disciplines.

To forge a career in research requires continuity of funding. While in the early years of my career continuity of funding was made possible by the Department of Health's 'envelope' grant to the unit, in the later years funding was more difficult to secure. In the 2000s a number of bids for large-scale projects to the European Union (EU) and ESRC which I wrote or co-authored bit the dust. The reasons for research bids' lack of success are often opaque. However, I recall the feedback that accompanied the rejection of one proposal in particular. The proposed study concerned the work and family lives of the UK's Members of Parliament. The project was dismissed out of hand by the reviewers as being of 'no societal interest'. I was amused when, not long after, the scandal broke concerning MPs' expenses and MPs' private lives were in the spotlight.

In order that contract researchers can contribute to research proposal writing after a project's funding has ceased, bridging funding is critical. In the 1980s and 1990s bridging funds were often granted by the Institute to the unit's research staff.

In addition to bridging funding, study leave is a requirement for contract research staff if they are to make a full contribution to publications and develop their writing. However, they had no such entitlement. In 1983, shortly after my arrival, Basil Bernstein, the Pro Director of Research for the Institute, supported by Barbara Tizard, took up the case for study leave that had been put forward by some of the unit's research staff. Unlike research staff, permanent teaching staff in the Institute of Education were entitled to one term of sabbatical leave for every five years of service. Those who had been in the unit for a long time, like Peter Moss and Charlie Owen, had gone from one project to the next with no time to consolidate reflection and writing in between. In 1987 study leave for research staff was mentioned as an area of concern in the Institute's submission to the University Grants Committee and discussed in two of the Institute's main committees. In 1990 a paid study leave scheme was extended to those research staff who had been in continuous employment in the unit for more than five years (Tizard, 2003: 51).

By the beginning of the 1990s, the 'golden years' in the unit were coming to an end. In an article in *The Guardian* on 16 July 1987 the journalist Polly Toynbee wrote that TCRU:

> has frequently produced some of the best research on children. Future such work is now under threat with the withdrawal of grants from the Economic and Social Research Council and the DHSS. Yet it is the DHSS who should be looking with the greatest interest at research such as this, which shows that simple statistics on family income can never begin to gauge the real nature of family poverty.

Her concerns about the unit's future research were well founded.

In September 1990 Barbara Tizard retired and a new director and other new senior staff were appointed. In 1991 the unit moved to Woburn Square, leading to greater integration and interaction with the Institute of Education, the main buildings of which were now our near neighbours. Because we moved into a tall early 19th-century house the unit's physical space was now vertical instead of horizontal and so much of the old daily sociality of the unit was lost. By the early 1990s, the rolling contract system and 'core funding' under the Department of Health from which the unit had benefited hugely were under review. In March 1994 it came to an end and the unit was offered a five-year fixed-term contract, renewable for a further fixed term with the Department of Health (DH as the DHSS had been split up).

Several of us submitted research proposals and received DH funding in the 1990s. But by the early 2000s, the DH units were a thing of the past. Writing in 2003, Barbara Tizard regarded even fixed-term contracts for the unit as 'a retrograde step': 'A fixed term contract offers much less expectation of continuity than a rolling contract, and "envelope" funding of statistical and computing costs must inevitably lead to project directors economising on these services in order to keep their budgets down, rather than seeking full advice and support throughout the project' (2003: 61). While Barbara Tizard reserved her criticism for statistical services and IT, she may have regarded with some dismay the shortening of project timetables and the patchwork of projects and teaching that make up many of today's research staff's responsibilities, together with the loss of other local support to the unit.

As I reflect on the institutional contexts of my fellow funded researchers today, I am saddened on their behalf. I have seen whole cadres of research colleagues come and go. Increasingly, those that stay as funded researchers are scrabbling around to find small pots of funding to retain a foothold in research. Indeed, however small the funding available, management encourages researchers to apply, while at the same time it adopts an overly cautious approach when vetting a bid for a larger grant that does not attract 'sufficient' overheads. For example, in 2017 a mid-career research colleague in the unit who was employed part-time but wanted to increase her hours, was encouraged to apply for a small pot of funding under a scheme that seeks to foster 'new and intense collaborations across a whole range of disciplines at the university'. In the event, she was told that her time could not be covered on the project. It was, moreover, suggested that a senior academic or senior researcher should 'front' the project, thereby potentially infringing the researcher's intellectual property. In research development terms this denied her the opportunity to direct a small project with a view to writing an application for research on a larger scale.

Yet, despite the organisational and funding difficulties for research and the disparities suffered by research staff, paradoxically research became more important in universities' competition for prestige. Dating from the first Research Assessment Exercise in 1986 the quality of publications, especially those based on externally funded research, was central to the amount of funding that universities received and the processes by which university reputations were made.

However, in recent years, many senior researchers who forged careers in research have been 'encouraged' to take early retirement as they were put under intense pressure from management to cover their time and, because of seniority, were too expensive to be covered fully in research bids. In addition, they experienced greater work intensification as the time frames for the delivery of research became shorter, with more focus on short-term policy concerns. The pressure on research staff to cover the costs of their time was further augmented by changes to university accounting rules, so that researchers were no longer permitted to carry over funding they had raised in one year to the next. This was punitive for those who covered more than 100 per cent of their time in any one year.

For less senior researchers the current structures and climate are equally tough, even though most are far better qualified than those of my generation who came into research. The culture in universities is highly competitive and considerable management pressure is exercised to 'produce outputs' that meet the criteria of 'global and international excellence'. Early career and mid-career researchers face increasing demands from management to cover their time in the form of piecemeal contributions to teaching, tutoring and student seminars for which they lack responsibility and are given insufficient recognition. Many have either moved over to teaching altogether or been replaced by new lecturing staff. They also compete with new teaching fellowships for which new staff are employed, usually part-time.

As I write, the status of researchers in TCRU has diminished. The changes in the wider institutional environment have played a not insignificant part in this. In 2015 the Institute was taken over by University College London (UCL) and as a consequence researchers no longer have the parity of status with teaching staff that they once enjoyed under the former Institute of Education's Charter and Statutes. Although at the time of the merger it was agreed that research staff would continue under the same conditions, this promise was short-lived, with a reduction in the conditions that were fought for and gained in the 1980s and 1990s. Those researchers who are promoted must move to UCL contracts that offer shorter holidays and lower status compared with 'academic staff'. Since the merger researchers have discovered that the opportunity for research staff to apply for study leave was not one of the conditions carried over in the merger. In 2017 a research colleague in the unit was refused study leave despite having spent the best part of 20 years in the Institute of Education. In the letter of complaint I sent on her behalf to the director of the Institute I wrote:

> When I came to the Institute as a researcher in the 1980s I found the system to be open, democratic and supportive. Certainly my own career would not have progressed and I would not have developed an international reputation and produced a large and diverse collection of books and refereed papers without the opportunities afforded in the Institute to research staff. It seems that we are now going backwards. There is nothing to suggest that the research staff is not of equal calibre to the academic staff. Indeed the quality of outputs for the Research Excellence Framework is dependent upon the efforts of research *teams* as well as

individual scholarship. It is therefore paramount to the success of the institution that the research staff as a whole is highly motivated and not discontented with its position.... Research funding rarely offers adequate time to produce four star publications and to develop new research proposals. Study leave is also a critical resource in creating and sustaining a critical mass of researchers, as we have managed to do in TCRU over several decades. The retrograde step to remove it cannot be right. (13 February 2017)

This was the reply I received from the director:

On arrival to the UCL Institute of Education I was very surprised to hear that researchers had previously been entitled to sabbaticals. In my experience this is unprecedented elsewhere in the sector, and I would suggest with clear reason. In my experience (including in self-sustaining research centres), if a researcher colleague is struggling to write and publish, that likely signals a challenge with the project team, or a lack of personal development provision (e.g. mentoring). Working on significant research projects often offers access to data and scale – and thus opportunity for world leading publication – that is hard to attain for many of our other colleagues. (Personal email, 16 February 2017)

Following subsequent interventions by the union (the Universities and Colleges Union), this refusal has been seemingly revoked although the decision to grant study leave has been declared 'a matter for department heads' and given only on condition that the person taking study leave can persuade another person to take over their duties. Such provisos do not bode well and, to date, to the best of my knowledge, study leave has not been granted to a member of research staff. Indeed, the grounds for study leave that used to apply, namely time to write up research, appear to have been questioned for those who already have a 'good' publication record.

Research teams and practices

Most externally funded research is team based. Research teams are organised in different ways even within a research unit or department, with some more hierarchical in structure and culture than others. In some hierarchically run teams researchers are still hired only to carry out the fieldwork, usually considered a lesser skilled and lower status research activity compared with analysis and writing (Roth, 1966). The result is that they feel they lack a stake in the research, with potential consequences for the quality of the work, and they lack opportunities to develop their expertise in other aspects of the research process. In less hierarchically organised teams researchers are encouraged to extend and develop their skills. In the past, many were apprenticed in the craft of research by working alongside and learning from more experienced researchers.

Research teams are also contexts in which ideas are exchanged and knowledge created. As Ann Phoenix argues, social research as an activity is necessarily intertextual in the sense that any text is affected by the meanings established in other previous or contemporary texts; 'language and thought are part of the process of re-describing the world and are always in dynamic interaction with previous and future thought and language' (Phoenix, 2014: 110). At TCRU I was fortunate in the teams I worked with in the formative years of my research trajectory; they afforded generative environments for the exchange of ideas and the creation of knowledge.

Team leaders are lynchpins in creating the conditions for such environments to develop. They are also crucial in determining whether team members are able to make an input into the study's ideas, methodological practices, written outputs and the oral communication of the research findings. While academic institutions are rarely democratic, within the web of administrative and bureaucratic constraints they place on researchers, opportunities depend to a large extent on the management of the lead investigator.

In this respect at TCRU I was particularly lucky. In 1982 I was recruited to work for, and later with, a researcher who not only came to believe and write about democratic practices in education but also was democratic in his research practice. As Peter Moss wrote, with Michael Fielding: 'We understand democracy as a multi-dimensional concept, with many different forms and practices; formal and procedural democracy, democratic governance, is important, but so too is democracy as a way of thinking, being and acting, of relating and living together, as a quality of personal life and relationships' (Fielding and Moss, 2012: 2). The way Peter Moss led projects at TCRU was always imbued with a democratic approach to being, acting and relating. Researchers with whom he worked were encouraged to take part in decisions concerning research strategies and for those working full-time to take part in all aspects of the research process, where possible. A collaborative way of working as a team, with all members participating in every aspect of the work, welded the team in ways that overcame disciplinary differences and hierarchies.

Learning to write up research is an important skill. I found writing with Peter Moss a liberating experience that freed me from the initial fear that what I had written was not 'good enough'. Our method of working was to allocate relatively short blocks of time to writing a draft and to bat it back and forth between us. In all the projects I worked on in the unit, publications were co-authored by all the research team's members if they had contributed to the data analysis. Regarding the order of authors, Peter stuck to the principle of alphabetical order, a practice that more often than not benefited me! I learned a great deal in my first years in the unit from Peter's democratic and collaborative approach and, in the last decade of my research life, I have tried hard to practise this approach and to transmit it to the generations of researchers who come after.

Learning the craft of research is like serving an apprenticeship. The science and art of research do not primarily depend on formal learning via lectures and training courses. Indeed, few textbooks and methodology courses were in existence when older generations embarked on social science. Even for the few in my generation who did a Master's degree in social research much of what we learned was through the practice of research in the many small projects we undertook as part of the degree. Moreover, apprenticeships in research do not have discrete endings. In the course of working in teams it is easier to learn and experiment with different research practices, techniques and technologies than working as a lone researcher.

My early years in TCRU confirmed my view of the importance of a rigorous approach to research design, data collection methods and analysis while leaving open the possibility for introducing new ideas and approaches in the course of projects. In the 1980s, when I joined the unit, a particular style of research dominated in the unit: studies with moderate to large-scale samples, employing interview and observation methods and analysis methods that relied primarily on the quantification of the data. When I sought to pose new research questions that required the addition of methods that generated qualitative data and analytic methods to do justice to these data, this was not only welcomed but facilitated.

Although the unit was dominated by psychologists when I joined, I was made to feel secure in my background as a sociologist. Peter Moss's flexibility and openness to new concepts, research methods and ways of doing research enabled me to make a major contribution to the Daycare project (Chapter 3). For example, we introduced a mixed method approach, although we did not refer to it in these terms at the time. This initially meant inserting open-ended questions into the interview schedules, and transcribing large amounts of interview data manually on to huge coding schedules that were organised according to both the questions asked in the interviews and a set of conceptual themes. This also involved cross-referencing themes in the margins of the interview coding schedules that came up under other responses. The analysis was complex – a mix of quantitative analysis on the whole dataset (N = 255 mothers and children at wave one) and qualitative analysis of the material on a smaller subset of cases (n = 70). The analysis process was further complicated by the fact that the study was longitudinal with four rounds of data collection.

Good research is produced when researchers are encouraged to communicate and work with others beyond the projects they are hired to work on. In the 1980s the unit was facilitative in that regard. Under the 1980s 'customer–contractor principle' that was set out in the Rothschild Report (HMSO, 1971),[1] government departments agreed that in buying research for their needs they had some responsibility for the 'health' of research. DHSS units interpreted this to mean that research staff were permitted one day a week outside their projects, for example, to complete other writing, go to conferences or organise research-related activities. My first years at the unit were productive and fruitful, enabling me to embark on a number of 'projects' due to the supportive context and those to whom I was accountable. In any case life was less pressured in those days with far less multi-tasking than is now required. The unit's director, Barbara Tizard, together with Peter Moss, gave me the freedom to expand my horizons: one project was to set up the Resources in Households Group with Gail Wilson, then completing her PhD at the Institute of Education where the group's meetings took place. The aim was to create an international network and discussion forum involving a wide range of researchers around a single focus: to open the black box of the household and examine how resources are distributed between family members (see Chapter 4).

Such opportunities brought home to me the potential for expanding intellectual and research horizons through wider collaboration and discussion. In particular, making connections with researchers in other countries enables a researcher to see their own society through strangers' eyes, a process central to social anthropology. Following contact with several Scandinavian researchers I met at international conferences, I saw that the research issues we were examining in the Daycare project – the return of women to the workplace following maternity leave and their children's daycare provision – were already established and commonplace practices in Denmark and Sweden. In contrast, it was not until the late 1980s that many mothers in the UK returned to employment following maternity leave. So, in 1984, I successfully applied for a British Council scholarship to visit Denmark and Sweden where I met researchers studying early childhood provision and visited several daycare centres. This gave me an early taste of what it means to take an international perspective and was the start of a long association with researchers in Scandinavia and other European countries. These experiences not only fostered my interest in international research, they also formed a basis for developing research proposals and collaborations under the EU funding that became available in the late 1990s and 2000s.

Other forms of activity are also important to researchers' intellectual development. These include service to the wider academic community, for example, reviewing journal articles and editing journals. In 1998 Rosalind Edwards and I founded a new journal on methodology, the *International Journal of Social Research Methodology* that I continued to co-edit until 2015, although this work was not officially recognised in terms of my time allocation (full time equivalent status). The work of editing and reviewing articles, while adding considerably to my workload and carried out in our own time, was another key way in which a research apprenticeship and collaboration between researchers are sustained. Opportunities also arise to participate in the shaping of decisions relating to national priorities for research funding and overseeing the practices and progress of other research centres. Between 2005 and 2010 I served on ESRC's Research Resources Board (later renamed Methods and Infrastructure Committee); this was an important way of understanding the wider context in which research is carried out, as well enhancing a critical approach to methodology. Despite the onerous and time-consuming nature of the work however, no time allocation was given for this. I doubt that this institutional failure to regard this work as a key part of a researcher's role would have happened a decade earlier.

Since being appointed to a readership (in 1994) and then a chair I have been classified as an 'academic'. In addition to research this has meant engaging in postgraduate teaching but rather more time in doctoral supervision and service within and beyond the Institute of Education. However, as I look at the current changes in academia I am less inclined to identify as an academic. Rather I prefer to see myself as a researcher in a research unit. Research based on strong 'communities of practice' helps weather upheavals in the wider university contexts that surround research. While some may argue that the *precarité* that goes with being a 'pure researcher' acts as an incentive for an individual to overcome the hurdles and to take risks, for me it has been the solidarity of the research environment and the teams that I have worked with that has sustained me.

Mentors

Looking back, I have become increasingly aware of the importance of mentors, especially in the early years of my research trajectory. Mentoring can be built into a research environment and it may also arise serendipitously through collegiality. While in my first two research positions I was somewhat isolated I can readily point to people who were important sources of encouragement at the time, in particular Jean Collard (at the Marriage Research Centre) with whom I worked closely on my first funded project. I also remember the constructive comments on my first publication, a journal article, made by a professor of social work who was carrying out a similar study to our own. Given that our research projects were potentially in competition, his helpful comments on my draft were not only generous but formative in helping me develop my writing of journal articles.

TCRU provided a generative climate for mentorship from peers and, from senior colleagues, for both mentorship and sponsorship (O'Connor, forthcoming). The unit's director, Barbara Tizard, while she could be formidable and a little intimidating, was a strong ally of, and advocate for, researchers who worked hard. Without her encouragement I am not sure that many of us would have achieved what we did. In my case she spotted the links I was making in the Daycare project between quantitative methods and qualitative approaches. In 1988, it was her idea, and with her support, that I secured a commission from the DHSS to write a paper for the department on combining qualitative and quantitative methods. This led to a one-to-one meeting with the Chief Scientist to discuss the merits of this approach. (As support I wisely decided to take along with me a prominent social science methodologist, Professor Martyn Hammersley.) She also encouraged me and offered support in the organisation of a two-day seminar on the topic with social science researchers from other units and took an active part in the seminar. Within work time and using the unit's resources I subsequently produced a book in 1992, *Mixing methods: Qualitative and quantitative research* (Brannen, 1992b) that proved to be one of my most widely read publications. Barbara was also instrumental in suggesting that I use the data analysis that I had carried out for the Daycare project for a PhD. The Institute of Education did not require their staff to pay fees in the 1980s.

In addition, I was fortunate that the distinguished feminist sociologist Ann Oakley joined the unit as its deputy director in 1985. Ann was an important role model for many of us. She was supportive in supervising my PhD in 1989, and crucial to securing funding for a new project on which we both worked. She made an important contribution to the volume that came out of the study (Brannen et al, 1994). Ann's formidable writing skills were always a source of great inspiration to me, especially in the years I worked with her.

Another key figure in my research life was the famous sociologist Basil Bernstein. I have already noted that, as Pro Director of Research in the Institute throughout the 1980s, he championed the cause of contract researchers in the Institute enabling us to set up our own organisation and to work towards better conditions. Basil was undoubtedly unique in taking up this cause given that he was a member of the Institute's senior management. Such a role in today's managerialist culture of universities is almost unthinkable. After Basil acted as the Internal Examiner for my PhD in 1990, he became a personal mentor and, henceforth, until his death in 2000, he exercised a watching brief over me. He was inspirational, encouraging, and always on hand (usually involving long lunches) to offer advice.

Unlike conventional models of apprenticeships, doing especially good research is as much dependent on one's peers as it is on those who are senior. While the unit provided much continuity, over the years many colleagues joined and left. Those, like me, who stayed greatly benefited from the experience of others. Although there were ups and downs, as in all organisations, the unit encouraged collegiality in which the contribution of everyone who was part of the research enterprise was recognised. Key people were administrative staff, statistical and computing staff, the finance officer, the tea lady and the wider group of research colleagues outside one's own team. I owe much to my colleagues, to whom I pay tribute in the acknowledgements at the start of the book.

Constraints and opportunities

This sketch of my experiences of a research unit covers four decades. The period has been one of considerable change in the policy and political context in the areas I research. Britain has seen the growth and near hegemony of neoliberal ideas and practices and the introduction of the market into central areas of the state, including health, education and social welfare. In relation to funding for social science research however, there have been opportunities that arose from Britain's increasing involvement in Europe over the period. Nationally one set of opportunities from which researchers have greatly benefited has been the decade and more of funding made by ESRC to the National Centre for Research Methods (NCRM) that enabled groups of researchers across the UK to develop methodologically oriented projects in ways they would never have otherwise been able to do. Our own unit was granted NCRM funding for a three-year programme on narrative methods that involved many members of the unit and collaboration with other institutions. Another key opportunity was the growth in the internationalisation of research, with opportunities to bid for research projects and engage in networks with colleagues in other countries. EU framework funding was particularly important. If Brexit means the withdrawal of these funding opportunities, as seems likely at the time of writing, UK social science research is placed in grave danger.

A particular and major change in the climate in which research is carried out today, as opposed to when I started out, concerns the demands of funders on researchers to create what they term 'impact'[2] – assessed largely in relation to the immediate or short-term economic and societal influence of research. Increased accountability of researchers to make their work accessible to different audiences is to be welcomed. However, the 'impact culture' also carries risks. It can take away resources from a project for which funding is already tight. Some of the 'impact events' that researchers build into their bids can be tokenistic and instrumental, for example, with a view to fulfilling the demands on universities to produce 'impact case studies' for the university Research Excellence Framework (REF), the successor to the Research Assessment Exercise. The kinds of skills that researchers possess may not match those that are required for the task of communicating the research findings to lay audiences, or universities may insufficiently support this work.

There is furthermore a danger that impact is interpreted in relation to the narrow time frames of policy makers, and underplays the important contribution of strategic and blue skies research. The journalist David Walker and former chair of one of ESRC's key committees is clearly an exponent of a narrow version of the 'impact' model, that 'social science must generate knowledge that is 'directly – and rapidly – translated into specific policy outcomes' (Scott 2017: 501). As the author of a recent history of the ESRC, he excoriates the ESRC, arguing that since its inception it has been a conduit for passing money to academics to define their own priorities and pursue their own interests and agendas (Walker, 2015). Such judgements demonstrate misconceptions about social science research: that it is not only a matter of individual academic scholarship but is founded upon the requirement that research is a collective activity that seeks to create and expand knowledge, while also seeking to be of interest to policy.

Earlier I argued that a critical aspect of the research environment is the research team. In today's academe, hierarchies within research teams are increasingly underpinned by institutional rules about whose work is most valued in the universities' REF submissions. There are negative outcomes to these ranking procedures which tend to be downplayed. One is their tendency to discourage interdisciplinary working. Another is that they downgrade the collective contribution that a research team makes to the success of a research project. This is because in the REF publications from research are allocated to particular individuals and only the contributions of higher grade researchers 'count'.

The changes to the funding of UK universities, the hike in student fees and increased managerialism are also profound in their effects. The increased marketisation of the higher education sector affects research and teaching alike. A goal in my own institution but also in many others is to transform universities into 'global' organisations. This involves vast investments in infrastructure, a huge growth in courses and student numbers. The founding principle of universities, despite the claim to achieve 'excellence', appears more and more to be about turning universities into profitable businesses in which the vice chancellors' salaries have risen astronomically at the same time as the salaries of university lecturers and researchers have stagnated, as have the time and priority given to research.

The Institute of Education, until the merger in 2015 with UCL, was a relatively small postgraduate institution of London University. On the positive side the merger with UCL has the potential to open up opportunities for cross-disciplinary collaboration involving other faculties of UCL. On the negative side, the Institute has experienced constant change that has brought with it more layers of administration. The TCRU, as a research environment, is swamped by several bureaucratic layers with which it has to negotiate. Organisational change and personnel turnover in central services have been relentless with largely negative consequences for the administration of research bids and research grants.

Change is of course inevitable in organisations. It was ongoing in the Institute of Education well before the merger with UCL, with several departmental reorganisations and the requirement for each department to become self-financing. For several years staff have been subject to micro-management exercised through systems for allocating staff time in ways that fail to reflect the realities of research, teaching and other activities. As in the UK social sciences generally, researchers are experiencing increasing difficulty in finding project funding, and if and when Britain leaves the EU, access to most EU funding will end. Research centres have found it increasingly hard to 'balance their books' with the result that management has preferred to divert resources and personnel into teaching.

Universities have increasingly centralised the infrastructure for research and teaching – for example the administration of funds, libraries, IT, web presence and the physical environment – and then charge these costs to the research funding bodies. The institutional environment sets the priorities and the structures for research and also frames the cultures for the way research is valued. It also increasingly controls the funding bidding process – whether a research bid can be submitted at all as well as over the pricing of central resources and researcher time. In my own institution in the 1980s and 1990s, research support was located in the centres where it was needed. When I was recruited to the TCRU in 1982, the unit had jurisdiction over its own resources, including its own finance officer, statisticians, administrative and computing staff, much of which was paid for through a rolling grant from the DHSS. From a research perspective, this was an efficient and effective model. Gradually this support was whittled away as senior management centralised these functions and operations and seized research overheads to buttress its own power and control. Today research units and their projects possess almost no localised support services of their own. The consequences of this mean that relationships with relevant services and support persons are remote and are typically conducted online. In addition, centralised structures and personnel frequently change, and their priorities and time frames are different from, and sometimes in conflict with, those of research projects. This leads to dysfunctional and asymmetric relationships, often resulting in delays and researcher frustration about what appears to be a lack of institutional responsibility.

As my experience illustrates, the value placed upon research has diminished. This happened to coincide with the merger with UCL, a time in which teaching has become more profitable compared with research. Research is seen to be 'too costly' and needs to be subsidised by teaching and increased student numbers.[3] Even so-called 'fully costed' bids, such as those submitted to the ESRC, are not necessarily encouraged. Researchers are required to adapt by making up the shortfall in their time and salaries when research funding dries up. In the Department of Social Science in which the unit now sits, an undergraduate course (in social sciences) was introduced in 2016 and new Master's courses have also been set up. These courses offer opportunities for researchers to participate in teaching and tutoring. However, the pressure to take on teaching competes for research time and takes researchers away from preparing research bids and writing up their research. Furthermore, these teaching opportunities have served to underline the disparities in status between lecturers and research staff.

The relocation and rebranding of the Institute of Education under the umbrella of UCL, which aimed to protect it from the vagaries of the market and government policy, is paradoxically also leading to greater exposure to market forces. Internally, the process of merger created organisational chaos, more tiers of management and increased bureaucracy. The competitive climate of university rankings and the contest for lecturers as well as students with the 'best' qualifications are part of the context – the spaces and places in which research is done. In the research unit where I have spent much of my working life, a whole cadre of new lecturing staff has been recruited that far outnumbers its research staff. Although many of these staff wish to engage in externally funded research, this is not their central responsibility. More importantly, the interests of some teaching staff do not coincide with the TCRU's long-standing remit concerning research on children, families and services. In my view, the unit's research identity and its original *raison d'être* are in jeopardy if not terminally undermined. As a centre for research it is struggling for air. Whether it can survive, only time will tell.

In 2019 further reorganisation was proposed. The head of the Department of Social Science, within which the TCRU currently sits, sought to move the department to another faculty of UCL on the grounds that its interests would sit more comfortably elsewhere and that the department's teaching and research would acquire greater visibility. This leap into the unknown would have meant severing the historic link between the Institute of Education and the TCRU. This would have brought more uncertainty, pain and disruption for gains that were unspecified and not guaranteed.

To suggest that doing social science research in the past was easier than at present would be to downplay the political and funding context of the times. It is important to remember that the Social Science Research Council (SSRC), as it was named at its start, was founded in 1965. In the 1970s and 1980s, the occupation of social science researcher was relatively uncommon and precarious. Project funding was then, as it is now, granted for fixed terms and researchers employed on temporary or short-term contracts. In 1983, social science went through a difficult time. Under Margaret Thatcher's premiership, the government was hostile to the value of social science research and SSRC centres were closed and funding for postgraduate funding severely curtailed. As a family we moved house five times in the course of ten years on account of the research positions of my husband and latterly my own, with the attendant financial costs.

In the past a job in research was rarely a route into a lectureship. Today far more people have PhDs in social science but both research and teaching positions are highly competitive. Yet, on the surface, today's researchers are in a stronger position to build research careers. It is now supposedly inadmissible in law to employ staff on fixed-term contracts after staff have worked for an organisation for four years, although few research grants last as long as that. This may well change, however, following the UK's departure from the EU if working conditions are no longer subject to EU standards and regulation.

Even if researchers succeed in gaining a succession of grants, these rarely cover them on a full-time basis and may not provide continuity of employment. Research bids have to be highly competitive in a market-driven economy while the research is assessed on the grounds of its current economic and societal 'impact'. In times of change and austerity universities, as self-financing organisations, are seeking to claw back as much as they can for their overheads with the result that researcher time is cut to the bone. With mortgages to pay and families to support, the salaries and pensions of researchers are increasingly unstable. The 'culture of impermanence', as Basil Bernstein called it, looks set to continue.

I have painted a rather pessimistic picture of research at the present time, perhaps not surprisingly given the state of the country at this moment and following a long period of cuts to public expenditure. However, I want to stress that practising social research and applying all the particular skills that it demands is a highly rewarding and creative occupation compared with most. For me it has offered considerable freedom to study issues of societal importance that in most cases I chose to study. It has been a great privilege to be party to the stories of so many adults and children whose lives I would otherwise never have encountered. In the following chapters I hope to share something of the excitement of this enterprise as well as the methodological and other challenges it has thrown up.

Mothers and the Labour Market

This chapter reflects on the shifting public discourses in Britain concerning mothers and the labour market from the end of the Second World War and shows how the framing of research questions reflects these changing public discourses. History is constituted through events and diverse intersecting and colliding interests that are shaped by the actions, resistances and discourses of those with less power, as well as those holding the reins of power. While these processes are complex, our understanding of history is often influenced by particular narratives that appear to provide a coherent account of events. One such narrative is that, at the end of the Second World War, women were ejected from many of the jobs in which they had worked in wartime to create work for returning servicemen and that this ejection marked a watershed in women's lives and a backward step in female emancipation. As Denise Riley's (1983) historical analysis of motherhood and childcare suggests, the reality was more complex, involving political, economic and social elements, and the labour market orientations of women themselves.

One major element of political concern in the post-war period was low birth rates and their economic and social consequences. An important priority of medical authorities was to improve the health and nutrition of families and to regulate mother craft (Riley, 1983). Public nurseries had been established in wartime to accommodate children whose mothers took on jobs in armament factories and other work that men had previously done. After the war these nurseries were regarded by some health experts as a potential site for health intervention: to 'free' women, especially poor women, to give birth to more children and as opportunities to cement marriages (Riley, 1983: 172). The government, however, was afraid that the continuing provision of nurseries would obstruct the creation of jobs for returning servicemen. Its view prevailed and a large proportion of public nurseries were closed. As the Ministry of Health circular 221/1945 sets out:

> The Ministers concerned accept the view of medical and other authority that, in the interest of the health and development of the child no less than the benefit of the mother, the proper place for a child under two is at home with his mother. They are also of the opinion that, under normal peacetime conditions, the right policy to pursue would be positively to discourage mother of children under two from going out to work.

However, women made their own decisions about their labour market participation (Riley, 1983). Many younger women, according to contemporaneous evidence (Thomas, 1944, 1948), welcomed opportunities to leave employment in the context of the uninviting nature of much of the work, the low level of skill required, and the 'saving grace of marriage' and motherhood that life after the war appeared to offer (Riley, 1983: 190). In the first three or more decades following the Second World War the refrain 'my mother never left us' became the canon of a 'proper' childhood and the key condition for providing children with psychological security. The fear of giving children too much space, that is, if children came home to empty, motherless homes, replaced the pre-war generations' experiences of too little space due to overcrowded housing and poverty.

Despite government policy the numbers of women in paid employment after the war continued to rise. Yet, over twenty years later in 1968, a government circular reiterated the view 'that whenever possible the younger pre-school child should be at home with the mother... because early and prolonged separation from the mother is detrimental to the child' (Ministry of Health 37/68). As I shall later discuss, the government's stance did not change until the mid-1980s when, under the influence of neoliberal policies, government sought to reduce 'dependency on the state' and to cease to 'interfere' in what it considered to be 'private family matters', apart from health and education (Brannen and Moss, 1991: 31).

In the late 1970s I began research on mothers in the labour market for a Master's dissertation. At that time, home was still promoted as the 'best place' to rear young children and mothers the best people to do so. Those few mothers who stayed in, or re-entered, the labour market following childbirth were regarded with suspicion, at least by policy makers and practitioners. Most of the research relating to the topic of 'working mothers', as it was known at the time, was done by psychologists and focused on the effects of mother–child attachment and separation (for example Ainsworth, 1979, 1989). Only a handful of social scientists framed women's paid work as a matter worthy of study but they mainly focused on the reasons why women worked (Jephcott, 1962; Myrdal and Klein, 1965; Hunt, 1968). They thereby contributed to the gender ideologies surrounding 'women's role', despite the reality of women's increasing presence in the labour market: that women's employment was optional and secondary to men's. The Rapoports (1971) were unusual at the time in identifying the phenomenon of 'dual-career families' as a focus of study, albeit their research was limited to upper middle-class families.

The research that questioned the normative assumption that home was the best place for mothers and children was carried out by women sociologists (Gavron, 1966; Oakley, 1974). In the early 1980s the Women and Employment Survey, commissioned by the Department for Employment (Martin and Roberts, 1984), was a path-breaking initiative that provided a thorough overview of women's employment histories, attitudes and the gendered structure of the labour market. I should declare an interest here as my husband, Peter, established the Social Science Research Branch in the department and at that time was its head. The survey afforded significant opportunities for secondary analysis (see the stream of work of Shirley Dex and Heather Joshi) and an impetus for further research in the field as mothers of young children increased their share of employment.

In the late 1980s the narrative shifted, reflecting not only the rapid growth in the employment of mothers with young children but the increased emphasis placed by government on market forces and the notion of 'individual choice'. While the state offered no support with childcare, it proposed that the decision of 'parents' (mothers) to engage in paid work was up to them to decide as 'private individuals'. The issue of 'working mothers' was redefined. Under the new choice ideology 'parents' were charged with managing family responsibilities and work commitments, and with making their own compromises concerning 'work–life balance'. Childcare became a matter for the market and the number of private nurseries burgeoned.

Reflecting these changes the social research agenda also shifted. In the 1960s and 1970s, motherhood was a small field of inquiry occupied mainly by those concerned with family life or child development. Gradually much of the territory of 'family studies' was taken over by feminist sociologists whose work threw the spotlight on to patriarchy and women's oppression. Some of this research sought to make visible women's labour in the home and gender inequality in childcare. As more women remained in work, attention next turned to understanding how paid work and responsibilities for children and family life intersected, and to the conceptualisation of public and private realms as interdependent. This new focus began to draw in some male researchers from the fields of labour market studies, most of whom had previously shown little interest in the fields of either family life or children's lives.

Both Second Wave Feminism and the 'working mothers debate' shaped the three pieces of research that I will focus upon in this chapter. The first study was a longitudinal project that examined the experiences and effects of employment on mothers who returned to work after childbirth in the early 1980s. The second jumps a decade to focus on the significant changes taking place in the workplace in ways that put strain on the boundaries between work and family life and undermined notions of work–life balance. My third example is a multi-level cross-national study carried out in the 2000s. This study took a European focus to examine the differences that welfare states, workplace policies and practices, and family support made to the lives of working families – mothers and fathers – in different countries but in similar sectors of the economy and in similar occupational statuses.

In describing these studies, I will also point to the insights they generated and outline the methodological approaches adopted and their respective benefits and drawbacks. In the first study of mothers returning to work after the birth of their first child we adopted an 'evolutionary' research strategy in which a qualitative methodological approach was added to a quantitative approach within a longitudinal research design. The second study employed a case study approach to examine to provide a 'thick' description of an organisation in the process of rapid change (Geertz, 1973) and how its workforce negotiated their work and family lives. This was a shift from analyses of patterns and themes across a dataset to an examination of the conditions that applied in particular cases and families. The third study of working parents in Europe adopted a comparative approach in which, by matching organisations and parents within those organisations, it was possible to identify some of the specificities that created differences and similarities across several European countries with a range of different welfare regimes and histories.

Mothers returning to work: the Daycare study

In 1973 Britain became a member of the European Community and, in 1975, Parliament passed employment protection legislation whose provisions were implemented over the following two years. In June 1976, under a section of the Employment Protection Act, it became illegal to sack a woman because she was pregnant. The right to maternity leave was also written into legislation although the introduction of the provisions for maternity pay had to wait a further year. However, as Peter Moss and I wrote in 1988: 'The tenacity with which the male-dominated pattern of work is defended is demonstrated by the history of maternity leave legislation' (Brannen and Moss, 1988: 17). The conditions of eligibility for maternity leave were stringent. Women had to have worked for two years for the same employer, with the result that half of all pregnant women were excluded from entitlement to leave. The total leave period was only 40 weeks and less than half the leave (18 weeks) attracted any benefit. Only 6 weeks were compensated at 90 per cent of earnings and the remaining 12 weeks of paid leave at a low flat rate. Further, mothers were expected to resume work full-time; there were no options to take longer leave or to go back part-time. Moreover, employment protection rights in the event of childbirth did not amount to much. Women had no right to return to the same jobs they had held before maternity leave so that when they resumed work they forfeited non-statutory benefits that might have accrued in their absence: pay rises, promotion, leave and bonuses. No changes were made in relation to childcare. As John Patten, Parliamentary Under-Secretary of State at the DHSS said: 'Day care will continue to be a private arrangement between parents and voluntary resources except where there are special needs' (*Hansard*, 18 February 1985: col. 397).

In 1982 I joined a team of researchers at TCRU led by Peter Moss on a six-year programme of longitudinal research funded by the DHSS that was called the Daycare study (1982–87). The programme was commissioned at the end of the 1970s before neoliberal ideas took hold in government, with consequences I have discussed earlier for the structure and funding of research (see Chapter 2). The project's aim was to examine the experiences of first-time mothers who resumed full-time employment under the maternity leave provision after the birth of their first children and the effects of different types of childcare on their young children. At the time there were still relatively few mothers who had returned to work when children were young and far fewer who were covered under the maternity leave provisions. In 1986 only a third of women with a child under five were employed at any one time (OPCS, 1989: Table 9.11). While the Women and Employment Survey (Martin and Roberts, 1984) found that women were returning to work increasingly between births and returning sooner, most mothers with 'dependent' children interrupted their employment careers and were working part-time, at least half of whom were working under 16 hours per week (Martin and Roberts, 1984: Table 2.8). Women's work careers were discontinuous; most were returning to different jobs and/or different employment conditions than those held prior to having their children, despite the maternity leave legislation, as we were to discover. However, the period was a generally a time of economic growth in south-east England where the research was carried out. There was also a substantial demand for women to take up employment as a result of the decline in the numbers of young people entering the labour market. It was estimated that 80 per cent of the increase in employment in the period up to 1995 would be accounted for by women (Department of Employment, 1988).

The initial aims of the Daycare study, as set out in the original research proposal submitted before I joined the study, were 'to describe the histories and experiences of the mothers and children; to assess their welfare and development, including the type and stability of nonparental care'. A variety of (quantitative) methods were to be used, including interviews, observations and developmental assessments (Brannen and Moss, 1991: 18). The study had a medium-sized sample at wave one (255 women of whom 60 were not intending to return to work – the comparison group) and four waves of data collection.[1] 'The original proposal assumed the project would be entirely oriented to a quantitative approach with statistical methods of analysis' (Brannen and Moss, 1991: 18).

At my suggestion, significant changes were subsequently made to the study. In any event the conditions of the grant afforded considerable scope in time and funding for further development. One change was to shift the focus from mothers to a focus upon the household. In exploring the reasons why mothers were employed (or not) in children's early years, we therefore sought to include the contribution of fathers and the ways in which mothers viewed men's breadwinning and contribution to fatherhood, care work and domestic labour. However, we did not have the resources to interview fathers. Furthermore, we conceptualised women's paid work and household work and childcare in terms of a 'negotiated accommodation' in which women's lives in public and private spheres were integrated and interdependent. In short, instead of seeing mothers as being caught psychologically between 'dual roles' in separate domains, we assumed that the tensions were also structural.

The implications of a change in conceptual focus meant that a qualitative component was added to the study in which we explored how mothers made sense of their situations and responsibilities, and the ways in which they and their households organised employment and parenthood. Given that going back to work when a child was a few months old was relatively uncommon in Britain at that time and full-time motherhood was still prioritised in public discourse, it was important to tap into any ambivalence mothers might express about going back to work (Brannen, 2004). These changes were translated into changes in the study's methodology, in the method of interviewing and the analysis of the data. The interview schedule was designed to combine structured questions (the responses to which were categorised according to predefined codes) with unstructured interview questions and flexible probes (the responses to which were transcribed and later subjected to qualitative analysis). A flexible, in-depth mode of interviewing was adopted in which research participants were encouraged to speak at length and to introduce and articulate their own concerns. The approach, while time-consuming, was so successful that when, at later waves of the longitudinal study, we decided to return to a structured interview approach with some of the sample, many of these mothers continued to respond in the way they had done in the earlier semi-structured interviews.

As we described in *Managing mothers* (Brannen and Moss, 1991), on the one hand we sought to elicit through indirect questioning narratives of motherhood and the return to work situated in women's experiences. On the other hand, using direct structured questions, we examined their present evaluations of their situations. In effect, as we argued, we were creating different types of data: 'the inter-penetration of ideology and practice … the mechanisms by which women reproduce and integrate contradictory elements of their beliefs, actions and the situations in which they find themselves … beliefs and practices … [which are] part and parcel of larger ideological debates concerning gender roles and the practice of everyday life' (Brannen and Moss, 1991: 7). The examination of interviewees' responses to different types of questioning was fruitful in exploring contradictions in the data.

The changes to the study's conceptual focus and fieldwork methods had far-reaching consequences in terms of time and money since we were committed to interviewing the mothers at four points over their first three years of motherhood. (We later decided at waves three and four to do a structured interview with those women who were no longer employed full-time and the complete two-and-a-half-hour interview with the 66 women who were still in full-time employment.) Moreover, with the changes to the fieldwork method, it was necessary to train the research team in a wholly different interviewing approach that required a high level of commitment, flexibility, concentration and listening skills. The fieldworkers had to be trained to code the data and transcribe responses by hand on to the interview schedules. This meant taking account of the research concepts, which were referenced on the interview schedule in relation to each interview question. It also meant cross-referencing different parts of the transcription where the material referred to concepts which were not explicitly linked to a particular interview question. Since this is a classic scenario for coder error (Crittenden and Hill, 1971), a great deal of time was devoted by the senior members of the research team to checking the transcribed material, coding and cross-referencing.

In this study, the context of enquiry (Kaplan, 1964) or data collection phase involved quantitative and qualitative approaches to be integrated into the investigation via a single research instrument. In the data analysis phase, we analysed the quantitative material (N = 255 at four waves) and we carried out qualitative analysis of the transcribed material for a subset of the sample (n = 70 women at three waves).

While different types of data had different benefits, in the context of justification (Kaplan, 1964) – the analysis stage of the inquiry – we sought to bring them together. In writing up the research both data analyses were given similar weight and both types of data analysis proceeded in parallel. In some instances the different types of data addressed a particular set of research questions and in others the two datasets were combined to address different questions. Detailed quantitative analysis of mothers' employment histories showed considerable change. Comparing their occupations before and after childbirth, nearly one quarter of women were downwardly mobile (within or between jobs) – with the majority staying at the same level. Most of the downwardly mobile resigned prior to the birth or after returning from maternity leave. Where they found new jobs, over half moved into sales or manual work with fewer hours and lower pay. Only those who were continuously employed full-time were upwardly mobile but, while staying with the same employer after childbirth increased women's promotion chances, few had long-term career plans in the event of having a second child, for example.

The qualitative data enabled us to identify the particular conditions under which upward or downward mobility occurred. The reasons for downward mobility *between* jobs included: the needs of children, the long time spent in travelling to work, and the need to find a different job locally because of changes in husbands' employment. Requests for hours reduction *within* jobs typically automatically entailed demotion; some said they felt under pressure to reduce their hours, for example, because of being unavailable to do overtime. The qualitative data fleshed out and added to the quantitative data in ways we did not anticipate. It became clear, for example, that the decision to go back to work after maternity leave was a mother's own decision and not a couple or household decision. Moreover, the group of mothers who did not return to work after maternity leave did not regard giving up their jobs at childbirth as decisions; they simply accepted that this was the 'normal thing to do'.

The qualitative data also offered insight into the significance of mothers' financial contributions from their employment. Mothers engaged in a mental accounting exercise, estimating whether the cost of working was 'worth their while'. This cost–benefit exercise was based on the assumption that the child and childcare arrangements were primarily their responsibilities. When mothers went back to work they mentally 'earmarked' their income for childcare costs and 'extras'. This had the effect of marginalising their financial contributions to the household, even though they contributed significantly to many essential items of household expenditure, rendering them secondary earners. Had we not employed open-ended questions, involving probing and follow-up questions, such insights would have been lost (Brannen and Moss, 1991: 19).

A further way of integrating the quantitative and qualitative data was to explore contradictions between women's responses to different questions. One example of this related to women's satisfaction with partners' contributions to housework and childcare that was tapped via direct questions that we coded. These coded responses were compared with women's narratives of childrearing and everyday life. For example, asked directly if they were satisfied with their husbands' contribution to housework, women were more likely to give positive, albeit qualified, answers. But, in giving accounts of particular experiences and situations, they were less positive. These conflicting accounts raise important methodological questions concerning how questions are asked. We wrote:

> Examination of the qualitative analysis of women's comments suggested a more complex conclusion. In many cases a good deal of criticism or ambivalence was expressed, especially when women recounted particular incidents. Critical comments, however, were often retracted or qualified in response to direct global questions concerning satisfaction with husbands' participation ... the strategy adopted was to examine the contexts in which women's responses were located, together with a content analysis of responses. In this way the contradictions were confronted,

and the processes identified by which dissatisfaction was underplayed or explained away. (Brannen and Moss, 1991: 20)

The Daycare study highlighted the problems as well as the advantages of working both quantitatively and quantitatively. Tensions arose between competing theoretical interests and around the allocation of resources. There was a tension between carrying out an analysis across a large number of cases and an in-depth analysis of a smaller set of cases. This tension is particularly difficult to manage in a longitudinal study, with several contact points as well as a large number of substantive issues to be addressed, and the requirement of repeating the same questions over time. We were aware that more analytical work might have been done to understand how, in particular cases and subgroups in the study, different dimensions came together in particular ways (Platt, 1988). Such an approach would have required a process of analytic induction (Bryman, 2001). Ideally, such case-by-case analysis proceeds during fieldwork and not *post hoc* (Lindesmith, 1947). In this particular investigation, to have proceeded along a path of analytic induction in which theory is developed and refined case by case was not possible. For one thing, a large amount of funding had been invested in achieving a large sample over several time points so that we were committed to quantitative analysis and explaining outcomes, for example relating to children's development and mothers' well-being. The tensions between the different levels and types of analysis had to be managed in the analysis phase and the result was inevitably a compromise.

These ways of combining qualitative and quantitative data within one fieldwork instrument were unusual. Moreover, in today's marketised research world, with tightly specified research contracts and considerable demands upon researchers to meet users' requirements, such an evolutionary research strategy is unlikely to be funded. It happened under particular conditions: in a period when funding was less market driven and when it was possible for researchers to have more control over the nature and direction of their research, and in a particular research environment that supported long-term team research (Chapter 2). It happened in a particular kind of investigation, in which particular ideological orthodoxies concerning the appropriate care for children and actions of mothers were influential and which undoubtedly contributed to the reasons why the research was funded (in the late 1970s) in the first place! However, in many ways the project was ahead of its time. The return of mothers to the labour market did not escalate until the end of the 1980s, after the project ended and before the topic of mothers' employment was widely discussed. The project took place among a particular group of researchers at a particular point in their research careers and with a particular interdisciplinary mix of sociology, social policy and psychology.

Combining approaches in this context was generative. Intellectually it was challenging because it brought together different perspectives and disciplines. The project's research strategy was unusual at the time but presaged the growth of 'mixed methods'. It expanded the skills and competencies of researchers in both data collection and data analysis, bringing out the best of both approaches as well as tensions between them. It highlighted the importance of spelling out the concepts that undergirded the study and the taken-for-granted assumptions that we as human beings brought to it. It underlined the importance of posing both exacting and open-ended questions to research participants, notably in respect of issues to which we sought specific answers. But it also counselled us against the risks of precision for its own sake (Sell, 2000).

Work–family issues and the changing world of work

Over the 1990s and 2000s a culture of self-reliance and individualism prevailed in Britain, with priority given to profit and economic prosperity. With the rise of the New Right under Thatcher, the upbringing of children was construed as a non-gendered practice, a consumer preference and a moral responsibility (Brannen, 1992). Lone motherhood was targeted and regulated (Duncan and Edwards, 1999). Parental responsibility was enshrined in a range of social policy domains: the labour market, childrearing, children's education, and support for young people (Edwards and Gilles, 2011).

The nuclear family consisting of two parents, a full-time at-home mother and a breadwinner father was becoming less and less representative of British society (Crompton, 1999). Changed circumstances required new public discourses. As Lewis (2002) argues, a discursive shift took place from male breadwinning to individual contractualism. While the language of the New Labour government (1997–2010) in its programme A New Deal for Lone Parents was about 'helping' lone mothers into work, in practice, it aimed to reduce the numbers on benefits. Government was less concerned with the quality of the jobs that mothers were being encouraged to fill, although it did invest heavily in children's centres and in tax credits for working parents, with the result that the probability of being on a relatively low income declined for working-age adults with children.

From the time of entry into the EU in 1973, the EU played a key role in limiting some of the damage done to employment conditions and employment protection by government's pursuit of neoliberal policies. However, British people's attitudes to the EU appear to have discounted this, as evidenced in the result of the 2016 referendum that resulted in a majority of the population voting in favour of withdrawal. The 'reconciliation of work and family life' and equal opportunities appeared on the EU agenda in the 1990s. Through the EU's treaty provisions and directives important protection was afforded concerning health and safety at work and equality in the workplace. Although the UK had its own laws in these areas, EU action extended workers' rights, making it more difficult for UK governments to undermine them unilaterally. In some cases laws that resulted directly from EU directives are now well accepted in Britain, for example, around sexual orientation, age, and religious discrimination. But other rights would have been difficult to secure and will be particularly vulnerable to attack if and when the UK leaves the EU. For example, UK governments have consistently resisted equal treatment rights for agency workers, working-time limits, and rights for workers to receive information and be consulted on changes in the workplace that affect their jobs and terms and conditions.

On the one hand, EU measures were underpinned by the EU's aim to promote economic prosperity and competitiveness (Walby, 1999; Hantrais, 2004). On the other, they were further stimulated by the recognition that ageing workforces and the diversification of families have major consequences for the sustainability of pensions, care and health services. In the 1990s the EU was concerned that the potential for labour supply was not being used to full effect because younger and older workers, and women of working age, were not participating in the labour market to their full capacity (Rubery et al, 1999). However, while the EU's employment strategy focused on access to training and conditions governing employment, it was left largely to national governments to introduce their own legislation on these and related matters (Hantrais, 2004: 101).

In the late 1990s the nature of work was continuing to change. Whole industries were being exported to Asia and product and service markets were increasingly internationalised, leading to rapid changes in the private sector. In the public sector, employment contracts were being flexibilised bringing increased job insecurity. Public services were being outsourced and permanent employment contracts in the public sector were increasingly rare. In addition, workers experienced workload intensification and feelings of time pressure (Brannen and Moss, 1998; Esping-Andersen et al, 2002). These experiences were no longer confined to those on piece rates and assembly lines but became common among those in non-manual employment. This period was also marked by longer working hours in some jobs and among some groups of workers, notably fathers (O'Brien and Shemilt, 2003).

Against this backcloth of rapid economic and social change the research literature on the work–family interface grew. In the US, scholarship on work and family topics, initially narrowly focused on 'working mothers' (Perry-Jenkins et al, 2000), expanded in scope and coverage during the 2000 to 2010 decade. In Britain, social scientists paid increasing attention to 'work–family' issues, later to be reframed as 'work–life' issues. Attention was also paid to the gendered segregation of the labour market, in particular women's concentration in particular sectors and lower level occupations. In the 2000s the implications of workplace change for mothers and fathers began to surface.

A case study of workplace change and family life

In order to deepen understanding of these changes we turned our attention to the workplace. In 2000 we carried out a study of banking that was small scale and exploratory (Brannen et al, 2001). The study was funded by the Tedworth Trust with the cooperation of two banks. It aimed to capture changes taking place in banking and the ways they affected the experience of work and family life.

The study's theoretical underpinnings focused on tensions between the short termism in the 'new capitalism' (Sennett, 1998) and the longer term vision and commitment required in family life (Sevenhuijsen, 1999) and the negotiation of work–family boundaries. In undertaking this project we did not appreciate just much how the study of changes in the banking world anticipated the financialisation of the British economy and the unravelling of capitalism that took place later in the decade. The workplace where the TCRU team members (Peter Moss and myself) did field work was a telephony department in a bank's call centre in the south east.[2] The banking industry was undergoing major change with the result that the physical location of staff and face-to-face contact ceased to play a part in bank–customer relationships. Both management and employees regarded change as inevitable but also relentless and out of control. While work was experienced as stressful and intense, employees valued the sense of personal autonomy provided by management's techniques of self-regulation. Against this the old values of trust, service, solidarity and continuity that characterised old-style banking were undermined by the lack of job security and the new emphasis on 'selling' that conflicted with the ethos of customer 'service'.

Focus groups were conducted in the workplace and some managers and supervisors interviewed. As focus group moderators we encouraged participants to reflect on different aspects of their work and to consider how they impacted upon their lives outside work. To some extent this line of questioning worked well although, given the workplace setting, the focus was more on work than family life.

The focus groups also provided a sampling frame for selecting a small number of employees with family responsibilities. Separate home-based interviews were carried out with employees and their partners. At the beginning of the interview research participants were invited to talk about their lives and to give a 'moment by moment' account of a recent working day, focusing on the content and structure of the day, social interactions, and feelings and reflections at transitional moments in the day, particularly in crossing physical and mental boundaries between home and work. Work intensification was major theme of both the focus groups and the interviews. To manage this some employees suggested they blurred the boundaries between work and her family life while others imposed strict boundaries.

The following is an emblematic case of a woman who experiences work intensification and who finds it difficult to manage to impose boundaries around work (Brannen, 2005a). Although only one case it speaks to a larger story of the effects of social and economic change, but also to continuities in employees' lack of control over their time: how in a seemingly self-regulating workplace the worker is expected to meet time-related targets. Such targets are not new, as E.P. Thompson (1967) described in 'Time, work-discipline and industrial capitalism'. Early modern agricultural labourers were expected to meet time-related targets in mowing fields irrespective of the type of terrain they were required to work and, in this context, time no longer 'passed' but was 'spent'.

> Those who are employed experience a distinction between their employers' time and their 'own' time. And the employer must *use* the time of his labour, and see it is not wasted: not the task but the value of time when reduced to money is dominant. Time is now currency: it is not passed but spent. (Thompson, 1967: 43)[3]

JJ was in her late 40s, married to a sales director. She and her husband had two daughters, one of whom was still living at home. As an only child, JJ had responsibility for her frail elderly mother who lived nearby and whom JJ visited and cared for most days. JJ was a call centre supervisor in a bank. She had seen many changes in banking: the disappearance of the old protective paternalism of the bank manager; the demise of 'jobs for life'; the replacement of the ethic of service with the ethic of sales; the introduction of individual responsibility for staying employable. JJ thought her employer better than most. She readily took responsibility for keeping up to date with changes: "these days there is so much to know". At interview she was doing a 30-session course in the evenings at the same college as her daughter. Her promotion to supervisor occurred at the time when the bank was under pressure to retain a competitive edge and to engage in cost cutting. Whole tiers of management had been removed and target times for answering calls at the call centre were constantly being reset – down to two minutes per call.

JJ described her daily life as a constant state of busyness – at work and in fulfilling her family responsibilities. Her account has many of the qualities of the 'extended present' (Nowotny, 1994) – a sense of busyness combined with a feeling of autonomy. Yet JJ often felt that her life was "out of control". At the start of her day, JJ said she was already 'mentally at work' as well as attending to domestic matters. At work JJ had to answer calls from the public as well as supervise her team's performance. Such was the pace of the day she forgot to take breaks, ignored lunchtime, and even put off going to the loo. Yet despite the pressure JJ still took charge of collections for colleagues when they left the bank. In taking on this extra work, JJ sought to inject a sense of care and community that had once typified the everyday rhythm of the bank. Most nights, JJ stayed late at work. When she got home she cooked supper, did some housework and then visited her mother. Often she swotted up on work manuals and memos because she had no time to do this at work. JJ took these manuals home each night in a large box, a symbol of the close connection JJ forged between home and her job. JJ's husband was also work driven.

In effect, JJ's experience of time was subject to intensification both at home and work, even though there was no overt means of controlling what she did. Moreover, work and care flowed across the boundaries into both settings. JJ's expectations of time exceeded what was realistically possible to do (Nowotny, 1994). In this case, the boundaries between work and family life were weakly drawn. Work and care were experienced as compulsion in both contexts as emanating from the *self* rather than from the bank. Significantly, JJ blamed *herself* for not managing her time better. This internalisation of control was rooted in the invisible structures by which the organisation exercised power over its employees' time and disconnected them from a collective experience of time: through the practices of human resource management and a set of techniques that depended upon communication rather than bureaucratic authority. The 'new bank' seduced employees like JJ by giving them the feeling of job autonomy – JJ could decide within limits how to manage her time and how to organise her different work tasks. This feeling appealed to JJ and generated commitment to her job that in turn created a sense of self-actualisation (Rose, 1990). But JJ had little real power. The call centre's senior management retained control centrally, chiefly through the call-time targets that it was JJ's job to ensure her team adhered to.

While JJ felt fulfilled in her work, she also felt driven, experiencing time as "stretched out". JJ was caught in a present crammed "full to the brim" and where the job seemed never done. So much so that JJ felt she had no proper "family time". Significantly, the work–life and family-friendly policies, which the bank advertised, played little part in enabling JJ to meet her caring responsibilities. Seduced by her busyness, JJ found it difficult to think about the future or take time off. JJ's ability to envisage a different way of organising her work and family life or to think about leaving her job was impaired by the experience of an individualised, demanding, and multifaceted present (Daly, 1996). In this context the sense of control over her work and the feeling of being increasingly dominated by it are not so paradoxical.

In its focus upon an individual's experience of time the case suggests some of the linkages between biography and the wider historical context (Mills, 1980 [1959]), especially seen from the present vantage point of the crisis of capitalism. It also speaks to the experience of time in 'work-busy' households (Daly, 1996). As Bauman (1998) wrote, those in the 'work world' live *in* time while space matters little to them. By contrast, those in the workless world live *in space*; in their time 'nothing ever happens' and space dominates time. For if you are poor you must choose cheaper modes of transport, for example, that cost less precisely because saving time is less relevant and being on time does not need to be guaranteed. In work-rich households, lives are driven by Marx's notion of 'time as commodity' with an economic price aimed at the production of profit and efficiency (Daly, 1996).

On the other hand, those who manage family life, whether they live in work-rich or work-poor households, are expected to live according to the 'moral economy of time' in the belief that their time ought to be given freely to family members; ought not be costed or measured; and should be driven by the rhythms relating to care and the needs and expectations of family members. 'Family time' and 'quality time' are today's symbols of a 'proper' family life, but are contingent largely on the contributions of *women*. Whether this notion of family time existed in the past is debatable (Gilles, 1996). Even so, family time carries connotations of process rather than commodity; for social interaction *is* the purpose and outcome of spending time with family members and is not simply a means to an instrumental end. Yet commodity time – what Daly (1996) calls 'a new kind of impatience' seems to be gaining the upper hand.

The gendered assumptions that underlie the allocation of responsibilities for family life also underlie workplace family-friendly policies; it is women who are expected to make compromises concerning 'work–life balance' (Lewis et al, 2009). While the term 'balance' suggests an equal time division between paid work and life outside the job, it also assumes a settled accommodation (Taylor, 2001) which is in practice ephemeral or unsustainable. Family commitments require different time frames compared with those of workplaces. In family life, commitments persist over whole phases of the life course and involve long-term relationships. They also require flexibility when family crises occur. In modern flexible organisations capitalism demands short-term financial gain that instils similarly short-term commitment from the workforce.

Gender, parenthood and the changing European workplace

As described earlier, in the Daycare study we looked for inspirational models for combining childcare and paid employment, in particular focusing on the Scandinavian countries. In the early 1990s Peter Moss and I did a small piece of work on gender equity in dual earner households with young children in Sweden (funded by the Ford Foundation) where, with the assistance of Swedish colleagues, we interviewed key officials in the Swedish government on gender equity issues and a number of families where both parents had taken parental leave. By the end of the 1990s, larger funding opportunities were opening up for European research. The EU was becoming a significant source of funding and had a strong policy interest in the matters to do with gender equity and what was termed the 'reconciliation of employment and family life'. The EU's aim in setting up its 'Framework funding' was also to create collaborative research teams that would develop researcher capacity across the countries of Europe as well as identifying key priority areas of EU policy for research. Because of the dominance of the English language, this funding meant that those with English as their first language had a significant advantage in writing research bids and in becoming project coordinators. UK researchers had moreover a flying start over their continental counterparts: they were used to the pressures from government and other funders for research to be 'useful' and policy relevant. Policy relevance was also a key element required in writing a successful EU research bid.

In the 1980s I was in contact with Professor Suzan Lewis at Manchester Metropolitan University who had carried out a study of dual-career families and had similar interests to my own in the work–family field. In the late 1990s we identified funds to organise a couple of meetings around our mutual interests and decided to seek further funding for an international project. In our first research collaboration we identified an issue in the work–family field that had not been explored: namely to examine how young people considered their futures as workers and parents. The time for such a study seemed ripe: considerable changes in employment for young people (growing job insecurity in particular); demographic change (fewer young people relative to elderly people in the population); the extension of the youth phase (through prolonged periods in education); and the closure of the gender gap in education (Brannen et al, 2002). We were successful in gaining funds from the EU's Directorate in Employment and Social Affairs (DGV). In its focus on young people, the project was ahead of its time, signalling what proved to be a current and increasingly problematic trend in many European societies. It prefigured the ongoing uncertainty that accompanies the social transitions of many young people today in terms of finding jobs commensurate with their qualifications; the difficulty of getting on to housing ladders; and hence the implications of these trends for embarking on parenthood.

The project on young people's futures in work and family life involved five countries. It became a launch pad for a later ambitious large cross-national collaboration, this time to investigate the experiences of working parents across Europe. In 2002, under the EU's Framework 5, we gained a grant for a large cross-national study that involved the UK, Norway, Sweden, Portugal, Slovenia, Bulgaria and France (Lewis et al, 2009; Nilsen et al, 2012). (Slovenia joined the EU in 2004 and Bulgaria in 2007 while Norway is not part of the EU but is permitted to take part in EU-funded research.) The study set out to compare the experiences of mothers and fathers in six of these countries as they combined paid work with responsibilities for young children. The title of the project was Gender, Parenthood and the Changing European Workplace (known as Transitions). Suzan Lewis coordinated the project, assisted by Janet Smithson, and I took the lead in methodological matters. We employed what we rather grandly termed an 'embedded contextual design'. Like a Russian doll the project encompassed different layers of data collection methods and analysis – one embedded in the other. The outer shell of the doll included mapping the national demographic trends and policies, examining public discourses on work–family matters and conducting literature reviews of the topic in each country. The second shell was to select the same two organisations in each country (social services and finance companies) and to study their policies, practices and cultures in relation to 'family friendliness' as seen from employees' and managers' perspectives. Focus groups were conducted with employees who were parents while interviews were carried out with managers at different levels. The third shell involved the selection of samples of working parents (mothers and fathers), matched by organisation, occupation, gender and marital status. In this phase of the project we adopted a biographical perspective to understand the ways in which employment and family responsibilities were organised over the life course. We also examined the sources of support available to parents – both formal and informal, and how supported they felt. While both the organisations and individual mothers and fathers were matched across countries, the countries inevitably differed in terms of their welfare regimes and histories.

The process of finding colleagues to collaborate with on the project was organic. Partnerships grew out relationships already forged, especially those in the earlier cross-national study on young people. They were not marriages of convenience. However, the EU required a particular mix of countries, including from east, west and southern Europe. But as we moved from one international project to the next we learned the value of putting in bids with those with whom we had already tried and tested relationships. Comparative research has its particular challenges, not least of which is managing and working in a large team with little face-to-face contact for much of the time.

The Transitions team encompassed different research traditions, theoretical perspectives, interests and expertise. The types of setting in which the members worked also varied; from university departments in which some tenured academics had teaching responsibilities to those non-tenured researchers employed in research institutes and who were used to team working. Some junior team members were on Master's and postdoctoral programmes. Such differences within the cross-national teams influenced expectations concerning contributions to publications from the study. In cross-national teams it is rare to be able to match the expertise of researchers. Therefore, training had to be provided for those unfamiliar with a particular methodology. Under EU funding rules, the teams' access to financial resources varied according to the position of their respective countries on the European index of economic prosperity. This created funding disparities and therefore further inequity across the team. In addition, researchers were differently supported by their own institutions/departments in the respective countries, again another potential source of tension and difference (Lewis and Brannen, 2011).

Comparative research necessitates rigour and transparency, requiring careful justification of choice of countries, organisations and individuals, matching like with like and specifying the limitations to case comparability. For example, in selecting cases of working parents, criteria were set concerning workplace, occupation, gender and marital status. However, in some organisations, it was difficult to find people working in the same jobs. In some workplaces and countries there were few lone mothers (Brannen and Nilsen, 2011).

A key objective was to find ways of integrating the different 'levels' or layers of data that were collected (Brannen and Nilsen, 2011). Comparisons were made at different levels. In comparing Bulgarian social services with Swedish social services, for example, account was taken of the different societal contexts. Bulgarian social services – set up after the fall of state socialism – have a relatively short history as unemployment rose under capitalism. The quality of its public childcare services that existed before the fall of state socialism was poor and the hours inflexible. However, as part of the state sector it attracted considerable employment security (in contrast to the private sector) with the result that recruitment and turnover of staff was not an issue in Bulgaria. Employees were, however, much less highly qualified and much lower paid compared with those in the Swedish social services. Bulgarian social services complied with the state legislation on parental leave and leave for sick children for its staff, although mothers had no entitlement to part-time or flexible working (Kovacheva, 2009). Swedish social services afforded their employees the generous policies of the state's parental leave scheme and its high-quality childcare services. However, unlike in Bulgaria, employees were required, and trusted, to sort out their clashes between work and family with their managers and their team members (Plantin and Back-Wiklund, 2009).

In the analysis of the individual-level data, we took account of the organisational and national contexts. One reason why these data were so important was that parents did not always refer to the structural conditions of their lives in their interviews. In analysing the interviews we also drew upon other team members to eliminate any blind spots or taken-for-granted assumptions concerning interpretations both of our own data and those of other countries. By bringing together all the levels of data sources we were able to examine the different types of support working parents drew upon, and the ways in which mothers and fathers exercised agency in the context of the opportunity structures available – structural, institutional and informal (Brannen and Sadar Černigoj, 2012; Nilsen et al, 2012).

A central feature of a comparative approach is that cases are conceptualised as 'cases of something' (Hammersley et al, 2000) and that it permits theoretical extrapolation. For example, it can show, 'how different causes combine in complex and sometimes contradictory ways to produce different outcomes' (Ragin, 1994: 138). Case-based research can generate explanations for social phenomena in relation to hypothesised sets of conditions; thus what holds for a particular case in a particular context and location may *not* be generalised to a country but may hold for a similar case in a similar context or set of circumstances (Brannen, 2005b: 2).

Through thick descriptions of the individual cases, and analysis of the organisations and the national data, we were able to tease out the specificities of the resources available to particular parents (or not) – public policy, workplace policy and practice, family and kinship networks. We thereby identified differences and similarities in the support available to the matched cases of parents. While we did not seek to address 'outcomes' as such in a systematic way, the material provided insight into how particular parents evaluated the support available to them and their sense of well-being, as well as indicating the different combinations of support in each case. Depending on the country, public policy provision concerning paid parental leave and leave for sick children were important to some parents/ mothers together with affordable flexible childcare. Workplace policies, cultures and practices were significant in some contexts, though they did not appear to be 'sufficient causes' in the sense of helping parents to feel supported. In other cases and contexts, childcare provision and domestic support from the child's father, the availability of intergenerational family help and decent (affordable) housing were critical. However, which of these conditions, and in which combination, made a difference depended on the context and the individual case. The difference these resources made to women's lives also varied according to how they valued them, for example, how they saw their lot in comparison to that of their peers. The following cases of a Bulgarian mother and a Swedish mother will, I hope, demonstrate some of the value of comparative case analysis of this kind.

Rosa (aged 24) lived in Bulgaria, the poorest country in the EU at the time. Rosa worked in social services and, like others in social services in her occupation, she had no formal qualifications. Rosa and her husband lived with her in-laws. After her baby was born she had a great deal of childcare assistance from them and from her own mother. Rosa saw it as "normal" to take the full two years of paid parental leave available: 135 days at 90 per cent of salary and the remainder of the two years at a flat rate. Rosa was convinced by her family that returning to her old job (there were no part-time options) in social assistance at the end of maternity leave was best because a public sector job offered security and very reasonable working hours. When her daughter was ill, Rosa was allowed to stay off work without problems because of the sick leave policies. When Rosa's daughter was three, Rosa also depended upon affordable local daycare provided by the state (for children aged three to seven years), even though the quality was not high and the hours inflexible. Unsurprisingly, Rosa felt herself "lucky" to have a job in a country with a high unemployment rate; she compared herself favourably to many young people she knew, especially those who were migrating for economic reasons. She also felt fortunate in having a healthy child, an emotionally supportive partner, and generous parents on both sides. In general, Rosa found her work and workplace conducive. Her work did not impinge on Rosa's home life and Rosa had low expectations of promotion (there were few opportunities), which in turn supported her decision to take the full amount of the extensive parental and child sickness leave then available. Unsurprisingly, Rosa described herself as happy with her lot.

We can compare Rosa with her counterpart, Susanne, who lived in Sweden and see the ways in which Susanne was supported in a country with a higher standard of living and very good conditions for childcare and parental leave. Susanne (aged 28) worked as a care worker in a centre for people with disabilities, work that she enjoyed greatly. Susanne, rather atypically for a Swede, did not go on to further education and got married aged 20 to have children. Her son started attending the high-quality, affordable public daycare that was near their home when he was 18 months old. Susanne and her husband shared the long period of paid parental leave: "We were very poor during that time but it was worth it. That's why I could stay home for nine months and my husband seven months." This way of extending and sharing parental leave is increasingly common in Sweden. Susanne and her husband had no parents living close by to provide additional support, something she regretted. She also lived far from the city where she worked, which added to the length of her working day. Because the couple had recently moved to a new area they had few friends in the neighbourhood to help with babysitting.

However, in terms of support, Susanne was fortunate. Her husband took their son to, and collected him from, daycare. The couple also shared the household work fairly, with Susanne conscious of how rare this was, even among Swedish couples. She also suggested that becoming a mother had improved her relationship with her partner. Under Swedish law, Susanne was entitled to reduce her hours on her return to work, which diminished the time pressures on the family. Susanne worked four days a week, having a day off in the middle of the week. She also negotiated informal arrangements with her flexible manager, who allowed Susanne time off when needed and to leave work 15 minutes early each day and to arrive 30 minutes later than her colleagues *without* a reduction in wages. This enabled Susanne to catch a train without having to wait a long time for the next train. Therefore Susanne felt highly committed to her work colleagues and clients, and kept strictly to this arrangement, and, because she was a frontline carer, she placed clear boundaries around her job, leaving it behind when she went home. Conversely, Susanne's enjoyment of motherhood helped her, she said, to empathise with her clients. In order to manage competing time pressures and to distinguish between work time and family time, she created "special times" to be with her son. Yet she still felt she spent insufficient time with him and regretted putting him into daycare so young, something they had to do because of the need for two salaries.

The cross-national research design and the use of a comparative approach enabled us to situate the two cases of working mothers in the context of public policies in their countries, with their contrasting national living standards and in the mothers' workplaces. Rosa in Bulgaria was less materially advantaged than Susanne in Sweden, where work in social services was much better remunerated and daycare of much higher quality. Employment practices were also particularly supportive and adaptable in Susanne's case. In Rosa's situation part-time or flexible working was not possible. While we see similarities in terms of informal support – considerable parental support was available to Rosa and a supportive husband in Susanne's case – the ways in which the two mothers valued the support available to them differed. Susanne set store by gender equity in her marriage while Rosa was grateful for an emotionally supportive husband, reflecting wider but differing discourses concerning gender relations in their countries.

Unlike Susanne, Rosa did not aspire to a gender equal partnership but was comforted in the availability of her mother and mother-in-law to care for her young child. Susanne regretted the absence of local kin and friends and, unlike Rosa, wished she had not returned to work so early despite shared parental leave. Rosa counted herself "lucky" in a society where economic migration and unemployment were high.

Carrying out this study brought home to us the importance of avoiding the trap of focusing on the 'national' aspects alone in making cross-national comparisons. The advantage of an embedded case approach is that it offers insight into the specificities of people's lives, cultures and contexts. The organisational case studies demonstrated how workplace and public policies worked in particular contexts for particular sectors, occupational groups and genders. The individual interviews showed the range of support available (or not) to mothers and fathers in the particular conditions in which they found themselves. The biographical approach highlighted the importance of adopting a temporal frame to understanding mothers' and fathers' trajectories, extending understandings of the changing institutional and historical contexts in which their lives were embedded. Together these layers of analysis helped to explain why and how parents valued and experienced their situations.

Conclusion

This chapter has suggested that the research issues we study need to be historicised. It has set the research questions concerning the place of mothers in the labour market in Britain in the history of the period – from 1945 to the present. It has argued that public policy concerning the care of children and the work patterns of their parents – or rather mothers – has shifted from a moral discourse about the 'need' for mothers to stay at home with their young children to a neoliberal discourse in which the state has shed its post-war responsibilities for the welfare of parents and children and, increasingly, left them to the vagaries of the labour market. The chapter has shown that these issues play out differently in different contexts; for example, in Sweden from the 1970s women were encouraged to remain in the labour market following childbirth and parents and children were provided with high-quality, affordable state-funded childcare.

Empirical social science captures moments in history and takes a particular slant on the world. The three studies discussed cover different periods and differently framed issues. The first focused on 'working mothers' in the 1980s who were expected to give up work to have children and, if they returned to the labour market (usually when their children started school), to be secondary earners to men. The second study, conducted in 2000, a period of neoliberalism and globalisation, focused on the rapid changes taking place in the workplace: the changing nature of work, and the subjection of workforces to increasing work intensification. At the same time, the discourse of 'work–life balance' came into vogue among employers and in public policy, introducing practices whereby workers were expected to take responsibility for their own work–life 'choices'. While employers appeared to offer employees 'flexibility' to determine their hours and patterns of work, in practice this meant hiring workers on the employers' own terms. Further, while 'work–family' and 'work–life' policies were framed as non-gendered, they were targeted at mothers and, more often than not, the policies did not amount to a great deal for those seeking to fulfil their responsibilities to their children.

The third study, carried out in 2002 to 2005, took a European perspective. It set out to examine whether general trends in the world of work spanned the same types of public and private sector organisations in several EU countries, and how far they were moderated by different welfare regimes for working parents. More specifically, it examined the experiences of mothers and fathers employed in similar organisations and in similar occupational statuses in different countries as they sought to manage their family responsibilities. In adopting a comparative approach, the study was able to capture the variety and combination of formal and informal resources that were available to working mothers and fathers, not only from their employers and the state but also their families, friends, and neighbours. As demonstrated in the comparison of Rosa and Susanne, the approach shows the resource mix for particular individuals in particular contexts and the consequences for how supported they felt. The study speaks not only to how parents negotiate their work and family responsibilities but also to some of the changes taking place in the intimate spaces of family life (see McCarthy, 2017).

Another way of reviewing these studies is through the lens of time. The period that these studies have covered suggests the ways in which mothers' biographical time has changed as increasingly women have maintained continuity in the workforce. But the studies also point to changes in the experience of time. When women assumed they would stop work to have children this was a collective experience, albeit often taken for granted. In the 'new' discourse of individualisation, women are required to see their own time, biographical time and work time, as matters for each person to determine (Hochschild, 1997). However, this apparent change hides underlying continuities. While globalisation and economic change affect how people work and live their lives outside work, they also represent continuities in the way capitalism has long transformed the passing of time into commodity time.

4

Inside the Household

The topic of this chapter is the household. It begins with a focus on women: how they were consigned to the home and how their status and power over household resources have been historically shaped by men. As I described in the last chapter, during the Second World War many women had taken the place of men in the workplace. As Elizabeth Wilson (1980: 26) contends in *Halfway to paradise* 'the housewife was the heroic figure of the Second World War and additionally so because she was often a worker as well'. However, while women had achieved a degree of emancipation and the role of housewife a degree of status and importance previously lacking, the return of male servicemen to their homes and communities following the end of the war raised policy issues on several fronts. A number of needs had to be met: servicemen had to be found work and the demographic decline needed reversing, requiring women to be child bearers and homemakers. Furthermore, the lack of domestic servants during the war meant that the middle classes began to experience the drudgery of housework and there were a variety of demands throughout the political system for support for housewives including community services, state financial support and a Housewife's Charter (Wilson, 1980: 21–3). Beveridge and other policy makers turned their attention to these, often competing, policy demands. But ultimately the sexual division of labour in the household was not questioned; so men remained the main breadwinners and the principle prevailed that first and foremost women should devote themselves to their families and be dependent on men's earnings.

The 1950s saw no resolution to the problem of women's financial dependence on men. Indeed, housekeeping money was 'the dark secret in the family' (Zweig, 1952). In the early 1950s, Michael Young (cited in Wilson, 1980) noted that full employment and inflation led to a loss of real income for housewives. He further noted men's failure to increase their wives' housekeeping when an extra child was born into a poor family (Wilson, 1980). This resulted in greater financial burden *not* on the household as a whole but on the mother and her other children (Wilson, 1980: 31). In this context public provision such as school meals, the National Health Service, and food subsidies were important in helping to reduce the effects of housewives' lack of and reductions in real income. In the 1970s, with the rise of the Women's Movement and the growing numbers of women in the labour market, housewives and housework were again on the public agenda. The unfairness of the unequal distribution of domestic work began to be recognised and housework understood as a form of labour (Oakley, 1974). When Family Allowances were first introduced in 1946 this had produced fierce debate in the House of Commons as to which partner in a marriage should be paid the allowance. Eleanor Rathbone MP eventually carried the day in mothers' favour. In the late 1980s, just after the start of Margaret Thatcher's third term in government as prime minister, the Family Allowance was again a matter of public contention. Child Benefit, as it was renamed in 1975, was made available for each child in a household. But under the 1988 'Fowler reforms' this universal benefit was frozen. For families with low earnings a means-tested benefit for children was introduced, named Family Credit, and made more generous. This policy change had the effect of taking money away from the control of mothers because it was paid to the earner (Glennerster et al, 2004). The journalist Polly Toynbee was quick to recognise this and, in an article in *The Guardian* in 1987, she wrote:

> When people talk of the redistribution of money and power in society, they concentrate almost exclusively on the broad class bands.... There are studies of poverty and relative poverty. Incomes are compared, benchmarks for family poverty are set – and disputed. But most such studies stop short at the door of the household.... Now a new book prises open the front door of the family, and examines what happens within. (Toynbee, 1987)

The book in question that sought to open the 'black box' of the household was *Give and take in families* (Brannen and Wilson, 1987). Up till then, social science research, most of it statistical, had treated the family/household as a unitary concept and assumed that all its members shared equally in the same standard of living (Arber, 1993). Attention now increasingly focused on the household as a more precise way of looking at families but without the normative connotations of families as consisting of two married parents and children. From the 1970s there was a major conceptual shift in the social sciences as feminist researchers deconstructed the 'family' in order to counteract dominant discourses surrounding a single family form as both desirable and the norm (for example, Barrett and McIntosh, 1982). In this process households in all their variety began to be identified in the context of rising rates of lone motherhood and step-families. Moral diktats surrounding the normative model of 'the family' were being destabilised, although new family forms were not necessarily seen as having equal merit in the mass media and government policy.

Resources in households

In the 1980s women's responsibilities for, and contributions to, family life began to be made more visible. As part of the refocusing of debates around gender inequalities within the household, in 1982 Gail Wilson and I set up a research network at the Institute of Education that we called the Resources in Households Group: the group was funded at various times by the ESRC. One aim was to bring together researchers with diverse interests and theoretical concerns to focus on the distribution of power and other resources *within* households. As we wrote in 1987, in order to understand the processes by which resources enter and are distributed within households it is necessary to trace their different sources – employment, the state, kin and communities (Brannen and Wilson, 1987). This involved examining how cultural, economic and institutional structures, and the interplay between these, shaped resource distribution inside households. The resources we considered took many forms, from human services (care, housework and other assistance) to material goods such as money, food and other material transfers. Later, attention began to focus on the transmission of less visible resources – notably time and the transmission of cultural capital and emotional resources – across more than two family generations (Chapter 5).

In our introduction to *Give and take in families* (Brannen and Wilson, 1987) households were conceptualised as sites in which resources were transformed according to the status and benefit of their members. We also argued that the value that was placed upon individuals' labour and time had implications for the work they did in the household and in the labour market. This usually meant that those whose time was valued less – typically women – were likely to have more responsibility for, and to devote more time to, childcare and household work. Those whose labour was valued more highly (typically men) substituted their household work by passing it on to others, either other household members or by outsourcing the work to others (often other women).

We also discussed the ways in which resource distribution in households between men and women was governed by the normative vocabularies of the times. For example, as we described, men typically used non-gendered and non-contentious language such as 'sharing' in household work and women spoke of receiving 'help' from their husbands. In the 1980s it was rare for couples to explain how 'sharing' played out in practice in terms of who did most of the work or took most responsibility. The vocabulary of 'sharing' thereby avoided making visible the power differentials between men and women who, in the context of prevailing norms of companionate marriage, sought to avoid conflict or even hint at its possibility (Benjamin, 1998). As well as examining inequities in resource distribution and how couples negotiated unequal power relations, we also considered it important to analyse the different ways in which women and other household members created, dispensed and transformed the resources available to them. Given women's responsibility for household labour, it often meant that women prioritised the needs of husbands and children over their own.

While the Resources in Households Group had an intellectual purpose it also served to place relations in 'the household', especially between men and women, on the public and social science agendas. Family studies and gender studies were not high-status fields of inquiry in sociology at that time. Research questions of higher standing concerned social class and social stratification – inequalities *between* households. These were the topics that attracted much of the research funding and were largely studied by male social scientists.

In *Give and take in families* (Brannen and Wilson, 1987), some of the following questions were addressed: How do women manage the housework and what meanings do they attach to their (unfair) share of responsibility for it? How do parents (mothers) fare financially, or rather, fail to fare, following divorce? How do lone parents (mothers) manage with fewer material resources post-separation and how do they feel about their increased control over (limited) resources? Who controls money in the household? Who takes responsibility for the financial costs of the dual-earner lifestyle (when women return to work after maternity leave)? In what ways is access to food in households distributed, in particular in accordance with age and gender?

Up to that time my own contribution to the intra-household debate had focused largely on gender relations. Children's part in and contribution to the household was a rather neglected topic.

According to discourses of child development, children's family work was normatively acceptable only as part of children's preparation for adulthood and growing independence (see Goodnow and Delaney, 1989; Goodnow, 1991). Social science's approach to children (as in survey and official data) was no better, defining children as dependants of parents and a drain upon, rather than an addition to, household resources (Chapter 6). Given centuries of child labour up to the first half of the 20th century for the majority of Britain's children, this was not surprising; as government increased the age to which education was mandatory, taking care of younger siblings or sick or disabled parents was considered exploitative on the basis that it was likely to interfere with children's schooling.

With the 'turn to childhood' and the emerging sociology of childhood, conceptualisations of children shifted from seeing them only as dependents of their parents and in need of protection (Chapter 6). Children began to be understood as a social group occupying a minority status, and as having the potential for agency. Childhood was viewed in effect as a social construction that was open to transformation (see, for example, James and Prout, 1990). While the new emphasis on children's interests, competences and agency was welcomed, this still left open the question of where children stood in the generational order (Alanen, 2003; Mayall and Zeiher, 2003) and as key participants in families and households. In the 1990s, generation became a focus of my own research.

Resources in low-income households

Given my early interest in money and the household economy, it is perhaps unsurprising that in the 21st century my research path led back to the topic of household resources but this time to households living in highly constrained financial circumstances As Daly (2017: 451) notes: 'Focusing on circumstances in which money is scarce offers a vital opportunity to develop an account of money as a means of organising everyday lives, articulating relationships and framing worth and meaning for self and social action.' In recent years, poverty has reappeared in Britain on a scale reminiscent of Victorian society as portrayed by Dickens as well as early social scientists like Charles Booth. Estimates suggest that over 4 million children are currently living in poverty in the UK (JRF, 2017), with the poverty line drawn at 60 per cent of median income taking account of household type. At risk are households in work as well as workless households, with those most at risk headed by lone parents and families consisting of three or more children and in-work poverty rising dramatically (JRF, 2017).

In the period following the 2008 financial crisis, the 2010 Conservative and Liberal Democrat Coalition government, and the subsequent Conservative governments implemented 'austerity measures', freezing public sector earnings and cutting benefits to working and workless households alike. The reorganisation of the benefits system still under way in the UK is intended to get people into work and to rationalise the range of welfare benefits. It has been subjected to widespread criticism, however: that it is operating on a hugely reduced budget and creating significant time delays in payments to claimants (Butler, 2018). In addition, changes to immigration law are pushing migrant families who have been refused 'leave to remain' into absolute poverty leaving them with no recourse to public funds or to income of any kind (O'Connell and Brannen, 2019). Changes to disability benefits and the so-called Bedroom Tax introduced in the Welfare Reform Act 2012 (an under-occupancy penalty applied to those in public housing) also penalise those on low incomes. Alongside these policy changes is the continuing deregulation of the labour market increasing the number of the 'working poor'; low-paid jobs are not only often part-time but also, increasingly, guarantee no fixed hours. Of equal significance is the rising cost of rented housing upon which poor families increasingly depend.

During this period food poverty has been on the rise. This is evidenced in the growth of food banks (Loopstra and Lalor, 2017). As the UK Poverty Report 2017 (JRF, 2017) suggests, those on low incomes spend proportionally more of their household income on food and fuel. The UK Poverty and Social Exclusion study, conducted in 2012, found that well over half a million children were living in families who were unable to feed them properly, that is, provide at least one of the following: three meals a day; fresh fruit and vegetables every day; or meat, fish or a vegetarian equivalent at least once a day (Gordon et al, 2013). The latter study also suggested that if parents were not cutting back on their own food intake to protect their children, the number would have been much higher (Lansley and Mack, 2015: 39). Research based on the Joseph Rowntree Foundation's Minimum Income Standard (MIS) found that large families (households with three or more children) and lone-parent families were most likely to struggle to meet the budget standard for a socially acceptable, healthy diet and be at risk of food poverty (O'Connell et al, 2018).

How these trends and policies play out in low-income families with children were matters in need of urgent attention.

Families and food in hard times

In 2009 my interest returned to the topic of food, a focus of my earlier work with colleagues concerning the health of young people (Brannen et al, 1994; Brannen and Storey, 1996, 1998). Following a successful bid for funding in a competition run by the Institute of Education, I appointed Rebecca O'Connell, a new PhD graduate, to a postdoctorate to examine the food practices of young children at home and in early childhood services. Although for a number of reasons we did not pursue this particular focus it led to a succession of projects on food in families (O'Connell and Brannen, 2016). Following these projects, in 2014 the Families and Food in Hard Times study began, supported by a starting grant from the European Research Council.[1] The project was led by Rebecca O'Connell with my role as advisor and overseer of the project. The team included Abigail Knight, Charlie Owen, Antonia Simon and other TCRU staff, together with teams of researchers in Portugal and Norway. The countries were chosen to provide 'a contrast of contexts' (Kohn, 1987). Like the UK, Portugal was selected because it had been severely affected by the financial crisis while Norway was chosen because its long-term oil investments have protected its economic prosperity.

The project involved a two-tier research design. Data were analysed at the national level. At the local level, case studies of low-income families were conducted in each of the three countries. In order to reflect different types of environments for accessing food, the families were recruited in each country from two types of area: an area with high levels of poverty in the inner city (the three capital cities) and a less urbanized area. This decision allowed for different types of 'foodscapes' or commercial food outlets (Miewald, and McCann, 2003). Qualitative interviews were carried out with young people aged 11 to 15 years and their parents. Forty-five families took part in the UK, the same number in Portugal and 43 families in Norway.

In analysing the qualitative interview data we sought to bring all the material concerning each household together: the interviews with the parent (usually the mother) and the child aged 11–15; our extensive field notes; the questionnaire data completed by young people (based on the eating habits module of the World Health Organization's cross-national Health Behaviour in School-aged Children Questionnaire); and visual data in which a subset of young people interviewed were given cameras to photograph food, the places it was kept and the environments in which they consumed it. The cases were written up to reflect the narrative quality of the material and to capture the key themes of the study, with observations concerning the interview encounter, recruitment, neighbourhood and housing, together with notes on food practices evident in the interview.

A 'practice approach' was adopted to describe the taken-for-granted aspects and practices of food provision and consumption (Shove et al, 2012; Warde, 2005). The aim thereby was to capture the gap between what people do and what they say they do. The study also drew conceptually on Townsend's (1979) seminal definition of relative poverty: 'the inability to acquire or consume an adequate quality or sufficient quantity of food in socially acceptable ways, or the uncertainty that one will be able to do so' (cited in Dowler et al, 2001: 12). This definition emphasises the dimension of social participation that is intrinsic to the consumption of food and in which food is a significant vehicle for social inclusion and exclusion. Thus the examination of the food available to children in low-income households was not limited only to questions of food quantity and quality but extended to the ways in which children are able to take part in the essentially sociable aspects of eating, both in terms of inviting their friends to their homes and participating in sociality around food outside the household.

For the purposes of this chapter I draw on material concerning the UK families, a disproportionate number of whom were lone-parent families (O'Connell et al, 2019). Their low incomes meant they had to restrict expenditure to a bare minimum. For those reliant on state benefits, their incomes were often subject to fluctuation and deductions as state benefits were withdrawn or reformed. For those living in inner London in privately rented property, rents were high and the conditions of the housing often unsatisfactory. For households in work wages were generally low because of the lack of labour market regulation and because the benefits system precluded parents working beyond a certain number of hours. Their jobs were often precarious with the result that household income was unpredictable. Moving from work into the benefits system usually involved significant time lags in payment with no savings to fall back on.

For low-income households in the study, feeding a family demanded considerable time to shop around for cheap food and the skill, time, fuel and other resources (for example, a functioning oven) to cook inexpensive meals. Typically mothers managed to feed their children by going without food themselves, thereby protecting their children's share and ensuring that their nutritional needs were met (O'Connell et al, 2019). Such concerns contrast with those that women gave for allocating food to household members in the 1980s, in particular the priority given to the male breadwinner, as in his entitlement to the 'better cuts of meat' (Charles and Kerr, 1987). Given it was, and is, largely women who carry most responsibility for food work, it is also women who bear most of the worry and shame if they cannot manage to feed their children adequately. As Walker (2014: 102) argues, '[food and housing] suggest security but with limited resources they can instil a sense of insecurity and real fear of the future'.

Limited resources affected the study families' capacity to engage in social relationships with others, in particular whether they could offer hospitality to others and whether they could accept hospitality. Reciprocity is at the heart of social relations and sociality, and central to reciprocity is the idea of 'balance' (Finch and Mason, 1993). However, as Finch and Mason (1993) suggest, the way in which 'balance' is calculated is not a simple reflection of the value of the goods or services exchanged. 'A central theme in classic accounts of reciprocity is that exchanges of goods have a symbolic as well as a material value' (Finch and Mason, 1993: 37). As their study of kin care showed, those at the receiving end sought to avoid falling into a state of dependence and indebtedness which would disrupt the balance of power between them and the potential givers of resources. In social relationships that involve 'give and take' it is vital to the receiving parties – 'a matter of pride' – that they do not feel unduly beholden to the givers and are put in a position of being unable to reciprocate. At stake here are the *moral identities* of those who are unable to engage in relations that involve direct reciprocity.

The link between household resource allocation and children's opportunities to invite friends home or go to friends' homes for something to eat is conceptualised as relations of reciprocity. Fewer than a fifth of the young people in the UK study cases of the Families and Food in Hard Times study reported having friends over to eat at their homes and just over a third said they ate at their friends' homes, of whom only half were able to reciprocate. As children move into their teenage years they expect some autonomy from parents and to start to lead their own social lives as members of their own generation (Brannen et al, 1994; Zeiher, 2001) and in this process to develop new identities. Many young people's activities outside the home involve financial expenditure, and this is recognised as intrinsic to 'growing up' and developing competences of various kinds. Yet, the children in the study were, like all children in western societies, dependent on their parents for money to take part in extra-curricular and school activities. Where mothers' budgets were heavily constrained financially this affected children's capacities to participate at school and in their own social circles. A third of children in the study were given no money by parents apart from lunch money and this excludes the parents who said they could not afford to pay for children's activities. In such settings children typically engaged in 'social comparison' (Festinger, 1954) in their relations with their peers. Where they lacked spending money or where parents could not afford to pay for football training, for example, this had consequences both for their social participation but also for how children *felt* about their situations in comparing themselves with other children, affecting their social status in peer groups and their self-esteem and sense of belonging.

Shame is a seminal concept in understanding poverty. As Sen (1983: 342) argues, the poverty line needs to be set at a level at which people can 'achieve adequate participation in communal activities and be free from public shame from failure to satisfy conventions'. Some sociologists analyse shame in terms of the embeddedness of people in structures of power and prestige, while others (from a symbolic interactionist perspective) pay attention to shame as an emotion that drives individuals to maintain a positive self-image (Walker, 2104). Walker makes an important distinction here between the externalisation of shame or shaming and the internal experience of feeling shame or shamed. 'External shame', Walker suggests, concerns the perception of how others view 'poor people', notably in the media, wider kin, schools and other institutions. 'Personal shame' refers a sense of individual failure in not living up to one's own expectations and in not being valued by others (Walker, 2014: 106). External shame generates and reinforces feelings of 'internal shame'. In individualist cultures like Britain's, the experience of shame is circumscribed, generally affecting the person who transgresses social norms, as contrasted with collectivist societies where the shame attached to, and experienced by, individuals can cast a shadow over all members of the social group to which they belong (Walker, 2014).

The distinction drawn by Walker resonates with Janet Finch's (1989: 188–92) discussion of concepts of public and personal reputation. Public reputation refers to the reputation of a group as a whole, a kin group for example, that is accountable to and sanctioned by external audiences. A personal reputation refers to a person's identity. A mother feels she needs to meet her own standards as well as those of others in providing for her children, although personal reputation may become a matter of public reputation where a lack of capacity to care adequately for a child is brought to the attention of public authorities. Poverty and food poverty therefore carry the risk and fear of stigma (Goffman, 1970). Stigma affects identity. Lack of money is, in Goffman's terms, a 'discreditable' condition. (Goffman, 1970: 57). To avoid becoming 'discredited', parents and children may seek to conceal poverty from others. As the Food and Hard Times study shows, for many children, participation in activities inside and outside the home, many involving food, was central to their social inclusion (O'Connell et al, 2019). In this context, children and parents rejected or avoided situations where reciprocity was expected. When it was not possible to conceal poverty, for example in situations of extreme need, a 'discredited' identity led to internal feelings of shame.

In order to demonstrate the ways in which households managed under conditions of low income, I am going to discuss two cases from the study, both recruited in the inner London borough. They were chosen on the grounds of sharing similar characteristics. Both are lone mothers, of a similar age and with one daughter at home. One mother has no source of regular income and the other recently moved from benefits into employment and, in order to study, back into unemployment. The families demonstrate what it is like to live on a low unstable income with consequences for food expenditure and consumption and opportunities for social participation within and beyond the household.

Lone parenthood is more common in the UK than it was when the research discussed in *Give and take in families* (Brannen and Wilson, 1987) in the 1980s took place. While most mothers today expect to support their families, employed lone parents are much more likely to be low paid compared with second earners in couples (JRF, 2017). Lone parents not in work are in receipt of much reduced welfare benefits compared with lone parents in the 1980s. As Hilary Graham's (1987) research showed then, while the resources of lone-parent households were heavily constrained, mothers valued the sole control that lone parenthood gave them over family finances. By contrast, because income was so limited and stretched for lone parents in the Families and Food in Hard Times study they felt totally constrained by a lack of financial autonomy.

Sandra and Kasey

Sandra is 38, a lone parent of African-Caribbean origin who has a 13-year-old daughter, Kasey. At interview Sandra had just started a new job as a receptionist on 30 hours a week having lost her previous job (income around £1,300 per month, including £960 gross per month earnings plus Child Benefit, Housing Benefit and Child Tax Credits). Sandra had aspirations to go back to college. Mother and daughter live in a two-bedroom privately rented flat in a poor part of the inner London borough. The rent is very high (£1,200 per month) and

Housing Benefit only covers a small part of it. When her partner left Sandra incurred a lot of debt; during the few months when she was out of work she built up rent arrears. In addition, Sandra has debts on her credit cards. Every month she engages in juggling her debts, "So my current account is just to pay bills, but my savings is to hold the money to pay the bills. It's like you know like a little waiting room before they take it away ..."

Sandra's life has been precarious in other ways. In 2012 the family was evicted because the landlord raised the rent and the council would not help cover the extra payments. Sandra and her daughter went to live with Sandra's mother in a one-bedroom assisted housing unit. They were then re-housed. Because she was working, Sandra's benefits were cut and her daughter no longer received free school meals, "According to my gross [pay] they say I make too much money. I'm like – I was getting tax credit, they cut me off, they said I made too much money. So everything was – last year I was getting cut off – 'Well wait a minute, my child has to eat.'"

In managing the household budget, at interview Sandra says she now prioritises paying the rent, council tax and utility bills and other services. The food budget (£120 a month) is what is left over. Despite these major constraints on food expenditure, Sandra was keen to present herself in a positive light. She says she is a good cook – preparing Caribbean dishes that she learned from her mother – and prides herself in being a "good manager". Consistent with this claim, she says she is "not ashamed" about not buying expensive food,

> 'I buy things like in bulk. So let's say chick peas are like 38 pence, I'm buying you know enough so I can find a meal to make out of it. I stretch my hand with a lot of things 'cos you know I'm not ashamed, I don't mind eating you know food – as long as it tastes good I'm okay with it, I don't have to have you know steak.... My parents made do [with] what [they] had and – they were both working parents.'

In these remarks Sandra positions herself as "respectable" just like her "working parents" who managed within their means. She is thereby claiming that, in Goffman's terms, she is not 'discredited' (Goffman, 1970).

When she runs out of food Sandra turns to her mother for help, albeit reluctantly as her mother is a pensioner, "So my mother would have to give me you know little groceries. Whenever she goes shopping she'll buy double and give me the other half." However, Sandra believes that she ought to be able to manage on her own because she is working, "I'm able bodied, so, in my mind ... I'm qualified to work so why can't I pay my own bills? So when I do fall short I'll sit here and I will ration out whatever I have in my cupboards until the very last thing ... nothing in the house."

As a mother, Sandra prioritised feeding her daughter and, like many mothers in the study, this often meant sacrificing her own food intake (O'Connell et al, 2019). When Sandra is unable to provide adequately for Kasey, she feels her public reputation is put in jeopardy and that she is a personal failure (internal shame):

> 'I was sad that I couldn't do it myself, feel kind of inadequate, you know you're not able to provide for your own child.... like you know why can't I manage my own finances? But there's nothing that – I'm not splurging 'cos I don't have anything here that's you know outlandish, I live simple. But it's just the money wasn't ... my wages wasn't matching outside my rent.'

In terms of socialising with friends, Sandra says that she has no money to do this or feels too tired after work. But this is only part of her narrative. Sandra also suggests, somewhat defensively, that she likes to keep her distance from others, "[to be] home, it's comfortable, it's quiet". This disposition is also about concealing her situation from others and not wanting to ask for help, for example, when she and her daughter were evicted. Social withdrawal and concealment are ways to avoid shame and conserve public reputation. By 'avoiding overtures of intimacy the individual can avoid the consequent obligation to divulge information' (Goffman, 1970: 122):

> 'I wanted to keep it [the eviction] quiet, but I don't want to publicise my downfall, and then you have something to use against me. You know people are you know ... they just look at you, like "Mm, single parent", you know "you can't manage". You know everyone's married in the church you know. So I just left it – I didn't want to be bothered with ... you know stigma that "Oh single parent".'

Sandra's way of retaining her pride is to keep herself to herself, a practice that produces a negative self-evaluation and contributes to the family's social isolation. However, despite her travails Sandra is supportive of her daughter socialising with her friends and she tries to find money to give her. This is difficult and she says she finds herself saying, "But I keep saying to her like everything your friends do you have to do?"

Kasey was interviewed a couple of months later by which time her mother had resigned from her job and returned to being a student. While Kasey's account confirmed much of her mother's story it was clear that their financial situation had worsened. There was much less food in the house. Kasey had recently accompanied her mother to a food bank, which she described as a humiliating experience. She noted that she often had to turn down invitations to go out with her friends because of the cost and rarely invited friends home. Like her mother, Kasey professed not to be "too fussed" about this. She offered this excuse for declining to join her friend's birthday outing, "it was because I lost my sweater so she [mother] said I couldn't go until I find it. I had to like find it."

Kasey has very little money to spend when she is out with friends. If friends offer to share some of the food they buy Kasey says she is careful not to accept their generosity too often, "Like they'll share like chips. But I'm not like – obviously they paid their money for their food so I wouldn't like just eat it off of them." In this interview interchange, Kasey illustrates the dilemma involved in accepting "gifts".

Kasey:	'And then … like if someone offers me something it feels I ought to like give it back.'
Interviewer:	'Okay, okay. Have you been able to do that though?'
Kasey:	'Sometimes.'
Interviewer:	'What do you offer them?'
Kasey:	'Like if I have anything like I just give it back to them. Like, I give them some.'

In this case a lone mother sought to manage the difficulties and uncertainties of living on an unstable and insufficient income. Sandra had moved in and out of work and at her daughter's interview had returned to being a full-time student (with a large student loan). Her moral identity was under threat both from being seen as a lone parent who was "not managing" and from internal shame in falling below her own standards of motherhood and respectability. In order to maintain some of her reputation and self-respect, she hid her family's difficulties and did not seek help or accept gifts from others. She and her daughter also concealed their "need" from themselves as well as others by creating "excuses" other than poverty.

Aya and Amara

The second case, one of the most extreme cases of poverty in the study, is one in which the family had no access to welfare benefits or paid work. Mother and daughter were on the verge of destitution in the sense that they lacked the wherewithal to sustain themselves including food (Crawley et al, 2011). Aya is 37 and a lone parent. Originally from North Africa, she lived in southern Europe for many years, where her two daughters were born. Recently she moved to the UK with her younger child, Amara, who is 15 years old "to give my daughter education". After initially living with friends, mother and daughter were placed in temporary accommodation in a room in a very large hostel but at interview they were facing eviction. Aya was registered with Jobcentre Plus but had not been able to find suitable employment: "I ask friends, I ask people, newspaper – everything. So I try everything looking for a job but nothing happened unfortunately." Either the cost of travel was too much for her to get to the job or its hours were unsuitable. She also felt she could not safely leave her child in the hostel alone, "It's not a nice a place […] people they're fighting (inaudible) they stab each other, drugs, alcohol …".

Aya does not even receive Child Benefit. Asked how she manages, Aya said she relies on friends and sometimes does informal work: "I have some cash in hand." She says she is paid £3 per hour by people who say that they will eventually give her a "proper job on the cards" but she thinks they are lying. Because the work is informal she is not eligible for Working Family Tax Credits. Mother and daughter were literally going hungry, "We're really starving, me and my daughter." Both skipped meals and the little food they had they shared. Mother and daughter were living hand to mouth.

Aya and Amara also suffered from social exclusion; they were unable to invite friends to the hostel or to participate in any form of sociable activity (except school for Amara). Both mother and daughter experienced the loss of personal dignity from their dire predicament. As the mother said repeatedly, they had to be "grateful" for charity because they had no choice.

This case suggests both parental sacrifice and child altruism; mother and daughter prioritised the needs of the other. Because there was so little to spend on food or anything else, Aya went without food during the day and reserved what little there was for the evening when mother and daughter ate together:

> 'Sometimes like I don't [eat] nothing just – I wait for my daughter to come at home and we have sandwich which

we have, well tin of tuna or something like that, you understand? I can starve all day long waiting for her, like then we can share what we have at home. This is how it is, you understand? My days – morning, I had coffee and that's it really, yeah, soft drinks or something or some toast. This is my day, yeah.'

Amara showed solidarity with her mother and sacrificed her own food intake saying that,

'I skip meals to share with my mum (inaudible) ... for example ... I skip my meal to wait for her to come back and at least we can have the same amount of food (inaudible), starve together through the whole day, so at least we will have had something to eat.'

When her mother had no money Amara said she gave what she had to her mother, "I try to keep ... put money together and [we] just help each other, that's what we do […] just share them."

Aya was forced publicly to admit to being in severe need – her status and identity were thus 'discredited'. She sought referral to a food bank but soon found that she had used up her 'entitlement' because the number of referrals is rationed: "I said 'sorry well we have to eat' – well we're eating just three times a year [referring here to the limit on the number of times she is allowed to use the food bank] ... I'm sorry to say that, I'm sorry. Well, we're eating every day, [we are] humans."

Until recently, because Amara was not eligible for free school meals, she went hungry at school: "I used to starve in school because ... well I couldn't manage to make sandwiches at home or take crisps or whatever (inaudible) so I was just starving in school for the whole day." This affected Amara's school work, "When I'm hungry I just can't concentrate, it's really really hard for me to do that.... so I just need to make my mind up and know that I will eat after five hours, seven hours when I get home." Aya felt compelled to speak to the school so that Amara could be provided with a free school meal. However, the allowance (just over £2 daily) does not provide sufficient food to satisfy Amara's appetite, "a small sandwich is like £1.60". Amara would like to take cheaper food from home but this is not an option: "But when I don't have food at home what am I going to do?"

Like Sandra, Aya enjoys, and takes pride in, cooking. Having lived in a southern European country for many years, she cooks Mediterranean dishes as does her daughter. They prefer fresh home-cooked food even though, as many of the low-income mothers said, it is more expensive to cook from scratch than to buy ready-made meals. However, the situation of Aya and Amara left them little scope for cooking or shopping as they would like. In their one room they had no space and poor conditions in which to store or cook food (the building was overrun with cockroaches).

Opportunities to offer or receive hospitality were non-existent because of the family's housing situation as well as lack of income. The hostel did not allow them to have visitors other than social workers. Aya broke down in tears when she said that the hostel was "like a prison", an admission of her desperation and shame. Amara also talked about their housing and how it constrained her relations with her peers, "If I had my own place, my own room, I could say [to my friends] 'Yeah come over' but my mum … I don't have a room, I'm just sharing a room with my mum. Then we haven't very much with food so –."

Socialising outside the home was also severely restricted. Amara reflected on times when life was better – when her mother had some work – and the difference this made to her: "when [mother] used to work and give me money I was most of the time there [eating a snack on the way back from school] with my friends, but now I just walk straight home because I can't afford to spend money on … well let's say food outside." Asked about the neighbourhood where she lives that is full of trendy coffee shops and cafés, Amara comments, "Why would I spend £8 on a coffee and a cake when I could get like proper food.… Like food that can actually last me for a couple of days." Just to get out of their one room Amara said that she and her mother often went for a walk round the park.

The depths to which their family fortunes have sunk were evident. To salvage their self-respect both mother and daughter concealed their situation from other people. As Amara noted, "I don't really talk about my personal life with my friends." However, by turning to food banks Aya risked the stigma of being a 'discredited person'. Being beholden to charity is demeaning and brings a loss of dignity and a negative existential state or condition (Daly, 2017). While Aya expressed gratitude for being given food, this was premised on having no other choice, "It's better than nothing." Gratitude here is linked to acceptance and resignation, "You have to accept this is how it is … when I'm hungry, I'm hungry and I'm not in a position … I mean I can't complain at the moment, I just can't complain. I'm not in a position to do that." At the same time, Aya resisted the attribution of dependence and expressed criticism of the government about the lack of a safety net when people are unable to find work,

> 'if a person is working the person has a responsibility to take care of everything in general. And if a person isn't working I think people should receive help from different places and not once every seven months because they can't go [to a food bank] every day. And, yeah, we do get food from food banks, but the food finishes, you won't just have things for a year. Once the things are finished what are we going to eat? Well, people should receive help, but then sometimes they don't ... and when you ask for help they always say no.'

Food banks do not, and cannot, in her view fill the gap.

Conclusion

In this chapter I have returned to a preoccupation of the 1980s: that social science needs not only to examine the distribution of income and wealth between social classes and households but also to analyse what comes into the household and how resources are distributed according to gender and generational orders within the household. The initial focus upon gender inequalities within households arose out of an historical alliance between motherhood and the status of housewife and a context in which women were dependent on men as sole or main breadwinners. In the past 30 or so years, the growth in lone parenthood, serial partnering and divorce, together with the increasing participation of women in the labour market and in further and higher education, have radically changed many women's status in society. The focus on gender has to some extent been replaced by a concern with children's access to household resources, a trend simultaneously driven by the reappearance of child poverty and child hunger and an increased child-centredness in the practice of parenthood (Chapter 6).

This chapter has examined access to and distribution of resources, food in particular, within two low-income households and the consequences for the dignity and moral identities of parents and children, and their capacity to participate in social activity inside and outside the household. As the two cases discussed demonstrate, when income is insufficient for a household's needs, especially in the case of lone parents, and when income from welfare benefits and employment is poorly paid and unpredictable, families struggle to 'get by' (Lister, 2004). Where housing costs are high, especially in the rapidly expanding privately rented sector upon which many low-income families depend, and at a time when benefits are being reduced and the welfare system reshaped, and costs of energy and other consumables are rising, what is left for the family food budget is insufficient. The result is that low-income parents are unable to take care of and feed their children to a socially acceptable level.

The study offers a significant contrast with the period covered by *Give and take in families* (Brannen and Wilson, 1987). In the 1980s, families depended upon employment, the state, kin and communities for support. In some key respects this has changed. One change is the depletion of the stock of public housing. Another is that benefit cuts, austerity policies, changes in immigration law, and government ideologies have created a situation in which voluntarism is stepping into the breach left by the shrunken welfare state. It is now normative for low-income families to turn to the charity sector for food (Lambie-Mumford, 2017). This growth in the influence of the voluntary sector is creating a reconfiguration of welfare, with the voluntary sector taking over much of the state's responsibility for social protection (Lambie-Mumford, 2017). Further, voluntarism exacerbates differences between poor families: those who are able to turn to informal social networks to help them withstand adversity and those that lack such networks. Migrants are among those doubly at risk. The first risk to which they are exposed concerns the difficult conditions that many have sought to escape by migrating, while the second risk lies in the country of destination where they lack deep social networks to draw upon (Estevao et al, 2017).

The two cases I have analysed also suggest that poverty and food poverty are variable conditions both over the life course of families and across cases. As they demonstrate, food poverty is highly contingent on the predictability of income from employment and welfare benefits and in relation to life-course events and changes, for example, separation, eviction and migration.

Low income also prevents parents and children from making and sustaining friendships and being part of civil society, leading to isolation, marginalisation and exclusion from many social spaces. The constraints on family budgets are evidenced in the limitations placed on the social activities that parents and children can engage in, both inside and outside the home. Food is intrinsic to many forms of social interaction and social relationships. The strain on household resources deprives children in low-income households of the opportunity to invite friends home or to take part in extra-curricular activities that most children today take for granted as part of 'ordinary childhood'.

As they get older and begin to navigate the neighbourhoods where they live, they also lack money to spend on socialising with their peers outside home (Knight et al, 2018). Those at secondary school may also lack the means to supplement the inadequate allowances under free school meals policies either by bringing extra food from home or by purchasing more food in the school canteen or outside school. Children's right to social participation as members of their own generation is thereby infringed.

The cases also show how low income affects the moral identities of parents and children. Parents and children are fearful of accepting hospitality, help or gifts because they cannot reciprocate. Some respond by withdrawing, or have no choice but to withdraw, from social interaction, a response that leads to social isolation, and sometimes depression and despair. Both parents and children often conceal their household's poverty from others in order to avoid stigma and loss of reputation. Moreover, mothers in these situations experience internal feelings of shame: that they have failed to live up to their own and others' expectations in being unable to provide for their children. Money, and the lack of it, shapes identity, constrains agency and condemns both parents and their children to living in the present as they struggle on a daily basis to feed themselves.

Experiences of poverty are contextual. They also change over time. Conceptual approaches, research designs and methods need to take account of this. Even within one interview a parent or child adopts different viewpoints, reflecting different positionings in relation to the self, significant others and the interviewer. For example, despite the unhappy experiences of both families discussed, the two mothers were hopeful about the future. Sandra in her interview hopes that she will sort out her debts and that, by pursuing her studies in higher education, she will find a better paid, more rewarding job. Aya, as a recent migrant, makes a plea to be given a chance in a new country: "give me [a] chance to make myself, to do something, to have some future ... to give [a] future for me, for my daughter".

On the other hand, those in poverty are caught in an extended present (Nowotny, 1994) as they struggle with the daily grind of "just staying alive" and "making do". At 15 it is not surprising that Amara says she does not think much about the future in general, "I don't really live by the future, I just live by the present and whatever comes.... I'm not upset. Like I do hope my mum would have more money." Yet Amara also has clear goals for her own future. Like many migrants she places her faith in education. However, both Aya and Amara also suggest that poverty and the accompanying loss of dignity bind them into a daily struggle. While Amara aspires to a better future, she also makes the point that poverty constrains the present. I will end the chapter with her powerful words,

> 'If I'm in this country I'm here for a reason, I'm here because my mum wants to give me a good education, and that's what I'm doing, I'm studying hard, I'm improving my skills, I'm doing my best to get good grades. And then once I finish I'm going to go college, and if God knows and I do have enough money I'm going to university. Then I will do some courses and see what I really want to do in life. I have a few ideas but I can't focus on the future if I don't know what's going to happen from now till – like from now to the next hour.'

5

A Generational Lens on Families and Fathers

The conceptual focus of this chapter is generation. Generation brings into view the historical period in which a person grows up; in my case a child of Britain's post-war hardship, a young adult of the 'swinging sixties', and an activist in the 1970s Women's Movement. The popularity of the concept waxes and wanes, often coming to the fore in lay, policy and sociological discourse in periods of rapid social change. According to Mannheim, generations are formed in particular conditions: those 'who share the same year of birth, are endowed, to that extent, with a common location in the historical dimension of the social process' (Mannheim, 1952 [1928]: 290). In this conceptualisation temporality and social location are paramount. Mannheim further distinguishes between generation as actuality and as unit, 'We shall therefore speak of a generation as an actuality only where a concrete bond is created between members of a generation by their being exposed to the social and intellectual symptoms of a process of dynamic de-stabilisation' (1952 [1928]: 303). A generational unit is formed not only when peers are exposed to the same phenomenon but when they also respond in the same way as a collective. A generation is not therefore only a matter of belonging to a particular birth cohort but the cultures, subjectivities and actions that it forges. The concept has therefore strong elements of agency and generational identity as a potential basis for political engagement.

As those of us in the 'Baby Boomer' generation in Britain have come to understand, what marks us out from later generations are the benefits reaped from the post-war welfare settlement – free university education, greater equality for women in employment and education, and a free universal health service. At the time of writing (2018), major socioeconomic and political differences between generations are evident, creating a significant gap between the Baby Boomers and the Millennials. The year 2016, in which the British people voted by a small minority in a referendum to leave the EU, revealed considerable divisions between younger and older generations, with acute educational divisions the clearest sign of profound societal cleavages (Richards, 2017). The year after the referendum, in the 2017 British general election, the younger generation had their revenge on older generations that voted in large numbers for Brexit. The generation gap in the election results was the largest since polling began, with 62 per cent of 18–24-year-olds voting for Labour compared with 27 per cent for the Tories, while the positions for older people were reversed (Eaton, 2018).

The current generational divisions between young and old have been exacerbated by the present UK government's policies of austerity, for example its abolition of the Education Maintenance Support Allowance and the raising of university tuition fees to an unsustainable level, while state pensions for those in retirement have been protected. What has become clear is that young people today have far worse prospects compared with those of their parents and grandparents when they were young. In England young people leave education with massive debts, while many enter jobs that do not match their qualifications with the result that, generation on generation, the incomes of UK Millennials have experienced the most significant slowdown in income gains in any high-income western country (Resolution Foundation, 2018). UK young people also face difficulty in getting onto the housing ladder unless they have very substantial parental support. However, while few commentators suggest that these disparities have led to generational conflict (Attias-Donfut and Arber, 2002, Willetts 2010), there are growing forces demanding a new intergenerational settlement (Resolution Foundation, 2018).

Families through a generational lens

This chapter discusses the application of a generational lens to family lives with reference to the study of fatherhood. As children we constitute the next generation in our families (Pilcher, 1994) as well as being the products of a particular period and cohort. In adulthood we remain in a generational relationship with our antecedents and successors. The concept of intergenerational relations in family life therefore articulates a sense of relatedness that focuses on vertical ties. As Lüscher and Hoff (2013) suggest, generations are distinguished by their boundedness, while at the same time they are integrated in a cross-generational succession and relationship. Yet the concept of intergenerational relations as it relates to families has been employed rather infrequently in sociology. Traditionally anthropologists have been interested in generations largely as a dimension of kinship systems and genealogical relationships. By contrast, much family sociology has focused on parents' relations with 'dependent' children. More recently, the focus has expanded to include grandparents. In addition, with continuing change in family structures and the 'turn to intimacy' (Jamieson, 1998), kinship and kin-like relations are being brought under the conceptual umbrella of 'personal relationships' (Smart, 2007). Furthermore, families are increasingly understood in terms of what families 'do' rather than what they 'are' in structural terms. (Morgan, 2011). In Morgan's conceptualisation 'family' becomes an adjective to describe different sets of 'practices'. At the same time, 'family' continues to be a particular, but not exclusive, 'lens through which to describe and to explore a set of social activities' (Morgan, 2011: 5).

Placing an intergenerational lens alerts us to *what* is transmitted across generations, including a variety of phenomena from material assets and occupations to values, political beliefs and social status (Bengtson et al, 2002). Important also are the transmission and reproduction of moral and emotional bonds (Bertaux and Thompson, 1997). Transmission takes place in both directions – upwards as well as downwards. Transmission does not necessarily occur between adjacent generations; for example, it may occur between grandparent and grandchild, as when a grandchild teaches a grandparent how to use a mobile phone or a grandparent talks about family history.

Transmission is in essence relational and therefore can imply reciprocity so that what is offered by an older generation may be reciprocated by the younger generation, often at a later point in the life course, although what is given may not be matched in the type of help or amount returned. Some forms of reciprocity in families are what Sahlins (1972) and Gouldner (1960) term 'generalised': what is given is treated as a gift without expectation of return while the giver is compensated by satisfaction derived from doing 'good deeds'.

As a concept transmission may be criticised as weakly theorised. However, its broad reach has advantages encompassing the subjective and psycho-social aspects of human lives as well as material, cultural and social forms of capital (Wright, 2018). As Harriet Nielsen (2017: 10) suggests, it may consist in 'more or less articulated feelings of self and others or it may be a kind of knowledge embedded in everyday practices and relationships'. Transmission is of its nature temporal, taking place across the life course and at particular moments in time. Some forms of transmission from older to younger generations, for example the passing on of educational aspirations, have a short window of opportunity to shape the lives of the next generation, but over time they may have complex effects. Where there are disjunctures between generations in terms of social mobility, for example, when educational capital is transmitted from one generation to the next resulting in the next generation's upward occupational mobility, this transformation may not necessarily disrupt the social ties between the generations. The older and younger generations may remain emotionally or geographically 'close' despite differences in socioeconomic status.

Looking at families over several generations enables the researcher to see that the passing on of resources is not automatic but a dynamic and open process; what is passed on only becomes a transmission when it is received (Bertaux-Wiame, 2005 [1993]). As new generations come forward and old generations withdraw, a new generation may reject what is passed on as it engages with the social and cultural resources and heritage of a given society. Transmission produces breaks and ambivalences within families. Breaks between family generations may be acted out structurally and interpersonally (Lüscher and Hoff, 2013) and in emotions and feelings. Drawing on the work of Raymond Williams, Eric Fromm and Pierre Bourdieu, Harriet Nielsen (2017) shows how, in the Scandinavian context, 'feelings of gender' – patternings of identifications, desires and subjectivities – change and are transformed in particular social and historical contexts.

Further, the acceptance of transmitted resources may not be evident to the receiver or it may be taken for granted. Transmission, whether it concerns assets, cultures, habits or emotions can be implicit, in the sense that research participants do not articulate their receipt (Bernstein, 1996). Transmission is often what people 'do' and is embedded in routine everyday practices and relationships (Morgan, 1996). The notion of 'family habitus' (Bourdieu, 1990) denotes a set of dispositions related to particular practices which may lead to regularities in patterns of transmission across family generations but also to discontinuity (Wacquant, 2006: 7). In the sense that habitus involves 'produc[ing] history on the basis of history', dispositions are cumulative (Bourdieu, 1990: 56) and can live on in families. As the cases analysed later will show, emotional undercurrents in transmission channels can echo across the generations forming recurring generational narratives (Brannen, 2015: 106).

Placing an intergenerational lens on family life, as Bertaux and Bertaux-Wiame (1997) argue, also sheds light on the *ways* in which a successor generation makes its own mark upon that which is passed on to it and on the meanings that are bestowed. However, what the next generation makes of its inheritance may or may not constitute something 'new'. There is a considerable body of evidence demonstrating the transfer of assets and cash within families both *inter vivos* and on inheritance (see Kohli and Künemunde, 2003; Albertini and Kohli, 2013). Such material transfers serve to reproduce the life chances of younger people, replicating those of their parents or grandparents. However, while such generational family transfers may create solidarities within families, they also produce material inequalities between families. There is notably little trickle-down effect from older to younger generations among those at the bottom of the wealth and income pyramid compared with the accumulation of assets by those who are in receipt of transfers from family members at the top of the pyramid (Hills, 2014).

Therefore intergenerational research needs to be intersectional in its approach, that is, to examine simultaneously the ways in which transmission in families varies by social class, birth order and other social divisions such as ethnicity, gender and migration. For example, in China, despite a long patriarchal tradition, the one-child policy and China's rapid socioeconomic development enables parents to concentrate the investment of available financial resources, time and attention on their singleton children. (Fong, 2004). However, whether this leads to greater gender equality is contested when account is taken of family size, sibship structure, and rural/ urban divisions (Hu and Shi, 2019).

In short, an intergenerational lens on families directs attention to individuals, kinship lineages and the similarities and differences between kinship lineages in families. It offers a nuanced understanding of the types and processes of social reproduction and social change within families. It can point to continuities across an intergenerational chain while simultaneously identifying ruptures, dissonance and ambivalences. It can also illuminate the transmission of emotional undercurrents that echo down the generations forming recurring generational narratives, as well as other forms of capital (Brannen, 2015: 106). As Carol Smart writes:

> It is impossible to imagine a family without the sense that it is part of a lineage; that the people who are the current parent generation are the children of the previous generation and that they carry with them some sense or aura (not to mention genes) of those who have gone before. Being part of a lineage carries with it echoes of the past, plus an embeddedness in what went (or who went) before.

The past and the present are therefore intertwined and each
gives meaning to the other. (Smart, 2011: 543)

Studying multi-generation families

Towards the end of the 1990s, in the context of major changes taking
place in the world of work, an ESRC research initiative was launched
called The Future of Work. Peter Moss and I put in a successful bid
to examine the patterning of paid and unpaid forms of work and
care in men's and women's lives over several family generations.
(Brannen et al, 2004). The generational focus was apposite because
of increased life expectancy, with more family generations alive
simultaneously. Multi-generation families – composed of three or
even four generations – were increasingly common, with shrinkages
in the size of each successive family generation as the number of
children born declined. At the time of our study, conducted in the
late 1990s, three fifths of the British population by the age of 50 still
had a living parent and just over a third were grandparents (Grundy
et al, 1999).

We recruited 12 four-generation families that consisted of three adult
generations – parents, grandparents and great grandparents (Brannen
et al, 2004), with up to eight persons interviewed in each family
(N = 71). Our approach involved a strategic choice of similar and
contrasting families, an historical contextualisation of the material and
the use of an interview method (Wengraf, 2001) that enabled research
participants to tell their life stories (see Chapter 8). By understanding
the particular conditions of the 'case' (a family and those members
we recruited), we sought to build in-depth analyses and typologies of
intergenerational family relations and practices, and to identify patterns
of change and continuity concerning paid work and care across family
generations. The book, *Four-generation families: Working and caring over
the twentieth century* (Brannen et al, 2004), covered family lives from
the interwar period until the end of the 20th century.

This work led to a subsequent study, Fatherhood across Three
Generations (funded by the ESRC 2008–11), in which a new team
adopted a similar approach, this time focusing on changes in fatherhood
(Brannen, 2015). In the four-generation study migrants to Britain were
absent; great grandparents were born and brought up at a time of low
migration to the UK. The second intergenerational study aimed to
examine the ways in which migration, a major structural shock, shaped
relations in families in relation to fatherhood: this involved, inter alia,
examining the resources migrants brought to their new society, those

they acted upon and transmitted to younger generations, and those that were rejected or not taken up by younger generations.

The research team, that included Ann Mooney, Valerie Wigfall and Violetta Parutis, spent a great deal of time and energy recruiting the three chains of fathers and sons (Wigfall et al, 2013). As well as a group of white British, we selected two waves of migrants: Irish grandfathers who came to Britain in the mid-20th century and Polish fathers who arrived in the first decade of the 21st century. This provided us with 30 chains:

(1) 10 chains of white British grandfathers, their sons and grandsons (aged 5–17);
(2) 10 chains of Irish-born grandfathers who migrated to Britain in the mid-20th century, their sons living in the UK and grandsons (aged 5–17);
(3) 10 Polish-born grandfathers who were resident in Poland and their sons who migrated to the UK in the 2000s with their families, and grandsons (aged 5–17).

By focusing on different historical generations the objective was to explore fatherhood and masculinity in particular historical contexts as well as within particular families; and to examine the fatherhood practices that were transmitted across family generations.

In this type of study, case selection is critical in deciding who to include and who to exclude. Some selection criteria made little sense; selection on the grounds of social class, for example, even if it were logistically easy to do (which it is not), misses the whole point of an investigation into generational change and continuity. Because of each generation's historical situation, its life chances depend, in part at least, on the opportunities available in the contemporaneous context. In the study of migrants these matters become evident given that occupational mobility is often contingent on migration. A further issue in case selection that is often encountered in small-scale studies concerns exceptionality. Because of the study's focus, by definition both migrant groups had to be fathers. However, many Irish men of the1950s and 1960s generation never married or became fathers, while the Polish migrants typically came to Britain either as single men or without their families. Further, where the research design requires linking family generations to historical generations, compromise may be necessary because even within a family generation there is likely to be inconsistency; men are typically older than their partners. On the other hand, this is not necessarily a disadvantage: those on the margins of a historical generation may show something of the gradual nature of generational reproduction and change (Nielsen, 2017).

Transmission and father–son relations

One of the key social changes that mark the differences between family generations and that characterises men's lives as fathers and partners is 'the turn to intimacy' (Jamieson, 1998). As defined by Jamieson (2011), intimacy is 'the quality of close connection between people and the process of building this "quality"'. Families are widely understood as legitimate spaces for talking about emotions and relationships, although variations according to gender, generation, social class, ethnicity and (dis)ability are to be expected (Morgan, 2011). Historically, western masculinity has tended to suppress men's emotions, denied their vulnerability (Connell, 2000: 4) and foregrounded toughness, power and authority. On the other hand, fatherhood provides a context in which men learn about and recognise their emotional side (Dermott, 2008). In particular, the discourse of the 'new father', with its emphasis upon men's emotional involvement with their children, requires men to recognise and deal with their emotions (Seidler, 1997). However, emotion as practice is not the same as talking about it.

Given the increased sociological interest in intimacy in family life, the focus here is upon the emotional ties and ambivalences that are transmitted across generations of fathers and sons, and how they cement – and divide – relations between them. The two chains of fathers and sons selected suggest how feelings and emotions can repeat themselves over family generations, reflecting the ways in which men's relationships with their fathers shape the kinds of fathers and men they become. The two chains are chosen because they are 'emblematic' of men who articulate their feelings. Although reference was made to feelings in many interviews with the current generation of fathers, especially when they spoke about their relations with their young children, in these two chains the expression of emotions constituted a central or 'problem focus' suggesting its current importance.

In the interviews, fathers and sons (re)constructed their relationships through memory as both parties looked back on their lives and recounted their relationships from the vantage point of adulthood and fatherhood. In order to prompt men to talk more freely, we invited them to tell their life stories (see Chapter 8 for a full discussion of the approach) in the first part of the interview and used a more conventional interview in the second part or subsequent interview. We also employed photo elicitation methods. Photos can act as prompts to memory in which people 'make meaning *with* and *from* pictures' (Chalfen, 1998: 229). The idea was to make visible those spoken about, stimulating further reflection and enabling the past to be retrieved in the present (Harper, 2002). The photos were also used to 'break the frame' of normative and habitual aspects of family relations. We hoped that asking men to talk about photos of themselves with their fathers and sons would confirm, elaborate or raise new questions about what they said elsewhere in the interviews.

The first case – a Polish grandfather, son and grandson – is suggestive of close and affectionate relationships that, despite the son's migration, transcend their geographical separation. The second – a white British grandfather, son and grandson – is indicative of ambivalent relationships. Both men express regret and concern that their relationship will be repeated with the next generation (the grandson).

A recurring generational narrative of closeness: Kacper and Waldemar

In the relationship between Kacper and Waldemar, warmth and closeness run through both men's narratives. Compared with other Polish migrants interviewed, their relationship appeared to be particularly close. Kacper, a Polish grandfather living in Poland, was born in 1932. He grew up in a very large family and experienced a poverty-stricken childhood in the shadows of the Second World War and enemy occupation, first by Germany and then by the Soviet Union. His father was absent for much of his childhood, "The war started and so all of us, children, lost our fathers." When the war ended, Kacper's father was unable to return to his family. Although Kacper remembered little of his father, his narrative constructs him as a 'good father' and one that he wished to emulate:

> 'I don't remember much … my father was always a role model for me. Because all the other fathers were not as good as mine. I had respect for my father. He never smacked me. So what did I get from him? I got the warmth that I later missed.'

Kacper left school at 15 and worked in a state company. After three years in the army, he went back to the business. He was promoted to director of the firm on condition he went to university, which he did. Kacper worked hard, conscious that a "good salary" and secure employment meant that he could send his children to state summer camps and support them through university. He presents himself as a loving father: sensitive and responsive to his children when they had problems, "talking" to them and showing them physical affection:

'I knew that children needed a father. And I was a father for them in as much as I could. I would feel when they had problems. As a father I would feel this. Something is bothering him. I knew. I would first play with him, hug him and then he would tell me. "You see, no need to worry. That's why you have your father. He will help you to solve your problems. You should always come and tell me. You will always have my support." I never had problems with them.'

His son, Waldemar, largely confirmed this picture of Kacper: "My dad always understood me and he didn't tell me off but would say: 'try and find a solution'. Like this. Sometimes I think that he didn't want to get too involved since he had his own things and his own problems." On the other hand, he said that his mother was more involved in his upbringing:

'I think that let's say she [mother] was more involved in all this. Erm, this probably stems from her upbringing. My dad was brought up in the way that he would go to work and did necessary things for his family but mum I think did more. Always mums do more for their children. So in those difficult times the word "to settle" [zalatwic] was probably the best word. And with settling something mum was the best and she was always successful. I can't say that my dad wasn't but from today's perspective, as a child I would say I always looked up to my dad. But my mum was the active one.'

Waldemar valued his father for not being overly ambitious for him: "Dad always accepted it as my choice, and mum always wanted to improve something." Looking at the photo he brought to the interview of himself with his father when they were adult, Waldemar characterised their relationship as one of "relaxation". His talk around the photo centred on relationality – shared activities, interests and overlapping friendships but also feelings:

'Because it's a complete relaxation here when me and my dad sit. When I was still in Poland, we would go fishing and sit drinking beer and talk about politics and changes and so on. So I think this photo shows how we sit and debate, not in a sad way but always with a smile. My dad has friends who are also my friends in a way, in spite of age differences. And so this is an example of relaxed relationship between us.'

Waldemar was born in Poland in 1970. He became a teacher but, with rising interest rates and the high cost of living following the fall of communism, the family migrated to Britain in 2006 at his wife's instigation. In Britain, Waldemar became downwardly mobile, working as a security guard. In contrast, his wife retained her former occupational status as a qualified nurse. Because his wife earned the higher income and Waldemar was a shift worker, Waldemar took on the main responsibility for the care of their son. Yet, although Waldemar was actively involved in his son's care, he stressed continuities between his own fathering of his 12-year-old son, Kristow, and his own experience as a child. In particular, he mentioned that his father taught him 'respect' for others, especially elders. Waldemar, for his part, wanted to pass on "masculinity" embodied in his own father's relational practices:

> 'providing him [his 12-year-old-son] with masculinity. For me it's what I got from my father, a kind of peace and control and I try to grow this in me and build a relationship with my son on this ... it's about being, being by his side all the time.'

Just as his own father was an important influence on him, so Waldemar sought to influence his son and to earn his respect:

> 'So let's say I try to draw 40 per cent of things from what I inherited from my father and I think I demand more from my son. But I also try to calm him down and not to push him to do things he doesn't want. He is still young but he could already do some things. I think my wife has a stronger influence on my son than me. But similarly to me in front of my father, my son has more respect for me.'

Waldemar is affectionate towards his son, which he sees as an inheritance from his father:

> 'I tried to draw out his best qualities, his peace, and, I don't know, ability to look for solutions while being less angry. But I think that I also inherited the emotional side of him.

It's very important for me, for example, to hug my son, to have this physical contact with him, which I didn't have with my mum, she wasn't that emotional. And I would always run to my dad and I loved hugging him. So this was the place where I could always feel safe. I think this is what I try to pass onto my son, that he can always come to me with any problems he has.'

In this case, the narratives of each generation suggest strong positive identifications between fathers and sons – a similar patterning of gendered feeling across time and place. Kacper sought to be a 'good father' in the absence of his own father. Despite being a typical breadwinner father for his generation, Kacper and his son had a particularly close relationship. This picture is supported by Waldemar's narrative in which the 'softer' aspects of fatherhood in the form of a non-hegemonic form of masculinity are passed on and enacted. Waldemar's son, Kristow, also confirms that he had come to know his father much better since coming to Britain and is close to him. For example, Kristow noted that if his mother complained that his father had not helped him with his homework, that he tried to protect him:

'because most of the time, if we are talking about homework, most of the time it's my fault so I try to put the blame on me. But I want to take the blame because he's done so much for me. He devoted so much time for me that I simply want to try and pay him back, like this. (And what is the best thing about your dad?) Two things are most important: that he's so funny and also that he's such loving father. That he helps me so much and does so much for me.'

Echoes and emotions across the generations: Donald and Hugh

In this second chain of fathers and sons negative emotional undercurrents echo down the generations. They lie beneath the surface and do not overtly disturb current social relations. Both the grandfather and his son recalled past emotional tensions between them and feared these might be carried over in the latter's relationship with his elder son. Furthermore, the father's engagement in the interview encounter was imbued with considerable emotion suggesting regret and a desire to redeem the situation in his relations with his son.

Donald, a white British grandfather was born in 1931, an only child. He grew up in Scotland and went to the local state school apart from the last three years when he was sent to a private boarding school. Donald came from a comfortable middle-class business background. He portrayed his own father as a "family man" – who spent time with his family rather than in the pub (see also Brannen et al, 2004). In his childhood, he said he was very close to his father, probably more so than to his mother. His parents were described as "hands on", "we always did things together as a family". He and his father were "great pals" and did lots of activities together. After gaining a good degree at a prestigious university, Donald went into academia, an occupation that exempted him from National Service in the 1950s. He then began a career as a government scientist.

When Donald became a father, he talked about being "hands on" just like his father – "helping" with his son, changing nappies but "not often" (he supposed this was unusual at the time) and feeding him, "he was an awful boy to feed – oh dear. Present a spoon to his face and he would immediately turn it away. Anyway, I got involved with that." It was his wife, he said, who spotted that their eldest son, Hugh, was exceptionally bright, "I'm bound to say I didn't. He was fine – I didn't know how to judge him, I had nothing to compare it with. But I wasn't aware of how bright he was." His younger son was less bright but a talented sportsman and Donald and his wife became very involved in supporting his sports activities, a different form of middle-class 'concerted cultivation' (Lareau, 2002) from that afforded to their elder son.

Hugh was initially sent to the local mixed-sex comprehensive but, at 16, when his father's job required the family to move, Hugh was sent away to school. He went to a (state, single-sex) boarding school that afforded opportunities to secure a place at Oxbridge. While Hugh regarded the move as a major disruption and an unhappy time, in retrospect he said that the school had taught him to apply himself to his studies in ways that had continued to benefit him. He gained a place at Oxbridge and did exceptionally well thereafter.

With hindsight, Donald suggested that sometimes he had not made a good fist of parenting his son Hugh; in particular that he had not given him enough of his time as a child. He recalled going to his son's boarding school on open day when he was visiting the area for work and realising what it meant to get parenting "right":

'And I didn't realise at the time (pause), 'cos he seemed fine (pause), how much he appreciated that. I think (pause), whether he remembers that I don't know, but um I realised that I'd got it right – it was the right thing to do to spend the day with him.'

Donald reflected that because of the considerable time he and his wife had given to supporting their younger son's sports activities his relationship with Hugh may have suffered. This lesser attention and closeness to Hugh, he suggested, had continued into adulthood in part because of the history of their relationship but also because of the long distance between their respective homes, and because Hugh's high-powered job was so demanding.

Donald further hinted that their relationship was being repeated down the generations. He noted that he felt less close to Hugh's children than to the children of his younger son and that he found little to talk about with Hugh's elder, more academic son, Myles, who took part in the study. He also identified Hugh as having a similar problem with Myles and suggested a repeating pattern. Just as Hugh's brother had been less academic so Hugh's younger son was "more practical" than his older brother. In the same way that Donald recalled being more involved with his younger son, so he recognised that Hugh was spending more time with his younger, more practical son. At the same time Donald was anxious to claim that Hugh treated his boys 'the same':

'When we phoned and said "What are you doing?" "Oh [younger] and I did so and so", "He and I went for a Christmas tree", "He and I chopped some logs", "He and I ..." – it's never [older more academic] and him. Well Myles [grandson] is very self-contained, he doesn't need it. It's maybe [he's] closer to his mother.... But, yeah, you know I'm not suggesting in any sense there's a rift or anything of that kind – there isn't. And um (pause) Hugh will encourage, (pause) he'll treat them much the same as I used to treat him and (his brother).'

Hugh's own initial narrative (in the life story interview) was one of the longest in the study and his portrayal of his relationship with his father took 45 minutes. Looking back from a present vantage point at their relationship from the perspectives of a child and adolescent, his account meshes with his father's narrative. Hugh considered his upbringing unusual and male-oriented but "not a macho/male sort of upbringing – very intellectual, very bookish and very scientific". His relationship with his father was dictated by his father's consuming scientific work and by his own ability to engage at this level. He recounted a strong memory of being out with his father walking the dogs when he was six or seven and of "running to keep up … and dad would be talking. And what would we be talking about? Science. And so by the time I was early years of secondary school you know I was stuffed full of (pause) well context-free knowledge, no doubt, of science." His father, he said, 'wanted to teach' him. Much later in his narrative Hugh remarked that his brother and his parents interact differently. Even now, he said, most comfortable conversation with his parents, particularly with his father is:

> 'not talking about people, it's not small talk, it's not talking about (pause) it's nothing like the sort of conversation I would have with my wife or with my wife's family, or with my own children – it's a conversation in which one or other of us is educating the other person. It's a wholly (pause) is that didactic, is that the right word? I don't know, it's an educational conversation in which one of us is telling the other about something – and it's usually something vaguely (pause) it doesn't have to be scientific, but it often is.'

Hugh's ambivalence towards his parents came to the fore in his teenage years as he began to assert personal independence:

> 'a huge absurd irrational resentment feeling – I can't now tell you what I was resentful of, because I don't think there was anything specifically. But I really (pause) you know at the time if you'd have managed to ask me, and I was being honest, I would have said that I hated my parents when I was 16 – I would have said that. And particularly my father. Now why was that? It's very difficult (pause) now looking back it's very hard to say why.'

Hugh went to describe his father as having about him an "other worldliness", which he hated as a teenager and is still embarrassed by. "Why did I hate my parents? They really didn't understand me." While recognising this as a cliché, he still believed it to be true. Here he attributes his resentment of his father when he was younger to his father being an "older dad", even though Hugh was only a few years younger when his first child was born. As if in support of this narrative, Hugh brought along a photo of himself as a teenager looking particularly grumpy with his father and brother. Contemplating the photo he noted, "I remember that picture being taken, and I remember thinking (pause) as I looked at it, I thought it did actually characterise my teenage angst perfectly. (Laughs) With my father looking actually happy and slightly oblivious."

Hugh followed in his father's footsteps and became a high achiever though in a different line of work, a difference that may contribute to their competitive relationship. He developed a highly successful career in a male-dominated profession that generated very considerable financial rewards, while retaining an interest in scientific matters. Hugh reflected, "there is definitely an element of competition – no doubt about it…. I judged my life by (pause) I do, and I still do probably look at my life compared to what my dad did. And it's interesting how it's gender based."

Hugh repeated a rather similar script in the way he portrayed his relationship with his 17-year-old son. He recognised the repeating pattern and was very concerned that Myles might be feeling the same way about him as he did about his father:

> 'Uh yeah, so Myles? I mean it's a difficult business Myles. Because Myles of [all] my children, he is the one who is (pause) I don't know how to say it really (pause) it's so pathetic – Myles is the one that I want to like me. And I think it's because (pause) I think it's 'cos I know the others do (pause) and I know he does really. But um, it's funny – sorry (sniffing tearfully) um, yeah interesting.'

Hugh went on to compare his relationship with his sons with the relationship of himself and his brother with their parents:

> 'and I'm sure it was always because I was the first born and I was the troublemaker and I was the one who you know hated them, and he therefore could (pause) he didn't have to hate them because I did that, so he could be different from me by not hating them. And I see that with Myles and [my other son] … [other son] is great, and he doesn't have to despise his parents because Myles can do that perfectly well. And I don't know, I don't think Myles really does – but maybe he does, maybe he feels the same way I felt about my parents – I think, I see that sometimes.'

Hugh also brought along what he said was a rare photo of himself with Myles. The family photo taken on holiday was, he said, the first that

Myles had agreed to being taken for some considerable time. In the photo his son was of a similar age as Hugh was in the photo of himself with his father. Here his narrative takes a new turn in his suggestion that Myles's seriousness – Myles looked just as serious as Hugh did in the photo with his own father – resembles his own character. In examining the photo Hugh was also quick to smooth over any suggestion of family tensions during the holiday:

> 'We all travelled round and just had a great time as a family which we so rarely do, 'cos there's always the busy things in life – it was so unusual to get all of us actually in the same place for more than about a day – and it was glorious.'

Not wanting to frame their relationship in negative terms, Hugh went on to recount the companionable way he and Myles had spent the morning of the interview together. But Hugh became upset again in the telling. The expression of emotion and regret here may perhaps underline the tensions between idealisations of how father–son relationships 'ought to be' and the imperfections of how they often 'are': "It was lovely, he is so clever, so bright, and it's great."

The unresolved tensions and undercurrents in father–son relationships in this chain of men are undercut by similarities in that both had high-status occupations in well-rewarded male-dominated sectors. Hugh reproduced the high occupational status of Donald through a strong commitment to educational and intellectual success. While he did not follow in his father's professional footsteps he made his own successful pathway into a more financially successful fraction of the upper middle class. So too, and somewhat to his regret, Hugh saw Myles creating a different future for himself, having different interests and choosing a different field of study than he had chosen. Hugh was concerned that Myles was living in a much less secure world and might not be able to sustain a similar standard of living as his own or his parents'. There are, however, significant continuities in their constructions of masculinity and in their practices of fathering; both Donald and Hugh were highly work-oriented and absent from much of their children's daily lives. In their interviews they viewed fathering from the current norms of fatherhood; they regretted their past practice and the passing on of particular 'structures of feeling' to their first-born sons.

In his turn Hugh's son, Myles, was rather defensive about his relationship with his father, insisting that he did not miss out on anything because of his father's demanding career. But, interestingly, he suggested a similar relational pattern as that described by Hugh and Donald, one that is primarily intellectual:

> 'we kind of (pause) I suppose you could say we get on with sort of intellectual pursuits, you know we read similar books, we have similar-ish music tastes, we both go to the theatre sometimes – that's mostly more than my mother will, whatever.... sometimes about kind of quite heated political things, which is always good for a laugh.... Vent one's political anguish, I suppose. But no, I wouldn't say I've missed anything. I suppose I could have seen more of him, but I don't think there'd be like an immediate benefit.'

When Myles was asked about what it means to be a father, he confirms his own experience of being fathered in terms of the practice of hegemonic masculinity:

> 'I suppose kind of more [a] vague thing, a kind of strength and things like that you know. Kind of emotional strength, you know to be honest, I've never seen my dad cry – which, what little impact of that on me has had I'm not sure, but (pause) I guess ... (pause) you know, till about this year or the last year he's always been kind of the "big man of the house", you know, he's been my dad. And whilst my mum is engaged on kind of the daily running of life, it's been dad who kind of books the holidays and kind of does all the big kind of expensive, grand things that when you're 12 all seem terribly exciting.'

While Myles said he did not want to be just like his father he clearly admired him for his intellect and his ease in getting on with people. He also pointed to the transmission of self-esteem and classed confidence,

> 'he hasn't really taught me this, but he's imparted on me ... that you don't have to be kind of you know shy and retiring and dumb oneself down. And obviously I don't quite go around quoting Shakespeare and ... figuring out Einstein's theory of relativity, but it's certainly given me kind of a sense of pride I suppose in who I am, and kind of my intellectual pursuits which I do rather enjoy.'

Myles is also occupationally ambitious like his father and grandfather, "you know want to improve on what you've got. You want to strive to kind of do slightly better."

Conclusion

This chapter made the case for applying a generational lens to the study of families. It has discussed the concept of generational relations and its linkages with historical generation and kinship. It then went on to analyse two generational chains with the aim of demonstrating the relational ways in which fathers and sons negotiate fatherhood, their identities as men and how feelings of gender are transmitted in families. The two cases show that relationships can repeat themselves, but that intergenerational relations and feelings are not one-dimensional. Positive and negative feelings run alongside one another over long stretches of the life course; they can be acknowledged at particular moments, that is, when grandfathers looked back at their adult sons' lives and adult sons reflected on their fathers' lives and on their own parenting. Such feelings can become topics for reflection in a research interview. The expression of emotion and ambivalence take place when it is 'highly relevant for their interpretations of their own lives ... *in the present*' (Nilsen, 1996: 27, emphasis in the original). It may be that these interview accounts transcend, to some extent, men's habitual and gendered ways of expressing and disclosing feelings and experiences. On the other hand, reflecting on the past involves hindsight, and an opportunity to articulate how feelings change or remain the same.

The cases demonstrate different conditions in which closeness and ambivalence in men's gendered relations in families arise in the British context of societal and discursive changes in the so-called crisis of masculinity. These changes appear to have less resonance with the new migrant generations, as exemplified by Kacper and Waldemar. Their narratives suggest continuities in gendered feeling patterns in which the closeness forged between a father and son is not affected either by migration or by the son's downward social mobility that follows his move to Britain. In part the emphasis on closeness may be augmented by migration, as exemplified by Waldemar's and Kacper's insistence that Waldemar was not keen to leave Poland. As Parreñas (2014) suggests, the fact of geographical distance in transnational families does not mean that they cannot maintain intimate family relationships. Kacper's narrative may also be shaped by an emotional investment in his son for the future – the hope that his son and grandson, to whom he referred as his "dream grandson", will return to Poland. At the same time, Kacper cautioned against this interpretation – not wishing to give the impression in the interview that he was opposed to his son's decision to migrate despite feeling sad about it.

In the second case of Donald and Hugh regrets were expressed by both father and son about their relationship over the life course. Both men benefited from the transmission of considerable material and cultural capital manifest in their high educational and occupational achievements. Rather, Donald's intellectual cultivation of his son paradoxically fostered competition between them and affected their ways of communicating on an everyday level. This father–son relationship was overshadowed by its abstract, intellectual foundation that obscured and frustrated the intimate and ordinary (Frosh, 1997: 49). Further tension was fostered by Hugh's decision not to follow in his father's occupational footsteps, although both were high fliers in their separate fields.

Furthermore, the pain of emotional distance was registered by both father and son in the recognition that Hugh might be in danger of repeating the same pattern of distance with his elder son, Myles. Donald saw Hugh replicating what he did with his own sons, that is, in the greater attention he gave to his younger, less academic son. Hugh felt torn and regretful at the thought that his son might be harbouring similar feelings towards him as he did towards his father when he was a teenager. Hugh blamed himself for this. In his interview, Hugh's son, Myles, appeared unconcerned about a lack of closeness with his father and, paradoxically, was a great admirer of his father's "masculine strengths", notably the way that he concealed vulnerability.

The ambivalence expressed by Hugh concerning his relationship with his father, Donald, speaks to the tensions between changing norms of fatherhood and the ways that fatherhood is lived: Hugh was torn between the kind of father he has been to his son and the father he would like to be. Hugh realised that some of the groundwork of fatherhood has been missing because of his heavy investment in his career when his children were young. As studies of fatherhood suggest, contemporary fathers want to do a better job than their own fathers (Dermott, 2008).

Reflecting the emphasis on intimate relations in modern family life, Hugh wished to forge a more rounded connection to his son and wanted his son to "like" him. In their different ways both cases testify to the currency of 'modern fatherhood' defined in normative terms: showing feelings, talking and listening to, and understanding and encouraging children to communicate their feelings. Kasper represents a father who is 'outside his time'; he lived in a period when many fathers in Poland were absent or traditional. The close relationship between Kacper and Waldemar developed in a cultural and class context that was shaped not by notions of individualistic 'projects of the self'. It has withstood the major social and economic disruption that followed the fall of communism and rise of neoliberal individualism in Poland. While being close to his son when he was a child, Kacper's identity rested largely on the educational and occupational success he achieved under communism and on his role as the family's breadwinner. Waldemar's identity, although underpinned by the advantages of a university education and a professional occupation in Poland, was formed at a time of economic uncertainty, when many migrated for economic reasons. This meant that he was downwardly mobile in Britain and that his wife was better positioned to succeed in the British labour market. A positive consequence of this, however, was that Waldemar became an involved father through taking substantial responsibility for the care of his son, an outcome recognised by his young son. Given these exigencies, it is unsurprising that Waldemar's narrative is not presented as a canonical story of 'modern fatherhood', although his actions suggest that he embodies just that.

Thus we can see that fathering is being reshaped by structural conditions and new models of masculinity are being negotiated (Brannen et al, 2004; Brannen and Nilsen, 2006). However, in making sense of their current situations, fathers drew upon transmission from their own fathers – accepting or rejecting it – together with the resources and 'fresh contacts' (Mannheim, 1952 [1928]) of their current environments. A further dimension is that men were looking back to experiences lived in different periods of being children and teenagers as well as fathers, and that they did so from the vantage point of the present.

An intergenerational approach is methodologically difficult. The claims that can be made from case studies are largely theoretical concerning the processes, changes and patternings of the particular cases under study. In the study of three generations of fathers the research design offered a rich description of relatively few cases but, through recourse to contemporary and historical material that 'filled in' the contexts, it was possible to extrapolate from the particular to other similar cases, thereby generating transferable knowledge (Lincoln and Guba, 1985). Intergenerational family studies involve a great deal of analytical and interpretative work in making sense of the experiences of different family members. To take account of historical and life-course differences, biographical trajectories were mapped for each family member and contextualised in relation to historical material. Life events and transitions, however, held different meanings for different generations as well as for different individuals. Therefore a critical methodological concern was the narrative context of how stories are told and meanings made (Brannen, 2013). As Molly Andrews (2013) comments, all interpretation is partial, provisional and anchored on shifting ground. This is the focus of Chapter 8.

6

Children and Young People in Families

I turn now to focus upon children and young people in families. Throughout most of the 20th century, psychology and its associated field of child development were lead disciplines in the study of children and childhood, just as psychology led the way in youth studies. Both gave primacy to the life span paradigm. Child development was an influential force in policy and public discourse because it emphasised the effects of early infancy on subsequent developmental outcomes. What Donzelot (1997 [1977]) called the 'psy complex' shapes children's lives through the agency of parents, health and welfare and legal services (Mayall, 1994, 2013). In the 1970s child–centred parenting began to be critiqued as a process of 'intensification' (Hays, 1996) in which parental skills and behaviour were targeted as deficient and in need of expert guidance (Ramaekers and Suissa, 2011). Parenting remains a key site for social intervention with psychology continuing to emphasise the normative goals of producing the 'optimal child' (eg Landry et al, 2008).

These developments also emanate from wider structural and ideological changes as, in recent decades, neoliberal policy and ideas have offloaded much of the responsibility for children's welfare from the state and the community on to parents. One consequence is that those parents who lack the resources to fulfil their responsibilities 'adequately' have been regarded as social problems. As Dermott and Pomati (2016) suggest, a dominant discourse that some groups are 'poor' at parenting, typically families on low incomes, is sustained because the norms of an educationally advantaged minority are accepted as the standard against which all other parents are evaluated. On the other hand, these ideas are not new. For example, Barbara Tizard, a psychologist, who had earlier questioned hypotheses that what happened in early childhood necessarily led to negative outcomes later in life (1977), had also challenged the dominant discourse concerning the classed effects of parenting on children in the early 1980s. Comparing the conversations of four-year-old girls with their teachers in nursery school and their mothers at home, Tizard and Hughes (1984) found – contrary to commonly held beliefs that working-class mothers failed to stimulate children – a relative paucity of talk at school but a rich learning environment in the home. Talk in working-class families was often richer than in the professional nursery school setting. Yet many of the ideas of developmental psychology have continued to be influential in health and childcare, despite the research of those who have challenged them, a situation that arises in part from the different disciplinary silos from which critics speak.

In the first part of the 1990s, government was advocating a 'return to family values'. Lone mothers were particularly demonised and seen as a social threat – as rearing delinquent children and scrounging public housing and state benefits (Duncan and Edwards, 1999). At the time there was a call for more research on parenting from the ESRC, despite the existing considerable investment, notably the British birth cohort studies. In 1993, the ESRC invited Elsa Ferri at City University to prepare a research initiative on parenting. When the ESRC's Grants Committee did not support it, the torch was passed to me to develop the ideas further. Following a series of workshops, a new proposal took shape in which the parenting programme was reformulated to bridge the childhood and parenting fields. Rosalind Edwards joined me in preparing it. We decided to foreground children both in families and in other contexts. In 1995 a £3 million programme of research – Children 5–15: Growing into the Twenty-first Century – was funded by ESRC. Although I played no further part in the programme of work, in 1996 I was granted funding from the Department of Health to carry out a three-year study of children living in different types of families, in which children's views on, and contributions to, family life were the main focus.

The rise of childhood studies

Like many in the field of gender relations and family research, I first drew for theoretical inspiration on an action frame of reference that was influential in sociology from the late 1960s, with its emphasis upon the social construction of meaning (Berger and Luckmann, 1971). Qualitative research had already established a foothold in UK social science and, by the early 1990s, it was mainstream and pervasive. This rise of qualitative approaches occurred in the context of a shift from structural, variable-based explanations as provided by survey research. Instead the focus was also on understanding process, and exploring agency, subjectivity and identity. However, it is important not to overstate the case, given a long tradition in sociology, from Weber onwards, of the importance of understanding action in relation to meaning and seeing society from the perspectives of the marginalised and oppressed (Becker, 1967; Becker and Horowitz, 1972).

Gender and family studies, and later childhood studies, drew inspiration from human rights movements. In Britain, following in the wake of the 1970s Women's Liberation Movement, feminist researchers sought to make visible the inequalities in gender relations. In 1991 the UK ratified the UN Convention on the Rights of the Child, and around this time childhood researchers in Britain turned their attention to the invisibility of children as a social group. The methodologies they developed were informed by the political urgency of finding ways of 'giving voice' to those in positions of dependency. In this context considerable emphasis, especially in childhood studies, was placed on participatory research methods and children as competent social actors (James and James, 2004; James, 2007; Christensen and James, 2008).

In the 1980s and early 1990s interest in childhood as a field of study was already firmly established among Scandinavian and US social scientists; the UK was a relative latecomer to the field. These social scientists afforded children 'conceptual autonomy' (Thorne, 1987), identified children as a distinct group in society, and viewed childhood as socially constructed. They considered children as social actors within a diversity of social contexts, not only as family members. The approach of the Danish researcher, Jens Qvortrup and his colleagues (see *Childhood matters*, 1994), was path breaking. It drew attention to three social processes shaping children's lives: institutionalisation, familialisation and individualisation (Brannen and O'Brien, 1995b). The growing reach of institutional settings into the lives of children has been evidenced by the increase in early childhood services and provision and, for young people, the extension of education into early adulthood. The institutionalisation of childhood and youth has also proceeded alongside commodification – the creation of niche markets that target children (food, clothes, TV programmes, and other products and activities). This process has also led to the compartmentalisation of children's lives into separate and exclusive spheres, set apart from the adult world though in many respects imitating adulthood and cutting into it.

Familialisation has its origins in socialisation theory, in which children were seen as passive, even pre-social objects (Alanen, 1992), and as determined by the actions of their parents. These ways of framing children devalue them as less than adults (Mayall, 1994, 2013) and as adults 'in waiting' (James and Prout, 1990; Corsaro, 2005). Despite childhood studies' critique of the conceptual confinement of children within families, it is hard to dismiss families' importance to children, particularly in the current context in which household expenditure has risen disproportionately in relation to income and the reduction in state support leaves so many children in low-income families in poverty.

Although sociological vocabularies have shifted, attention is increasingly drawn to 'responsibilised' parents as the primary moral arbiters of children's lives, as the state and communities have divested themselves of many of their welfare responsibilities. Parents' organisation of children's lives in extra-curricular activities, increasingly a feature of modern childhood, has attracted much research attention (Vincent and Ball, 2007) and has been conceptualised as 'concerted cultivation' (Lareau, 2011). At the same time, parents have been subjected increasingly to the influence of experts but have been given the task of policing their children and protecting them from their parents (Lee et al, 2010).

In the third conceptual frame children are seen to exercise agency, a concept that appears on the surface to run against the themes of institutionalisation and familialisation. However, while individualisation has been a popular theory in sociology in recent years, especially in relation to youth, opportunities for individual action or agency are heavily structured and standardised in modern society by social class, gender and life-course phase (Brannen and Nilsen, 2005). While family life and other institutions appear to stress the importance of giving children autonomy, children's lives are practically and normatively circumscribed. Processes that purport to consult children are often pseudo-democratic, rarely affording them opportunities for individual or collective action. Furthermore, individualisation is not new. Western models of parenting have long emphasised individuality – the importance of enabling children to develop identities of their own.

These conceptual framings and the paradoxes that they raise concerning the interplay between children's structural, relational and ideological positionings are just as relevant today if not more so. They highlight issues arising from the position of children as family members and their locus in the 'parenting project' (familialisation); from the growth and extension of institutionalisation outside families (early childhood institutions, schools and educational institutions beyond schooling); and in the ideological construction of children as a social, emotional and economic good – 'the priceless child' (Zelizer, 1985).

Children now spend longer periods in education and care. In state schools attainment targets and benchmarks are increasingly ratcheted up. At the same time, in the name of 'children's rights', consultation has come into fashion but is often tokenistic. The neoliberal turn in which parents are expected to manage, and are liable for, the 'risks' that children encounter sits uneasily alongside the emphasis on individualisation and the social construction of children as agentic competent social actors.

Participatory approaches

One feature that characterises a significant body of childhood research is the use of participatory methodologies that are intended to give primacy to children. Participatory methods are not exclusive to childhood research but part of a more general trend in the social sciences that seeks to cede some power to those studied in the process of creating knowledge (Hammersley, 2017). Participatory methods date back a long time to action research and to social anthropology. In their contemporary usage, participation is transposed from the researcher, as in the case of *participant* observer, to the research participant. The approach has arisen out of a particular kind of politics (Freire, 1993) that is emancipatory and transformative. Within this framework the rationale for participatory approaches is to create social change by giving a voice to the disadvantaged and disempowered. As has been argued in the study of disability, for example, a non-participatory methodology serves to reproduce power inequalities between the disabled and non-disabled, while risking the perpetuation of a medical model of disability produced by non-disabled experts (Danieli and Woodhams, 2005). A participatory approach to disability is meant to counter such inequalities.

In childhood studies, participatory methods have been considered ethically preferable (Kellett, 2005; Nind, 2011, 2014) and an extension to informed consent (Hammersley, 2017). Many researchers in childhood studies also justify them on the basis of children's *own expert knowledge* of childhood which, they suggest, lends much greater insight than traditional non-participatory methods (see, for example, Alderson, 2001). Moreover, participatory methods are also meant to benefit research participants, 'Doing research helps children (perhaps disadvantaged ones especially) to gain more skills, confidence and possibly determination to overcome their disadvantages than adult researchers working on their behalf could give them' (Alderson, 2001: 151).

In practice, participatory methods embrace a wide spectrum of involvement: from researchers consulting their informants in some phases of the research process through to participants' involvement in fieldwork and data analysis. At one end, the aim is to create collaborative knowledge with children that is produced and owned by them. At the other extreme, researchers take the view that researchers can learn from children of whatever age and that their activities, interests, beliefs and experiences are worthy of being listened to and have to be respected (Thorne, 1993). The former position concerning knowledge as collaboration has implications for the value or validity of research knowledge as compared with lay knowledge. The latter position concerns hermeneutics – the importance of understanding children's own worlds. However, it stops short at the analysis phase of research, that is, it does not prioritise the actors' voices over that of the researcher. Instead the social scientist is beholden to generate knowledge by applying concepts that are sensitive and fitted to children's situations and experiences. In practice many participatory methods used with children are researcher-led.

For over 40 years, my own work on family life has consistently included the perspectives of children and young people. The rest of this chapter examines some of the studies in which children were involved as research participants. The discussion of the first study focuses on the methodological implications of foregrounding children's accounts of family life and the value and limitations of a participatory approach. In the second study, the importance of treating children and young people as a differentiated social group in data collection and data analysis is emphasised. In the third study, a case is made for applying a comparative approach and the use of different types of data to understand the multi-layered contexts in which children live and experience their lives.

Children's concepts of care: children as research participants

In the late 1990s, with funding from the Department of Health, Children's Concepts of Care, a three-year mixed methods study, set out to examine children's understandings and experiences of family life (Brannen et al, 2000). The research team, which included Ellen Heptinstall and Kalwant Bhopal, carried out a series of focus groups with children in the top year of primary school. These were followed by surveys, conducted in lesson time, in nine state primary and three secondary schools with children aged 10–12 in two local education authorities in multi-ethnic areas of South London. On the basis of the survey data we selected children living in these types of families: two-parent households (n = 15), lone parents (n = 18) and step families (n = 15). With the help of social services departments we also gained access to a group of 15 similarly aged children in foster care. The children and their parents/carers were interviewed separately. A number of different methods were employed to engage children: questionnaires, interview questions, vignettes, family maps or genealogies, and maps of significant others. In order to counteract some of the imbalance of power inherent in a one-to-one interview between an adult and a child, we were careful in seeking children's informed consent, for example, helping children to practise saying 'no' if they did not want to answer a specific question. However, we only went so far down the participatory route and to gain a fuller understanding of children's experiences we also drew on parents' accounts in the data analysis.

In order to fulfil our ethical responsibilities to the children, in the interviews we approached sensitively the topic of household change and children's relationships with their parents, especially those with whom they no longer lived. We invited children to complete family genealogies during the course of the interviews. Children who no longer lived with one or more parents typically did not remember when their parents separated or how old they were when they went into foster care. We also asked children to complete an exercise in which they placed 'significant others' in their lives in three concentric circles that represented the degrees of closeness they felt towards those they mentioned. Unsurprisingly, some of the foster children seemed not to want to talk about their parents. In addition, we asked children to comment on a number of vignettes. One depicted a mother and father in dispute and the father about to leave the house with a suitcase. In response to this vignette, a few children referred to their own family histories but most offered moral judgements about parental separation in general, saying that parents should first consider their children in making decisions about their relationships. In their responses to a range of questions and methods it was clear that children were reluctant to criticise their parents or cast one parent in a lesser light than the other. In this respect the survey questionnaire, because it was impersonal, may have made it easier for children to report on family matters than the one-to-one qualitative encounter.

Because of the sensitivity of matters to do with household change and parental separation, and the difficulty children had in talking about these, we also examined what their parents said about children's experiences and feelings on the matter. An illustration of the importance of the parent's account may be helpful here.

A white British, working-class girl aged 11, whom I shall call Anna, lived with her mother and stepfather and two younger siblings. Anna said she was resentful when her stepfather moved in but thought her feelings would change but "it never did". At the same time, she admitted that he "understood" how she felt about her birth father. Anna's mother expanded on this, describing how badly Anna had reacted when her father had left, so that she had asked him to let Anna live with him for a while. Instead, the father had suggested that Anna should be placed in care. Anna's mother explained that the father still showed no interest in his children (and paid no maintenance) other than a brief fortnightly visit. Anna, by contrast, gave no indication of being aware of her father's lack of interest in her.

Perhaps the most difficult interviews to interpret were those with foster children. Some children expressed either positive or negative feelings about being in foster care at the time of the interview but gave no sense of how their feelings had changed over time. By contrast, foster carers told us how children went through long and painful processes of adjustment. In our discussions with children about the people they placed on their maps of significant others, most foster children had little to say about their own parents while a few suggested ambivalent feelings. For example, some placed their birth parents in the inner circle of their maps (the most important people to them), while giving accounts that contradicted this elsewhere in their interviews. This raises a key premise of the participatory approach, namely that, in offering children the opportunity to be commentators *on* their lives, they were not necessarily inclined, or able, to be reflexive. Instead, they were getting on with the business of living their lives. It was therefore our ethical responsibility as researchers to create as little disturbance as possible to their daily rhythms and concerns. Thus the story we told, especially about the foster children, was in many respects a 'between the lines' story based on carers' as well as children's interviews.

In the dissemination phase of this study we sought to engage children by presenting them with some of the results of the study. We carried out a consultation exercise (Brannen, 2002a) for which we gained additional funding from the Department of Health. We returned to one of the schools where we had conducted a survey and found new research participants. We presented the main research findings to a group of children in the same age range as those who had taken part in the study (the original children were now several years older). We asked their permission to make a film of them discussing the results of the study and explained that we would be showing it to practitioners and policy makers as part of the dissemination of the research.

The final edit of the film was, however, my responsibility and children took no part in deciding what was included. While some of the material selected in the edit illustrated or expanded on the themes of the book that we wrote from the study, it was also chosen for its rhetorical impact. Indeed the whole point of the exercise was to make powerful points via visual media (Brannen, 2002a). From a participatory perspective, such an exercise risked increasing the power that adults exercised over children and constituted yet another form of surveillance that intruded into children's lives. In short, while adults could use the film as ammunition to promote 'children's best interests', it gave children no direct power. On the other hand, the film seemed to make a big impact upon adult audiences. However, it appeared that the audience seemed less impressed by children's comments about the research, and whether they agreed with the study findings, than they were in children's demonstrable competence and expertise in discussing the study in a public forum. But at least the film may have altered their perspectives of children's competence.

In reflecting on this study and the accompanying dissemination and engagement, the importance of involving children is not disputed. However, it is difficult to envisage or create situations in which children are primary authors, and audiences of research. When involving children, their involvement is of necessity limited; inevitably the researcher occupies a different position from the researched. This is equally the case in studying children as it is in studies of adults. I am in agreement with Hammersley (2017) that full participatory approaches may risk putting the researcher out of business but also relegating research knowledge to a relativist position, in which multiple conceptions of, or discourses about, the world are given equal value. Instead, we should be both sceptical about claiming certainty for our research findings while also not going so far as to claim that they are all equally likely to be false. As Harding (1990: 100) has put it, we should not give up on telling 'less false stories'. We should take care in making judgements about the interpretations we draw from our data; we should avoid making them only on the basis of validation by research participants or our own cultural communities. In short, scientific validity is not the same as 'cultural acceptability' (Hammersley, 2000b).

Children's perspectives on their fathers: children as a differentiated social group

The next study that I draw upon is Fatherhood across Three Generations, that was also discussed in Chapter 5. In this study of three generations of fathers and sons, we set out to examine understandings of fatherhood and experiences of father–son relationships. Here I will discuss issues relating to children's age and social competence – the importance of viewing children and young people as a differentiated social group. What came to the fore were the considerable differences among the youngest generation, whose ages ranged between 5 and 17, that were not necessarily to do with 'age'. Differences also concerned their ethnic origins, a key focus of the study and, for one group of children, their status as recent migrants. These differences influenced and challenged how we designed the methods and made sense of the data.

In the study we eschewed a one-dimensional view of our research participants. Rather, we conceptualised them and their social relations on the basis of several social categories – gender, age, social class, ethnic origin, migrant status. An intersectional approach analyses and explains the complexity and plurality of contemporary life (Phoenix, 2019). This means that different modes of social classification are not simply added together. Rather, social categories mutually reconstitute each other; they are dynamic and meaningful in relation to social contexts and other social categories (Phoenix, 2019).

How researchers categorise cases can change over the course of a study. In a case-based methodology, such as we adopted in Fatherhood across Three Generations (Brannen, 2015), different social categories came to the fore in different social contexts and relationships. For example, children were considered sons in their relations with their fathers while their ethnicity or nationality was usually a less relevant category in this relationship. In designing the study, particular categories determined who we included in the study. For example, when we selected groups of fathers we selected them on the basis of their ethnic origins – white British fathers, second-generation Irish fathers and first-generation Polish fathers. However, in the course of analysing the social relations of the Polish fathers, who we had initially defined in terms of their recent migration status, we came to define them and their families differently in the data analysis in relation to their 'transnational practices'. The fathers and their families regularly visited Poland and kept in frequent touch with family members through a variety of means and, significantly, did not necessarily see themselves as migrants who had permanently settled in the UK.

In the research proposal, age criteria underpinned the selection of the youngest generation in the study; we initially decided to select the boys within a narrow age range in order to limit the study's focus to a particular phase of parenting. However, this was not logistically possible given the study's remit to secure access to the older generations of fathers and grandfathers. Yet we found that the wide variation in the ages of the youngest generation was useful in making the research team question the category of 'age' in the conduct of the study.

Given the wide age range of the boys, we tailored our research methods according to ageist assumptions, thinking that some research methods would be more suited to the younger boys than the older boys. So we offered the younger boys, but not the older boys, a palette of visual materials. These included sheets of paper with drawings and text upon which children could write or tick their answers or place stickers on the items and pictures they selected. We also offered them the choice of a standard interview. In the event some younger boys said they preferred just to answer our questions rather than use the visual materials.

Age was also a category that we considered would influence children's participation in the interviews. As part of our ethical practice we first sought parents' permission to include their children in the study. We expected that parents of younger children might want to be present, and that this might affect what children would say. On the other hand, we thought parents would permit sons who were older to be interviewed alone. In the event we were unprepared for how the social category of 'recent migrant' might intervene, whatever the age of the boy. Despite the reassurances of the Polish researcher that the research team had no connection to any public authority, the Polish fathers were generally rather suspicious of research, and concerned about their children taking part. They were fearful about what their sons might say to us and so insisted on being present and on their sons being interviewed in Polish in order that they could monitor what they said. As one father explained later in his interview, it was acceptable to smack children in Poland but not allowed in the UK. He was therefore clearly fearful that his son might mention being smacked and the repercussions of a revelation. Another father was concerned that his son would mention that he and his siblings were at home on their own after school without adult supervision, again a practice that fathers did not want sons to mention in an interview. In gaining access to the Polish boys these tricky ethical matters had to be negotiated. The status of recent migrant was clearly more significant than the category of 'age'.

By contrast, most fathers who were born in Britain (the white British and second-generation Irish) expressed few such concerns and readily allowed us to speak with their children. A few mothers whose children were very young hovered in the wings and occasionally intervened, but most made themselves scarce, not wanting their children to feel constrained by their presence. For example, a six-year-old who was interviewed alone seemed quite unperturbed when his father left him with the researcher in the kitchen and went upstairs to get on with his work. Indeed, this particular boy also challenged our assumptions about 'age' in the way he took charge in some parts of the interview and asked a lot of questions about the study. One of us wrote later in a field note:

> I explained the study to [the boy] who said he knew what research was. But then he asked what would happen to what he told me and the activities he was being asked to do. This was quite challenging and I gave a very specific account of a particular activity. In the course of the interview I was quizzed about how many other children had taken part and their ages.

As some of our field notes suggested, irrespective of age the boys varied considerably in their competence as research participants. This was true of both the teenagers and the younger group of boys. One of us wrote after a long session with an eight-year-old:

> The boy took everything in, and responded seriously to all of the questions in the interview, sitting quite still without fidgeting. The interview took rather longer than expected (1 hour 16 minutes) because he was so attentive to doing everything asked of him, and giving full answers to all the questions. He even volunteered some information of his own, without being asked, as he became more comfortable, e.g. asking if the interviewer would like to hear about his girlfriend, telling me about dad learning to drive, etc. Coming before the interview with his father, the boy filled in a lot [of questions] about his parents' routines with him and his brother and their respective work schedules.

In contrast, some of the other children of a similar age were much less forthcoming.

The process of interviewing the boys also made us reflect on what it is to be an adult researcher in relation to children and young people. Our 'adultism' became evident in some of our field notes in which we adopted a maternal tone as we delighted in the articulateness of younger children, or felt protective towards them. One of us wrote, after interviewing a 12-year-old, '[The grandson] did indeed impress me with his maturity. He seemed entirely relaxed, talked very easily, expanding on his responses, filling in detail where appropriate. It seems unlikely that his father had primed him what to say before the interview.' Undoubtedly on occasion we betrayed a note of condescension towards the boys based on our own 'age' assumptions.

Despite evidence of some of the younger boys' considerable competence in the interviews, we still found that that we needed to contextualise what they said to us through recourse to parents' interviews. For example, a six-year-old boy readily provided a great deal of information about his life. However, the researcher wrote in her field note that she was a little concerned because he was giving his father a very bad press, claiming that his dad did not play, or do any activities, with him. It was only when the researcher chatted with the father before she left (the father had been interviewed some weeks previously) that she learned that he had recently broken his shoulder after an accident and was hampered in what he could do with his young children. In the field note we reflected on the importance of taking account of the short time frames of young children.

> He kept saying his dad did nothing with him and it emerged this was related to the period since his dad had a broken shoulder from an accident. When I talked later to the father, it turned out the problem with his shoulder was only 2–3 weeks old! His son's reference points were therefore very short term. In interpreting young children's responses, this is an important methodological point to bear in mind.

The significance of time was further underlined when the boy completed the sheet of household activities and how they were shared between his parents. The six-year-old discussed earlier had some difficulty completing the item on gardening. To the interviewer the reason seemed obvious as she looked out into their suburban garden on a bleak dismal winter day. In this boy's experience summer was indeed a long time ago. No wonder gardening had little relevance for him.

Assumptions about 'age' and its relation to competence were challenged by the study's findings concerning the boys' understandings of the pressures of employment on their fathers (Brannen et al, 2012). The younger boys' comments tended to be more insightful and indicated greater emotional intelligence than those of the older teenagers. For example, this eight-year-old gave a graphic narrative of the toll work took on his dad when he had to work late at the office (a narrative borne out by his father's own interview) and described this particular incident:

> 'when because once I was woken up in the morning and I went in (pause) when my mum was up I went into her room and I still couldn't find dad. And when I got back from school he had just arrived back home from work. He had been stuck there – there had been an argument and he came home sleeping. (Oh dear! And did you try to help him?) Yeah ... (pause) he just looked really tired. And so (pause) then he slept for like 14 hours and then mum just really needed him, so we went up and put an ice cube on him, and he woke up like that (clicking fingers).'

In contrast, a 17-year-old took it as given that his father worked very long hours. He told us that his dad was rarely home before 9.00 pm but his family waited to have dinner with him. However, the young man asserted that he did not feel he was "missing out" or lacking his father's attention. On the other hand, it was evident from his father's interview that the father regretted not having spent more time with his son when he was younger (Chapter 5).

In general in this study the tendency to judge children and young people in developmental terms was tempered by our awareness of considerable differences among the boys irrespective of 'age'. While we held the view that even very young children have competence and can participate effectively in research (Alderson and Morrow, 2011), we realised the importance of taking into consideration the constraints on children, for example, the duty of care of parents to children in protecting them from the potential intrusiveness of research. We were also careful not to over-interpret what young children said to us, for example, by taking account of the short time frames of young children. We needed also to bring into the analysis other data in order to understand children's experiences more fully and to provide context.

Children and food poverty: a contextualist comparative approach

The last section of the chapter draws upon the Families and Food in Hard Times study that was discussed in Chapter 4.[1] Here the focus is on its cross-national research design. The UK, Portugal and Norway were selected to provide for a 'contrast of contexts' (Kohn, 1989) in the aftermath of the 2008 financial crisis that led to a significant decline in household incomes across Europe and, increasingly, vulnerability to poverty (Matsaganis and Levanti, 2014) and food poverty in particular. Cross-national research lends itself to the employment of multiple methods and different types of data that can be used conceptually to capture multiple layers or levels of reality, as in macro, meso and micro levels. As Pawson (1995) argues, these different levels should be fused in our thinking and brought together in the data analysis, particularly in case-based research. Many of the studies I have done depended on more than one type of data or method. Further, the choice of methods was closely allied to the framing of the research questions the studies sought to address (Brannen, 2005, for example). The importance placed on fleshing out social context meant not only analysing the world through the perspectives of research participants. As Sayer (2000: 20) argues, understanding involves interpretation: 'Much of what happens does not depend on or correspond to actors' understandings; there are unintended consequences and unacknowledged conditions and things can happen to people regardless of their understandings.' The analysis of social structure and context typically necessitates collecting data about wider institutional and cultural contexts and national trends and policies.

A comparative approach that focuses upon cases, as in households or families, permits the researcher to move from understanding and interpretation towards explanation and generalisation (in a non-statistical sense). Ragin's (1994) qualitative comparative analysis approach (QCA) affords the opportunity to see 'how different causes combine in complex and sometimes contradictory ways to produce different outcomes' (1994: 138). Thus we may take instances of a social phenomenon and examine whether similar instances occur in similar contexts in different societies. For example, in the Families and Food in Hard Times study we examined whether the conditions that led to low family income were similar in different countries, and whether low family income led to food poverty in one society compared with another, and under which sets of conditions this happened. However, as in all case-based research, it was important to be clear about what is being compared: a country, a family, an individual, a particular practice. There was also a balance to be struck between being overly specific about the conditions or dimensions that were compared, so that those that had a common influence across countries were not overlooked (see Naroll, 1965 on Galton's problem). As Sayer (2000: 27) suggests, how we 'carve up and define our dimensions of study tends to set the fate of any subsequent research'.

The Families and Food in Hard Times study modelled itself in part on a multi-tiered research design employed in our cross-national study discussed in Chapter 3 (Brannen and Nilsen, 2011). It employed a combination of qualitative and quantitative methods to examine food poverty in relation to different layers of context – national, household, and the meso level of school and community. For the purposes of this chapter I will refer only to some of the UK and Portuguese data.

The national level

At the national level, large-scale datasets were analysed to identify which types of households with children were most at risk of poverty and food poverty in the three countries in the study in the period 2005–16. The European Survey on Income and Living Conditions (EU-SILC) was the only source of comparative data available to do this. The evidence is based on a direct question which asks about capacity to afford a meal with meat, chicken, fish (or vegetarian equivalent) every second day. For the UK, while households at risk of poverty were found to be also more at risk of food poverty, there is a difference by family type, with lone-parent households reporting more food poverty than couple families. For Portugal, families at risk of poverty also reported high levels of food poverty, but family type does not seem to be related to levels of food poverty, with lone-parent families reporting an only slightly higher level as couple families (O'Connell, forthcoming).

The household level

To understand the experiences of food poverty at the household level a qualitative study of 45 families in each country (43 in Norway) was carried out. Children were asked to complete the eating module of the Health Behaviour in School-aged Children questionnaire,[2] with one item about experiencing hunger – often, sometimes or not at all – when going to school and going to bed. In their interviews, some children and parents also talked about children going without sufficient food. Taking account of both the questionnaire responses and interview data, over half of the UK low-income families suffered food poverty and over three quarters of families in Portugal.

The case-based approach offers the possibility for analysing and comparing apparently similar cases in different social contexts. The following two cases suggest some similarities and differences in food poverty among *lone parents* living in food poverty in London and

Lisbon. While the cases were classified as lone-parent households, the Portuguese case demonstrates how the daily lives of a family may be lived across households: the home where the lone mother and children officially live and the grandmother's home.

Charlie, an English boy aged 15, lives in a two-bedroom council flat in a gentrifying area of inner London. His mother is an unemployed lone parent who has fallen on hard times; she lost her job two years before the interview. The family depends on benefits (around £660 a month) and was recruited at a food bank. They have no relatives in London and no other form of support to turn to. His mother is very angry about the cuts to benefits. In order to 'get by' (Lister, 2004) she often skips meals and keeps to a food budget of £20–25 a week, which she finds difficult because, as she says, her son is always hungry. She has difficulty paying the fuel bills. Charlie ticked that he 'often' felt hungry on his questionnaire both going to school and to bed. Although he is entitled to a free school meal he often uses his allowance (just over £2 a day) at break-time because he is hungry, having skipped breakfast. At lunchtime he can only afford a small sandwich costing £1.80; the cost of something more substantial would exceed his allowance. After lunch he often goes home where he typically makes instant noodles or pasta with pesto or butter. However "sometimes there's no food", he says. In the evenings, his mother cooks Charlie the kind of foods that he likes; he doesn't like the more healthy food she cooks for herself. As he says, he eats "pretty much the same thing" every day. But in the evening, as he says, he is hungry again and goes searching for food.

Pedro, age 14, is from a Portuguese Roma family. He lives in social housing with his three siblings (aged between 11 and six) in central Lisbon. His mother is a widow. She has a disability and has been unemployed for a long time. The family has always lived close to the breadline. They live on minimum-level welfare benefits and a very low widow's pension that together amount to less than €400 a month (though their rent is very low). Almost half of the mother's income goes on medication for herself and her children. Their access to electricity is through an illegal connection to a neighbour's supply. Access to food is entirely from charitable sources. Although entitled to a free three-course meal at school Pedro does not eat at school when he does not like the food on offer that day. The family has breakfast only if there is enough 'charity food' left over. Unsurprisingly, Pedro reports feeling hungry when going to school. In the evening, they usually eat at the maternal grandmother's house. Because the grandmother is also dependent on food aid they combine resources. But, as Pedro's mother explained, what, and how much, they eat depends on what the food bank gives them. Moreover, the food is distributed only in the evening and often there are long queues. The result is that they usually eat leftovers from the previous day and do not cook. They run out of food frequently, especially at the end of the month when Pedro's mother's welfare benefits have been spent. However, in some respects Pedro is better provided for than Charlie. Sometimes he eats at the home of his cousins whose father has a job and where the food is better and more plentiful. Pedro's family also shares the food that his grandmother is given. Unlike Charlie, he is reluctant to admit to a lack of food at home, "My mother will always manage something. My mother will go to the church when there is little money and the church will give her some."

In both cases the mothers' capacity to protect their children's food intake was heavily constrained. When income was short both went without food. Both families depended on a low level of benefit in the context of long-term unemployment. Both relied on food aid, although Pedro's mother and grandmother had much more frequent access compared with Charlie's mother. While Pedro's mother and siblings were living in very poor conditions, their situation defined as a lone-parent household is significantly different from Charlie's situation; they regularly eat and move between households and are embedded in a wider supportive kin network.

Cases can also be compared across contexts on other dimensions. For example, while conducting the fieldwork in the UK we recruited several families who lacked what is known as 'leave to remain' or whose migration status was under review by the authorities. In 2012 a significant change was introduced in the UK's immigration rules to discourage the settlement of migrants. As a result, a growing number of non-European immigrants and refugees with no leave to remain in the UK or those whose cases were being considered by the Home Office are no longer entitled to public funds (what is known as 'no recourse to public funds') (Dexter et al, 2016). While migration status was not a focus of the study we may compare the situation of families in similar situations across the two countries (Brannen, forthcoming).

Delilah, aged 14, lives with her younger brother and her mother. Her mother migrated from a former West African colony of the UK 11 years ago and is waiting for her leave to remain to be renewed. Her mother is not allowed to work and has no access to benefits. Delilah and her younger brother and mother share a council house in inner London, living effectively in one room with access to a kitchen and bathroom two floors below. The family is totally dependent on charitable organisations. They have no family in the UK to turn to. Delilah is not eligible for free school meals because the family's lack of a residence permit means they have no recourse to public funds. So she relies on money given to them by the church so that she can buy something to eat in the school canteen. Delilah commented on the little they have to eat at home, stressing the goodness of one piece of fruit, "After school and after clubs, [I'd] probably have something really small. I'd probably have like a noodle and then I have like an apple or a fruit after that. Just for like an evening meal, and then the fruit builds me up." At weekends the family relies on the food given to them by their church. Delilah also notes that it is "easier" to go without food at weekends: she needs less energy because she is doing fewer activities, "the energy stays in you a bit longer".

Maria, age ten, migrated to Portugal from a former Portuguese Central African colony five years ago. Her mother, an unemployed lone parent, says she had no choice but to migrate to Portugal if Maria was to receive treatment for a rare eyesight problem. This meant leaving her husband and, for a while, her young son behind. "I had my job, my house, a husband." For the first two years the treatment in Portugal was sponsored by government and their accommodation and expenses were covered. However, after this period of funding ended, Maria's mother had to choose between returning to their country of origin or interrupting Maria's treatment, which was not recommended by the doctors as it would risk further deterioration to Maria's eyesight.

Maria's mother opted to stay in Portugal, as a consequence of which their situation has markedly deteriorated. She has tried to get a job but says it is difficult because she lacks experience. They are reliant for accommodation on Maria's mother and her younger sister who had migrated earlier. The apartment is also occupied by her sister's two children. They live on a very low level of benefit – €412 a month that includes child benefit for Maria. Maria is entitled to free school meals and snacks in the morning and afternoon. However, her young brother is not eligible for child allowance or free school meals as he lacks the necessary documentation from their home country. Maria's mother visits food banks and tries to eat little food herself. "But I did not let them realise that I was not eating." While Maria indicated that she never went to school or bed hungry on the questionnaire, the interviewer noted Maria's reticence in the interview. Perhaps most revealing is the interviewer's fieldwork comment about the interview that took place in her research institute. After the interview the researcher bought Maria and her brother a juice and a sandwich each in the research institute's kiosk and noted how they both savoured the sandwiches and commented on their large size. They also told their mother as soon as she arrived to collect them what they had been given to eat.

Both lone-parent families are experiencing severe food deprivation as a result of migration. However, the cases point to some interesting differences between the two contexts. The first concerns access to the labour market and to benefits, albeit at a minimum level. Delilah's mother is not allowed to work and the family has no recourse to public funds, while Maria's mother suggests they have access to minimum benefits, free school meals and health care for Maria. She does not say that she is not allowed to work. The second difference concerns patterns of chain migration from former Portuguese colonies in which family members are supported by kin who have already settled in Portugal, as is shown in the case of Maria and her family. Portugal appears not to have severed its ties to its former colonies to the extent that Britain has endeavoured to do with its own former colonies.

The meso level: school policies and practices

We also examined schools' policies concerning food – the meso level of analysis. The school meals policies in the two countries operate at national and local level with different schools adopting different practices. School meals in the two countries afford an interesting contrast. In the UK, food in secondary schools is provided on a cafeteria basis in which children select particular food items, each costed separately. While there are School Food Standards, introduced in England in 2015, that endorse a 'whole school approach' to healthy school meals, they are not mandatory. As to free school meals that are meant to cover children from low-income families, around a third do not receive them (Royston et al, 2012). To be eligible, parents have to be unemployed and on benefits, which means that those whose parents are in part-time, low-paid work are not eligible. However, some schools that the study children attended covered the cost of school lunch even when the children were not strictly eligible.

Unlike in the UK, schools in Portugal provide a full three-course meal for all children at lunchtime, a policy that has continued despite the austerity measures placed on public spending because of the financial crisis. The importance of food in Portugal's schools reflects Portugal's general cultural and historical pattern of eating. Furthermore, schools are obliged to provide children with soup, a traditional component of Portuguese cuisine and emblematic of Portugal's food identity (Valagão, 2009), a mandatory element of a meal. Those whose families are on low incomes are in the main exempt from paying for school meals.

The few low-income Portuguese families in the study who were not exempt only paid 50 per cent of the already low price. At home, as in the UK, Portuguese children depended on similar cheap staple foods, namely foods that filled their stomachs such as rice, pasta and noodles. It is therefore clear that their diet would have been further compromised without the provision of a generous school meal. Because soup was an intrinsic part of both the school meal and often the evening meal at home (Lopes et al, 2006), children's intake of vegetables added to the quality of their diets.

While Portugal's customary eating practices and policies on school food may help mitigate the poor diets of many children in low-income families, in the UK by contrast the quality and quantity of food at school was less adequate. Few children were eating a full meal at secondary school. For those on free school meals, the allowance was so small that they could afford only to purchase a snack either at lunch time or at break. Several children complained that the allowance only enabled them to buy a small sandwich rather than a larger one, or that they had to choose between a drink and a sweet food item. Such food was clearly not very nutritious and did not fill them up. There was also variation *between* secondary schools in the UK study in the delivery of free school meals, with many secondary schools acting in potentially exclusionary or stigmatising ways (O'Connell et al, 2019). Only one child in the study who was eligible for free school meals ate a proper meal at secondary school. This practice was specific to the school and extended to all the children and was paid for out of its own funds.

Cross-national, comparative case-based research that is informed by data that address different layers of social context (global, European, national, local and family levels) can suggest how particular lives may be led if policy, economic and social conditions change and resources are differently distributed (Brannen and Nilsen, 2011). In this study it afforded layers of explanation that accounted for children's and parents' experiences of food poverty. A key aspect of the global and national context concerned the financial crisis and its effects in both countries. However, national policies, according to which governments in the UK and Portugal managed the economic crisis, and how their respective economies have fared since then differ.

In the period covered by the study, at the national level unemployment was higher in Portugal while the UK was characterised by low-paid part-time jobs with no permanent contracts or guaranteed hours (also common for those in employment in Portugal). Large-scale data suggest that those most at risk of food poverty were lone-parent families in the UK, while in Portugal family form appeared not to make a difference. At the micro level, the resources available to lone parents or to migrants living on a low income and seeking to combat food poverty are shaped by social context, for example kin networks and the availability of food aid. At the meso level, the provision of food at school in Portugal mitigated some of the effects of food poverty on children while in the UK it signally failed to do so. Portugal and the UK therefore provide an interesting contrast in this respect, although the more generous free school meals did not protect all Portuguese children from lack of adequate nutritious food, as analysis at the micro level of the household suggests.

Conclusion

This chapter has covered several studies of children's family lives in which I have been involved. It has reflected upon some of the tenets of childhood studies in terms of theorisations and methodological approaches. First, drawing on a study of children's perspectives of care and their experiences of living in different family forms, it considered some of the methodological limitations of foregrounding children's accounts of family change without recourse to data from their parents. It also considered issues that arise in adopting an approach that claimed to be fully participatory. In particular, it argued that as researchers we should take ownership of the claims we make from our research while doing all that we can to test the validity of those claims.

The second study the chapter discussed concerning three generations of men and father–son relationships involved selecting children and young people on the basis of family generation. This study suggests the importance of problematising the idea that children constitute a homogeneous social group, as implied or indeed proposed in some of the literature on childhood. The argument was made that we need to guard against defining children by 'age' in a simplistic way that accords with the developmental paradigm. Rather, children should be conceptualised as a socially differentiated group. Like adults, children's positionings are gendered, classed, and are shaped by the intersection of ethnicity, age and migration status. These categories are dynamic, mutually reinforcing one another in different domains (Phoenix, 2019). In short, how researchers categorise children and young people needs to be flexible and dynamic, including in the research design, the data collection, and the analysis and interpretation of data.

For a third example, I chose a study of children and parents in low-income families with a focus on food poverty. The cross-national design offered the opportunity to employ a comparative perspective to understanding the lives of children and young people in different societies and in relation to multiple layers of social context. As Qvortrup (2000: 81) argues, to ignore systematic variations between countries at a macro level 'increase[s] the risk for overlooking the reality and systematic influence of such large socio-economic factors, which presumably account for fundamental variations of everybody's life worlds and thus also those of children'. Here the case was made for understanding the materiality of children's lives by situating them at the micro level of households, the meso level of school as well as the macro societal level. In relation to low income and the risk of food poverty, it examined the resources available to families, how they employ resources and the constraints upon their lives of public policy, schools, the voluntary sector, and kinship, friends and neighbours.

7

Families through the Lens of Food

Food is central to family life and a key lens through which a sociologist may understand family relations in social context. Food provisioning has been, and remains, largely the responsibility of mothers. In the 19th century the meagre diets of poor people were blamed on their own actions and doctors (mainly men) sought to educate mothers in poor families on how to feed their children 'properly'. At particular points in history, for example after a war, governments have intervened to alleviate the poor nutrition of the population. In the first part of the 20th century, British children were seen as a direct route through which the nutrition and health of the next generation could be improved. Socialist feminists and other pioneering women were instrumental in putting pressure on the state to improve the nutrition of women and children (Mayall, 2017). In 1909 the Fabian feminist Maud Pember Reeves and the Fabian Women's Group set up an investigation into the causes of infant mortality. The London borough of Lambeth, where the study was done, was one of poorest parts of Britain at the time (Pember Reeves, 1988 [1913]). According to their report, mothers found it impossible adequately to feed a family on the pound a week that their husbands earned. The report, *Round about a pound a week*, recommended a set of reforms to improve the lives of children – child benefit, school meals and free health clinics. Later, in the 1930s, the work of the Women's Health Enquiry Committee (Spring Rice, 1939) was seminal in drawing attention to the diet, health and conditions of working-class women. The report demanded that the 'labour of the housewife' receive 'the acknowledgement and consideration it deserves' (Spring Rice, 1939: 27).

The school meals service in Britain was established as a consequence of public concern about severe malnutrition among children living in poverty. In 1904, a parliamentary committee reported that the poor physique of volunteers in the Boer War was a result of underfed children. School meals were introduced in England in 1906 and some school boards and philanthropic organisations began to provide cheap or free school dinners.[1] However, it was not until 1941 that a National School Meals policy was implemented and the first nutritional standards for school meals were set. 'These laid down levels of protein, fat and calories which should be provided by a school meal' (Evans and Harper, 2009: 90). However, school meals, including free school meals, did not become extensive until the 1944 Education Act (Gillard, 2003). In the 1980s school meals underwent major change when the 1980 Education Act designated them 'a nonessential service' and removed the obligation on local education authorities to provide meals except for pupils entitled to free provision (the parents or child must be 'dependent' on benefits) (Evans and Harper, 2009). The local education authorities were also given the choice to decide the price, type and quality of meals provided. Shortly afterwards in 1986 the Local Government Act's introduction of competitive tendering meant contracts had to be allocated to commercial caterers offering the cheapest price (Gustafsson, 2002: 688).

My own interest in researching food began in the 1990s, when several of us at Thomas Coram Research Unit undertook research on the health of young people and children. In one study we sought to examine how 16-year-olds and their parents managed young people's health broadly conceived (Brannen et al, 1994). At the time public policy concerning young people's health and welfare largely focused on health education programmes in schools. Our aim was to investigate health practices related to eating, smoking, sex, and drugs among a community sample of young people at a life-course phase when they were seeking to exercise greater independence. Subsequently, in the late 1990s, Pamela Storey and I did some research on children's health and food in relation to the transition to secondary school (Brannen and Storey, 1998). As mentioned, this was a time in which school meals services had been removed from the jurisdiction of local education authorities and contracted out to commercial caterers. In secondary schools 'meals' were replaced by 'food choices', in which young people selected items from a cafeteria on the basis of cost and often to the detriment of their nutrition. Government spending on school meals fell and there was a significant drop in the numbers taking school meals (Brannen and Storey, 1998).

In recent years food has provoked increasing attention from social science researchers in a context of increasing policy concern about the effects of diet on health. Policy makers and the health profession find it difficult to understand why people eat as they do, when the 'choices' available are against their interests in pursuing healthy lives. The increasing incidence of coronary heart disease, type II diabetes and cancer (Kirkpatrick et al, 2010; Lawlor, 2013; RCPCH and CPAG, 2017), together with overweight and obesity, especially among children, are a major policy concern (House of Commons Health Committee, 2018). The old chestnut of maternal blame is still part of this public debate, with some contested survey evidence concerning the effects of maternal employment on children's diet (O'Connell and Brannen, 2016).

Conceptualising food

As social anthropologists have longer understood, food is of profound symbolic significance (Douglas, 1981; Lévi-Strauss, 1969). A number of conceptualisations are employed in social science. Food is understood as a material resource in the sense that both the quality and quantity of food are the basis for energy and nutrition. (Najman and Davey Smith,, 2000). Food is conceptualised as 'work', requiring time, knowledge and skills in accessing and preparing it (DeVault, 1991). Food is also seen as a key dimension of social participation (Davis et al, 2012) and provides some of the material, social and emotional conditions for social inclusion. It is a means of organising the everyday and of orchestrating its rhythms (Sutton, 2001); it is central to celebrations that mark rites of passage in individuals' lives, points in the calendar related to family celebrations, and is implicated in the symbols and practices of each family, ethnic group, social class and the generation to which it belongs. Food and meal preparation are also pivotal in constructing home as a 'special place' (DeVault, 1991) and is an expression of 'who we are' (Fischler, 1988). It is also a site of punishment and of resistance and power negotiation, especially between parents and young children (O'Connell and Brannen, 2016).

Given that the meaning of food and its material form are subject to variation and change across time and place (for example, Warde, 1997), the concept of 'social practice' has been employed in its study (Warde, 2005). A practice approach engages with the habitual aspects of human behaviour that are not easily open to reflexive engagement. Many everyday practices, 'are often hidden from view; part of an everyday and mundane world frequently so taken for granted that their meaning becomes lost' (Punch et al, 2010: 227). The notion of practice as developed by Reckwitz (2002) and Shove et al (2012) makes a particular practice the primary unit of inquiry rather than an individual or institution. From this perspective it becomes possible to understand how practices are established and consolidated, and how they change. This theory of practice involves an ontological shift in which the focus is on the 'qualities of a practice in which the single individual participates, not qualities of the individual' and people are reframed as 'carriers' of practices (Reckwitz, 2002: 250). A practice approach, moreover, engages with the constitutive elements relating to a social domain, for example, cooking, eating meals and washing up, and the sequencing of, and the linkage between, these and other practices. Shove et al (2012) see practices as comprised of three elements – *competency*, *materials* and *meaning*. Competency refers to skills and know-how, materiality to the broad array of objects and technologies that are involved in or comprise a practice, and meanings refer to ideas, aspirations, norms and symbolic meanings surrounding a practice (Shove et al, 2012: 14). Practices have historical trajectories that provide for the study of social change through generating insight into how particular practices recruit and lose practitioners. Shove et al argue that 'practices emerge, persist, shift and disappear when *connections* between elements of [competency, materials and meanings] are made, sustained or broken' (2012: 14–15 original emphasis).

Another use of the term 'practice' is that of David Morgan (2011), who has argued that family life is what people 'do' (Morgan, 1996) with reference to other family members, in contrast to emphases on what families 'are'. As Morgan (2011) argues, family practices can be strongly or weakly bounded so that, in the latter case, non-related persons may be treated as part of the family; family practices may also constitute concentrated and closely linked sets of practices, or they may be diffuse, that is, carried out individually and with small, short-lived configurations of family members. Many family practices relate to food. In the case of cooking a family meal, a parent may engage in a number of other practices, for example simultaneously keeping an eye on children, monitoring their games or TV watching as well as feeding them. In this way food practices are understood as part of the performance of parenthood; they are constitutive of parenting. Following Shove et al (2012), parents determine a great deal of the *materiality* of what children eat. Typically, mothers decide which particular foods to buy and prepare. Parents inculcate in their children *competencies*, notably teaching them how to eat, for example, table manners. They may also teach them conviviality associated with meal times and impart nutritional knowledge. Parents convey food *meanings* symbolically, through suggesting to children notions of the 'goodness' and 'badness' of particular foods. Food is also a means of communicating love and maternal care.

Food as a means to examine family dynamics and power

In the period up to the early 2000s rather little sociological research had been conducted on food in families and early childhood settings, despite the rise in early childhood provision. It was still widely assumed that parents (mothers) were responsible for everything that their children ate. As noted in Chapter 6, an opportunity arose to compete for funding for a postdoctoral position for which my application was successful. Rebecca O'Connell was appointed and we developed some research ideas together. The possibility for some funding arose under a joint initiative by the ESRC and the Food Standards Agency 'to further explore and explain UK dietary decisions' and the circumstances in which they change. The Food Practices in Working Families study (2009–13) was funded in order to examine some existing claims that both parents being employed was linked to poor food practices and dietary outcomes for young children. The team leader was Rebecca; I acted as adviser and senior researcher with colleagues at TCRU playing other roles. In its first phase we analysed existing large-scale datasets in order to examine the effects of maternal/dual parental employment on the quality of children's diets. A second phase aimed to understand how food fitted into the lives of working parents and their children. To address this latter question we designed a qualitative study that involved taking a representative subsample from the National Diet and Nutrition Survey of mothers in paid employment and one of their children (analysed in phase one). Mothers or the main food providers in the household (N = 47) and a child aged 2–10 were studied at two points in time (with a two-year gap between interviews)[2] (O'Connell and Brannen, 2016).

Recounting embodied experiences inscribes meaning to food and food events. In addition it can evoke and reveal feelings and conflicts that lie below the surface of family relationships that have their origins in the past as well as those that express current practices and relationships. A focus on food can suggest the ways in which family experiences and practices are reproduced, are in tension, or in the process of change. In the course of the study we sometimes had a rare insight into family dynamics and the underlying conflicts and ambivalences around food practices. This happened when both parents and children were present at interviews and interacted with each other and with the researcher (Brannen and O'Connell, 2017: 107).

In the following family, both the parents and the child were present at the first interview of the qualitative study, with the result that a great deal of social interaction took place between the three of them. These social interactions added greatly to our understanding of the complexity of the 'food habitus' (Bourdieu, 1977) of this particular family and its power dynamics. They highlighted how each parent, while actively seeking to control their child's life and diet to positive effect, transmitted mixed and conflicting messages, intended and unintended, and provoked resistance from the child (Brannen and O'Connell, 2017).

Amelia was nine years old when the first interviews were conducted. She is an only child. Amelia's parents said they wanted the "best" for her and sent her to a private school. They lived in a detached house on a country lane on the outskirts of a northern city. Amelia's father was a self-employed salesman. Because he worked mainly in the evenings and at weekends, he did all the food shopping and cooking during term time. Amelia's mother was a teacher; she had a long commute to work and brought a lot of work home to do in the evenings.

At the first interview, neither Amelia's mother nor father considered Amelia capable of making "good" food choices, saying that "in fairness if she had her own choice she wouldn't be as healthy as she is, would she?" For her part, in her own interview Amelia strongly resisted her parents' attempts to control what she ate. According to both Amelia and her father, Amelia had little say about what she ate at home. Amelia's parents also attempted to control what she ate at school, instructing her about what to choose and trying to check up on what she had eaten. They both noted also that their attempts to ensure their daughter ate a healthy diet were often counterproductive. While Amelia's father took responsibility for what Amelia ate at home, his wife was highly critical of his cooking, suggesting he was not feeding Amelia what she considered to be healthy food. Elsewhere in the interview, Amelia's mother rebuked him for his choice of meals: "You can't actually get away from meat and two veg."

In the following interview extract we can see further tensions being played out between husband and wife in the interview about the healthiness of their daughter's diet.

Interviewer:	'And do you think Amelia has a healthy diet?'
Mother:	'No.'
Father:	'Yes. I would say in general, compared with a lot of children I would say yes she did.'
Mother:	'Not for the school she's going to and if you look at say socioeconomics, and you know actually I think that where she is, in the school she's at, actually her diet should be better.'
Father:	'yeah I mean – '
Mother:	'People from middle – yeah, so the environment that she's in, her diet should actually be better than it is.'
Father:	'Yes.'
Mother:	'And, most probably, her range of eating should be better than it is.'
Father:	'Yes, no, I agree with that, no, I do agree with that.'
Mother:	'So, no, actually think that – '
Father:	'But compared with the majority of children I would say, yes.'
Mother:	'She's never had things like an avocado, no, anyway.'
Father:	'Yeah, but compared with the majority of children – '
Mother:	'I suppose.'
Father:	'It's a minority that go to public school, private school, sorry –'

In this interview extract, the mother's points of dietary reference were the diets of the children at Amelia's private school that she felt Amelia's diet was failing to live up to. In this context it is important to note that the mother's job was not only more demanding than her husband's in terms of hours it was also higher status. Amelia's mother was, furthermore, both class conscious and a class riser (albeit she is hesitant to admit to her class views openly). This is evident not only in the decision to educate Amelia privately but also in the control she sought to exercise over her daughter's cultural tastes and her appearance. Note the coded mention of avocados as a desirable food, "She's never had things like an avocado." Amelia's father, on the other hand, felt that his daughter's diet was as good as other children's – "the majority of children" (his words). However, to placate his wife – perhaps because of the interviewer's presence – the father appeared to capitulate to his wife's assertion that Amelia was not eating as well as her peers in his ambiguous responses, "Yes, no, I agree with that, no I do agree with that." However, it is notable that he tried to have the last word reminding his wife that "it's only a minority" of children that are privately educated. Significantly, he then apologised for his uncertainty about his use of the term private education – "public school, private school, sorry" – which represents perhaps an indication of his own subjective social class insecurity.

On the one hand, Amelia's father asserted that he was "90 per cent happy" with Amelia's diet but would also like Amelia to eat a wider range of foods. His wife, on the other hand, considered that Amelia ate too much, noting that she was developing "fatty deposits on her bottom". Amelia had clearly taken her mother's views on board and focused on fatness and anorexia rather than 'health' in her own interview. Amelia's mother saw her husband's cooking as responsible for the unhealthy food that Amelia was eating, while Amelia's father blamed it on his wife:

Mother: 'I think she eats more than what you think she eats. Now I say that because I know that when I open this [freezer], we've got these [pulls out a frozen pie and shows interviewer]. And, I say well no, actually it's processed and it's not healthy and – '
Father: 'But that's one day a week.'
Mother: 'Yeah but – '
Father: 'The junk that Amelia eats is when she raids the cupboards and your handbag and things, that tends to be what it is, because she roots it out. If she knows it's there, she'll make sure that she sneaks out at some point and eats it.'

Thus in the above interchange it becomes clear that Amelia's mother did not always eat healthily and that she secreted 'forbidden foods' so that Amelia (and her husband) would not find out. In this context it is unsurprising that Amelia was rebelling by gorging on these foods and stealing from her mother's handbag. Given the inconsistent behaviour of her parents but also between what her mother professed to eat in public and how she ate in private, Amelia played her parents "off one another" (Amelia's mother's words). The power play, as both Amelia and her mother noted, also concerned Amelia not knowing which of her parents to keep happy.

Mother: 'I find her sometimes, she was heading a little bit towards the getting picky, playing us off against each other. [Father] [doesn't] buy brown [bread], all of a sudden she no longer likes brown bread. I will buy brown and tell her she starves if she doesn't eat it. 'Cos I know the minute that she will eat it she loves it.... So I am more –, aren't I? When it comes to food ... I am more, I won't let her.... But sometimes she doesn't know who to keep happy. Because she knows that [husband] only likes white bread. So sometimes she doesn't know who to keep happy, does she? ... If she chooses brown she'll keep me happy, if she chooses white she'll keep you happy.'

It also transpires in the interview that, despite Amelia's father taking more responsibility for cooking and food purchasing than his wife, Amelia's mother sets the household's standards and is the boss. The interview dynamics between Amelia's father and Amelia hint at how this played out in the household. In this next interview extract we can see how Amelia's father owned up to his failures to meet his wife's high household standards. He infantilised himself in confessing to his 'bad behaviour' – that is, not always following the methods of washing up set down by his wife. Amelia impishly acceded and was complicit in labelling her father as "naughty".

Interviewer: 'Who put the stuff in the dish washer?'
Father: 'We've got a dish washer, that's the truth of the matter (laughing).'
Amelia: 'Well basically you do wash them, because you have to rinse them out and then put it in the dish washer.'
Father: 'You're supposed to. Daddy doesn't always, does he?'
Amelia: 'No, not always. Naughty!'

It is relatively unusual to happen upon opportunities to observe the interplay of family relationships, because studies of parenting and family life have tended to use one parent's account as proxy. This is not to suggest that interviews with individuals are not useful. They may be necessary for practical or logistical reasons or because the focus of the study (in this case food) is the province or responsibility of one parent (usually the mother) more than the other. In Food Practices and Working Families it was more common for mothers to be interviewed because they were the main food providers. But sometimes fathers were interviewed, either alone or jointly with mothers. The siblings of the target children were also often present. Such opportunities, while challenging, in terms of managing the interview dynamics and making for inconsistent data (between cases), can provide important insights into family life in terms of understanding the negotiations of power and control between parents and between parents and children, both in relation to the study focus but sometimes other family practices.

Food, family memories and intergenerational transmission

A methodological benefit of studying food is the way it can provoke, indeed embody, memory (Sutton, 2001). Memories cohere around bodily experiences that stretch back into the past (Narvaez, 2006, citing Mauss and Halbwachs). As Proust wrote, '[t]he past is somewhere beyond the reach of the intellect and unmistakeably present in some material object (or in the sensation which an object arouses in us)' (cited in Narvaez, 2006: 51). While the past exerts a strong grip on embodiment 'so that the unfair spectres of tradition will thus have an incarnate presence in the body and thus become organically present in life' (Narvaez, 2006: 68), embodiment is also a 'structure of possibilities', a site of learning and change, where new practices emerge.

Childhood is a significant period in shaping adult tastes and dispositions (Bourdieu, 1973), and a period in which parents try to nurture their children's food tastes and practices. Although the emphasis on 'healthy eating' is encouraged in the context of contemporary professionalised discourses of active, 'responsible parenting' (Ramaekers and Suissa, 2012), early life-course experiences and intergenerational influences also influence the ways that parents 'encourage' their children to eat. Intergenerational transmission, conceptualised as the cultivation of 'habitus' (Bourdieu, 1977), refers to the passing on of attitudes, values and practices, and a 'system of dispositions acquired by implicit or explicit learning which functions as a system of generative schemes, [which] generates strategies' (Bourdieu, 1993: 76). Positive and negative memories of past experiences are themselves forms of transmission (Thompson, 1993). They can have unintended and unconscious consequences both for the individuals concerned but also for the succeeding generation. Through the medium of food cultural meanings are passed between family generations. Food evokes strong emotional responses including resentment, dislike, physical revulsion, security, love and nostalgia and is often associated with feelings of past powerlessness (Lupton, 1994; Uprichard et al, 2013; Knight et al, 2014: 310), and emotional responses that can be passed on. 'We do not simply put away childish things. Our childhood experiences continue, whether we like it or will it or not, to inform our present behaviour' (Morgan, 1996: 275).

In nurturing and feeding their children it was common for parents in the study to say that they drew inspiration from memories and traditions of their own childhoods and from their ethnic and family cultures. Some wanted to continue these traditions within their own families; they wanted their families to carry on food routines and tastes established by their own mothers in their childhood, reflecting culturally normative ideas (DeVault, 1991). Discussing the topic of eating together as a family, one white British mother, for example, described the importance of family meals when she was a child, especially at the weekends, "So yeah I think I've been brought up with that and that's what I want to pass on to my children. And hopefully it makes them closer as brother and sister as well in future life." One British Asian mother with a six-year-old son described the conscious and unconscious character of transmission, and how she told her son a story about how her mother made a special drink for her when she was ill. The extract suggests that this transmission was successful and imbued with emotional significance:

> 'it's conscious, it's subconscious, you cook the foods that you grew up to eat and then you sort of pass those foods down, the tastes and the cuisines down. So it's something we always grew up eating and sometimes I say to my son: "This is something my mum made, you know. And I enjoyed it so maybe you'll like it." And he may not like it but I'll tell him that story. The story was this, you know, when I was little, my mum used to make that 'cos I had a cold, or my mum made me certain teas for medicinal purposes. And she'd put aniseed in them and she'd put cinnamon and she'd put in cloves and she'd put all these different things and she'd brew them up. And you'd have them if you didn't feel well and had tummy aches and things like that. So if my son has a tummy ache he'll say to me: "Mummy make me the tea that your mummy made you, my grandma made you."'

Food may also create intergenerational ambivalence (Lüscher, 2005; Brannen, 2015) so that parents may carry and reconstruct negative memories of food in their childhood that make them want to change their own tastes and food practices and thereby to foster different tastes in their children. At the same time, despite such rejection of past tastes and practices, tensions that originate in the past may live on, and be expressed as current tensions in families. As the case of Amelia suggested, Amelia was exposed to different and conflicting messages about diet from each of her parents. We began to understand this better when it transpired in the interview that her parents' own food tastes and dispositions from their childhoods differed significantly. Amelia's father's recollections about what he ate as a child suggest continuities with his present tastes and demonstrate strongly conservative preferences in matters to do with food. He described himself as a "fussy child". He recalled how he grew up in a corner shop that he said gave him the freedom to help himself to food. When he did not like the meals on offer at home he made himself something else to eat. He also suggested that his own conservatism was passed on to him by his dad who, like him, did a lot of the cooking at home,

> 'My dad, he was very, he was a plain eater like me, my mum would eat anything. But because my dad used to do a lot of the cooking, in fairness he did, especially later in life ... and therefore I don't like different things. Er, and to some degree that's my fault with Amelia 'cos she ought to try more but my limitations stop her'.

Amelia's father therefore seems to have blamed his daughter's own food issues on himself. At the same time, he went to great lengths to hide his severe phobia of cheese from his daughter. He said he had to hold the cheese in plastic in order to grate it but that once Amelia had become aware of his phobia, he allowed her to grate her own cheese onto pasta. This deeply embodied food dislike made it difficult, therefore, for this father to break with past habits.

Amelia's mother was dismissive of the diet she had been brought up on and wanted to eat differently. She said she disliked eating the same foods time and again because she had grown up with her grandmother for many years when she had, "ham sandwiches every day for five years and it does get a bit monotonous". She also remarked that food practices had changed from her childhood when there was less variety of food, "that there wasn't the fresh fruit and veg ... and you used to eat your tinned carrots and your tinned peas, and your spam". However, this diet, she now considered "unhealthy" from the perspective of contemporary food norms, although she also said that her unhealthy diet was offset by having been brought up to take exercise: "Like I've been brought up with my dad going jogging. I used to go running with my dad, I use to play squash with my dad."

While Amelia's mother explicitly rejected the eating practices of her upbringing, she also admitted that her own food habits veered between extremes – between eating "rubbish" and eating "healthily" (vegetables and salad). What she ate, it seemed, depended on her "mood". She ate "junk" in the evenings when she felt bored with being stuck at home when her husband was at work. She also refused to eat with Amelia and her husband when she got home from work. On the one hand, Amelia's mother displayed her *current* cosmopolitan and class aspirational tastes for foods like "stir fries and curries" that contrasted with the monotonous food she ate in a different period in her working-class childhood. But on the other hand, Amelia's mother engaged in (unhealthy) food practices that were inconsistent with her dietary aspirations for herself and her daughter. At the same time, she appeared somewhat disenfranchised at home, unable to enact her preferred practices for preparing food for Amelia. As a mother she felt she ought to be responsible for her daughter's diet. In order to conform to the discourse of 'maternal responsibility', she exercised control in the interview by disparaging her husband's food tastes and cooking practices, despite his taking responsibility for cooking for their daughter.

Through having recourse to both parents' accounts and through observing family dynamics in the interview it was possible to see how Amelia's parents transmitted mixed messages to Amelia. Amelia's response was to rebel, caught as she was between her parents' mixed messages and their own struggles with the legacies from their own childhoods. Amelia was unashamed of her rebellious actions in her interview, even in her parents' presence. She admitted to lying about what she ate at school, for example, telling her parents she had eaten a roast when she had eaten pasta. She also confessed to stealing cakes and chewing gum from her mother's handbag, eating them in secret and stuffing the sweet wrappers down the back of the sofa. Amelia flaunted her refusal to go along with her parents' wishes. She completed a research activity in which she was asked to fill a supermarket shopping trolley; she drew a range of contraband – lemonade, bubble-gum, sweets and cakes.

At the second interview two years later, when Amelia was 11, the situation had intensified both in regard to parental control and Amelia's resistance to it. Both Amelia and her father (the mother was not present) were quite open about Amelia "gorging" on sweet foods, stealing food and hiding the evidence. When asked if Amelia ever helped herself to food, her father said: "Anything she can find in the cupboard if we're not around." Amelia commented "Junk food basically…. Ice cream, chocolate (laughing). Doesn't matter what type of chocolate, I'll gobble it all up." This gorging on food led Amelia to being hospitalised more than once for bad stomach pains. Her father wondered whether he and his wife were being too restrictive and Amelia seemed to agree, explaining that she lied about what she ate because she wanted to please her parents. As Amelia's mother explained in the first interview, "sometimes she doesn't know who to keep happy, does she?"

In this context, Amelia used food to control family relationships. Like other children, Amelia sought both to please her parents and, at the same time, to carve her own path through rebelling against them and engaging in the popular food culture of her peers. Amelia's interview responses also spoke volumes about family tensions. Amelia noted that her mother "skipped meals" and did not often sit with them at table. When asked about "the good and bad points of family meals" Amelia commented ironically, "Right, the bad points are, they have arguments because mummy thinks daddy slurps (laughs) and the good thing is, we're just one happy big happy family eating together."

In this case, by adopting an intergenerational lens (Brannen, 2015; see also Chapter 5), we see how food's materiality, sensory and normative character provoked memories of food in childhood that live on as a continuing presence in the lives of parents (Morgan, 1996). Both parents' food practices persisted over time, despite their efforts to change. Amelia's father expressed a desire not to pass on his own food tastes and phobias to his daughter and was under pressure from his wife to change the way he cooked. Amelia's mother developed new tastes in adulthood and wanted her daughter to eat healthily but continued secretly to enjoy eating in unhealthy ways. In this analysis we see how the competing legacies of each parent's past lives played out in the present, what they transmitted, consciously and unconsciously, to their child, and the effects on the dispositions and responses of the next generation.

Food as a methodological entry point into family life

A sociologist's foray into food presents methodological challenges. Much of the routinised, mundane and sheer ordinariness of living we must necessarily forget. If we were to remember, hour by hour, minute by minute, everything we do – to quote King Lear out of context – 'that way madness lies'. Part of the problem is that much of the research on food has relied on surveys requiring informants to report what they eat, with evidence suggesting that people significantly under-report the calories consumed.[3] A major challenge for researchers is to bridge the gap between what people *say* they eat and what they *do* eat. Therefore, increasingly, researchers employ methods that seek to take account of the materiality of food and food consumption as routine (Warde, 2005).

As already suggested, food can provide a significant window into family lives. On the one hand, asking people about food seems a relatively non-threatening topic. On the other hand, food has become heavily imbued with normative health messages while confessing to a lack of food invokes shame. Studying food is also methodologically challenging given its routine practice and the diversity of settings and activities involved (accessing, eating, and preparing food).[4] But what is intrinsic to the everyday and the 'normal' can also provide a lens on what is '*non-normal*' and the ways in which food practices are linked to other social domains beyond the household. As we found in Families and Food in Hard Times (see Chapters 4 and 6), research participants told us about times when, and the conditions under which, it was particularly difficult to manage to feed their families.

As many qualitative researchers have found, in approaching research participants we need to remember that they too have agendas when they agree to be take part in our studies. In choosing to study food we need to be mindful that it may not seem an important or interesting subject to interviewees. In my early research career when carrying out conventional semi-structured interviews, I noticed that there were occasions when people broke the rules of the 'question and answer' format of the qualitative interview and engaged in telling stories about matters in their own lives of importance to them. As Chapter 8 will describe, my interest in narratives was sparked by people who told stories spontaneously about topics that were not directly related to the focus of the study (Brannen, 2013).

Narratives are of their nature about temporality – stories of past experiences and events, told in present time with an eye to the future. A key assumption in analysing narratives therefore is that they are social constructions and should not be interpreted as if they were direct reflections of a 'real past'. Narratives are also co-constructions between the interviewee and the interviewer. They come in a variety of forms that range from the canonical narrative of a life story or 'grand narrative' to those that Bamberg (2006a; 2006b) terms 'small stories'. As Bamberg and Georgakopoulou (2008: 2) argue, 'Narratives, in our approach, are aspects of situated language use, employed by speakers/narrators to position a display of situated, contextualized identities.' These interactional forms of engagement tend to occur in thematically oriented interviews designed to focus on a particular research problem that the researcher is interested in.[5]

In this vein, we were open in the study of food practices among low-income families in the Families and Food in Hard Times project to listening to stories about people's lives as well as about the place of food in them. In being attentive to informants' agendas we learned much about the experiences and events in their lives that plunged them into, or kept them in, poverty as well as their daily food practices. Indeed such 'contextual material' is intrinsic to understanding families' current situations, cultural tastes and traditions, and the resources available to them. However, what people say in interviews, either as unprompted stories or as responses to researchers' questions, does not always give a full or clear picture of the historical and biographical contexts in which their lives unfold. In my view much qualitative research fails to do full justice to social context and history. Perhaps qualitative methods cannot do this alone? Or is it that we lack ways to bring a contextual understanding to our work, for example, because of the places and formats in which we are required to publish?

The way a study of food can provoke stories about people's lives is demonstrated in an extract from an interview taken from the study of low-income families from the Families and Food in Hard Times study (see also Chapters 4 and 6). Sharon is a white British lone mother. Sharon and her 11-year-old son, who had some learning difficulties, lived on income support in social housing on an inner London estate. She had been a carer for most of her life: first caring for her grandparents as a child and now for her son. She suffered from depression and both mother and son were overweight. Sharon admitted to using food as an emotional prop and as a way to please others.

Small stories: context and drama

Sharon's interview was punctuated by many small stories. These stories are part of interactional engagement in the interview but they are also in Bamberg's and Georgakopoulou's (2008) terms 'sites of identity work'. In her interview Sharon constructs her identity as she recounts significant events and difficulties in her life: her struggles caring for her grandparents as a child, with her marriage and its break-up, problems bringing up her older daughter, and her own battle with depression and overweight. Sharon also referred to incidents that she said had affected her son's health, notably her son refusing to go to the toilet on his own at night or insisting on sleeping in her bed.

Given the focus on food and low income, the interviewer had to balance asking a large number of specific questions, while also attending to Sharon's stories and making sense of them. At the point in the interview in which this small story was narrated, the interviewer struggled to bring Sharon back to questions about food. However, Sharon's divergence from the topic was not because she was not interested in it; in fact she provided a good deal of detail about her food practices. For example, Sharon recounted how, in the past when she had more money, she would feed 'all the children on the estate' but could no longer afford to do it. As well as pointing to her worsening economic situation, this fits with her self-identification and the claims she makes as an agentic person: how under difficult circumstances she is seeking to take charge of her life.

In the following interview extract, Sharon is responding to a question about whether she eats out in cafés or restaurants, one of several indicators of food poverty in relation to social exclusion that we used. Sharon mentions receiving a restaurant food voucher that she was given while on 'a course' which, thus far, she had not referred to. Asked about the course, Sharon explains that it was intended to help people in 'difficult situations'. She then breaks off to embark on a story about a violent incident on her estate thereby illustrating the kinds of difficulties the residents face on a daily basis. As the flow of the narrative shows, Sharon is less interested in talking about her referral to the course than she is in telling a story about life on the estate.

Interviewer: 'Oh great, which course have you been doing?'
Sharon: 'A family course, like strategies on – in situations when you're around people ... I have been in situations where I've been attacked around here, and I've had drugs spat in my face trying to help ... that's why I went to court not long ago with this old lady ... yeah, I was trying to stop this man from attacking this old lady. And then he left her alone and went for another old lady with her little dog. And he spat in her face and everything, and he kicked her dog and I had to say "Calm down, you're going to get yourself in a lot of trouble." ... and he used threatening behaviour towards me and stuff. And last week I went to court.... He thought I weren't going to turn up. And then they called him and he was walking – he said he didn't have the bus fare. They will pay for you to get to there as well, they've even said to me you know "We'll pay your bus fare." ... And I got a text message from the police to say that he's been found guilty and he's waiting on trial. ...'
Interviewer: 'So why did you have to go to a course that was linked to that?'

Sharon: 'No I was ... oh no, the course was ... yeah but
um ... being aware of situations around you. I've
been ... it's been an eye opener for me here. I'm
not stupid, but I didn't know what went on went
on. I had no idea about like drugs like that.... You
see it in a film but you don't think ... but actually
you're living it – you're walking down the street,
you're living what's going on. There was a gunshot
the other day round here. One runs in and I'm
picking the weeds [on her ground floor balcony],
and they were like to me "Aren't you going in?"
and I was like "No, it's nice." "There's just been
a gun shot." Everyone gone in, it's gone all eerie
and quiet, and I'm sitting there ... 'cos I don't
know what it is. ... They went through a woman's
window over there ... lucky she's in a wheelchair,
if she'd have been walking it would have hit her....
Well I had loads of flowers out there to be honest
with you ... I had the strawberry plants as well ...
but people was hiding the knives and stuff in my
plant pots, and my son was finding them. He was
like "Mum, look, gangs left this here." I thought,
you know what? "Enough's enough now!" And
I called 101 and I said "You need to get round
here now and you need to take this stuff because
it's not fair. My son has got a disability yeah, and he
will hurt hisself or hurt somebody ... he's finding
these things – it's not right, you know." And I did
give it to them. And the last thing I give them was
a packet of bullets I found (laughs). Thrown over.'

This story and many of the other stories Sharon recounted reveal much
about Sharon's life – as 'you're living it' (her words). The narrative
quality of the interview is thus intrinsic to understanding what it means
to be on a low income and a lone parent living on a rough council estate
in inner London. Sharon demonstrates her resistance to the violence
around her through her actions: she reported the violent incident to
the police, was prepared to go to court to testify against a perpetrator,
and defended the interests of her son. In addition, she demonstrates
agency in her resistance to the violence on the estate which she relives
through her graphic detailed account in the interview, for example,
how the old lady in her story avoided the line of fire because she was

in a wheelchair and how the plant pots were used as receptacles for the gang's knives. While this extract apparently tells us little about her food practices we do learn that she grows strawberry plants on her balcony as well as the difficulties she and her son face because of the gangs and the gun crime.

My point here is that we ignore the agendas of our research participants at our peril. The ways in which Sharon embarked on unsolicited and vivid stories suggest her need to talk about her everyday experience in the inner city where gangs were rife. Thus as well as telling the listener about the realities of her life Sharon used the interview as a means to communicate the *dramas* of her daily life: her active engagement and resistance to the violence. Her narrative style was therefore highly performative in the sense that she took charge of the interview and gave graphic accounts of particular incidents (Phoenix, 2013) in which she presented herself as a key protagonist.

Conclusion

This chapter has highlighted the significance of food, examined the ways in which it is understood by social scientists and how it figures in the lives of families with children. It has argued that the study of food generates opportunities for social science researchers interested in how family life is constituted and reconstituted. Asked to focus on food, research participants are required not only to report on the materiality of food in their lives but may also to narrate and sometimes display practices that constitute and reproduce their lives more generally.

The cases and interview extracts presented and discussed demonstrate some of the methodological benefits of food as a pretext for entry into the field of family lives. The first case (Amelia and her parents) shows how the interview context can be a site for observing family interaction and that focusing on food in the presence of both parents and child can becomes a window into family dynamics. The taken-for-grantedness of food as an integral part of family life may, therefore, paradoxically not only suggest its importance as a topic of inquiry in its own right but may also serve to highlight relationality in families and the dynamics of social relationships.

The recounting of embodied experience inscribes meaning not only in food and food events but can evoke memories and reveal feelings and conflicts that lie below the surface of consciousness and relationships, suggesting the ways in which family experiences and practices are both produced and reproduced over time. The case of Amelia and her parents points also to processes of transmission: how childhood dispositions and tastes developed in childhood can live on into adulthood and traverse family generations who in turn may resist or reproduce that which is transmitted. Such transmission can occur unwittingly or unconsciously despite, as in the case of Amelia's parents, their seeking at a conscious level to resist the repetition of past habits. It is also important to note here the relation between individual biography and normative food cultures of particular periods – the formation and trajectories of food tastes and habits developed in childhood. Food practices in childhood are shaped by individual tastes but also the availability and affordability of food for a family and the meanings attributed to it at particular periods and places – by practices related to social class, geography and culture. Such practices change over the life course and in relation to changing food norms and environments. However, the strong normativity that currently surrounds 'healthy eating' is likely to pose significant challenges for many parents today, bringing them into conflict with their own food habitus from their pasts.

The second case of Sharon demonstrates that semi-structured interviews that set out to capture the food practices of families may be subverted by research participants who have their own agendas and stories to tell. Asked to recount the minutiae of everyday food practices they may instead choose to talk about concerns that are germane to them at the time of interview. In Sharon's interview extract, the interview is used to give an account that throws light on the difficult environment in which the interviewee lives. It illustrates how the interviewee engages in small stories and, through the narration of critical incidents or dramas, seeks to convince the listener not only of the tough situations in which she finds herself but also her agency and resistance in combating them.

My intention here has not been to suggest that we use food as a ploy to enter, and engage with, the field of family life, which might be considered unethical. Rather we should think imaginatively about the research questions we ask, the methods we use, and how the data we collect enable us to think about and understand social relationships in relation to the contexts and material world in which they live: how people make sense of their situations and how they act on them and negotiate change. The data we analyse are only as good as the questions we ask and the methods we use. Thus, it is always beholden on researchers to consider and confront the production, analysis and interpretation of data. Attending to the ways in which food is a lens into family life alerts us to some of these issues.

8

Life Stories: Biographical and Narrative Analysis

Recent years have seen a growth in interest in the social sciences in the narrative form and it is the use of auto/biographical approaches that I discuss in this chapter. The narrative turn is also reflected in wider society, in the mass media and popular and policy discourse. My own interest in auto/biograpraphical narratives goes back a long way. In my long experience of interviewing people it became obvious to me that some interviewees decide to tell stories and recount testimonies and memories even when they are not invited to. I began to notice, and became increasingly interested in, the occasions when people broke the rules of the 'question and answer' format of a conventional semi-structured qualitative interview and embarked on unsolicited stories (Brannen, 2013).

Let me give some examples. In the very early 1980s, I was employed to do fieldwork for a community study of depression among a working-class sample of mothers in north London. The four-hour recorded interview included a standardised psychiatric research instrument, the Present State Examination (PSE), in which the interviewees were asked whether and how often they had experienced psychiatric symptoms of depression, anxiety and other disorders, as well as questions concerning marriage, family and other close relationships. Later we had to transcribe and code sections of the recording according to a large set of predefined measures on to different coding sheets. Although the study was about the aetiology of psychiatric illness, the methodology for data collection and analysis was not concerned with women's own understandings and attributions of their 'symptoms'. The interviews were never fully transcribed and the women's stories were lost.

What struck me at the time, and has stayed with me since then, was the way even the decontextualised questions of the PSE instrument provoked stories about people's lives and did indeed provide insight into the origins of mental illness. Sadly, I have forgotten many of the stories. In one case my memory of the first interview I conducted on the project was overlaid by my shock when the interviewee, a young black British mother, responded in the affirmative to a question that I found difficult to ask: 'Do you ever feel like you are falling off the edge of the universe?' While my memory of the details of her story has been erased, what has remained with me is the concern I felt as her small child busily took apart the sound system in the sitting room. So engrossed was the mother in telling her story that she seemed largely to ignore this.

Another interview that I recall clearly is that of a mother who was suffering from anxiety, brought on, she said, by her job as a night cleaner for the London underground. She vividly described what it was like to clean out the rubbish in the dark tunnels among the rats after the tube system closed down. Another mother admitted to a fear of heights and confined spaces that meant she was unable to attend interviews at the benefits office that was on the top floor of a local tower block. Her fear of heights also made her acutely anxious about her children's safety in public places and so inhibited their freedom. These and many other stories emerged, often early on in very long interviews and in response to specific questions in the PSE instrument. I have also often wondered about my own part in prompting women's responses; I told them that we wanted to hear what it was like living in Britain in the1980s (the early Thatcher years).

Interviewees were clearly making decisions about whether to tell their stories. In one instance, it seemed that an interviewee selected the timing of the interview as her own life was unfolding. After a number of phone calls we finally agreed a date and time for the interview. On arrival the mother told me that she now felt ready to be interviewed. Her explanation went something like this, 'I have bought a dog, dyed my hair and got rid of my husband.' Her willingness to be interviewed at this moment seemed to be prompted by a significant turning point in her life.

When I moved on to research projects with different foci and samples with more varied social class profiles, I encountered such experiences less often; however, I began to realise how unpredictable storytelling is. Contrary to Denzin's (1997) assertion that, as interpretive researchers, we *seek out* the stories people tell 'as they attempt to make sense of the epiphanies or existential turning point moment in their lives' (1997: 92), I seemed to happen upon them as if the stories sought out the interviewer. I will return to this theme later but first I want to say something about what constitutes narrative and how it differs from a life history which is made up of the events and transitions in a person's life.

What is narrative?

Narrative research and narrative analysis are umbrella terms that refer to data available in a variety of forms and produced for a variety of purposes. Such data can be spoken, written or visual. They also may consist of artefacts. Moreover, narrative approaches are not allied to any one set of methods of data collection or analysis. By contrast, life history methods are guided by the aim to elicit life course transitions, their ordering and their relationship to historical processes, social structure and social institutions. Elder et al (2006: 4) see the life course as 'consisting of age-graded patterns that are embedded in social institutions and history ... a view that is grounded in a contextualist perspective and emphasises the implications of pathways in historical time and place for human development and ageing'.

Narrative research can overlap with life history or biographical research. But we have to decide at what point an account of a life becomes a narrative. There are many schools of thought on the subject. While narrative usually involves the arranging and temporal sequencing of events, the linkages made by narrators between events and experiences are the building block of narrative (Franzosi, 1998; Salmon and Riessman, 2013). Event-based narratives, as in life histories, tend to emphasise past events that happened to the narrator, with an assumption by the researcher that they took place in actuality. Within a narrative approach, memories and representations of events and experience are assumed to vary over time and are not therefore considered 'true' representations. They are also understood as being recounted in accordance with structured conventions of narrative and performative genres (Denzin, 1989). However, the boundaries between the two approaches of biography and narrative are in practice often porous.

Narratives range from 'grand narratives' to what Bamberg (2006a; 2006b) terms 'small stories' or partial narratives. As Bamberg and Georgakopoulou (2008: 2) suggest, narratives particularly of this latter variety provide 'constructive means that are functional in the creation of characters in space and time, which in turn are instrumental for the creation of positions vis-à-vis co-conversationalists'. They may also go beyond conventional ideas of a 'story' in that they can encompass habitual narratives, topic-centred narratives and hypothetical narratives (Riessman, 1993; see Chapter 7).

Narrative approaches are guided by attention to plot, language, symbolic representations and cultural forms. Some of the markers of narrative are its storied structure; the use of direct quotations of speech as if the characters were on a stage; the production of closed significant anecdotes that have the 'linguistic and narrative marks of the process of fictionalisation' (Burgos, 1991). Other markers include dramatic character – a performance conducted for an audience with attention to aesthetics and emotions (Denzin, 1997). As the literature on narrative suggests, narrators do not discover the rules of narrative for themselves but follow some kind of model suited to their aims, albeit they are not aware of the narrative frames they are using.

The conditions for narrative in an interview

Fuelled by the 'discursive turn' in the social sciences, attention is being paid increasingly to the contexts in which narratives are co-produced, to the occasioning of stories, and to stories as sites in which individuals perform and construct identities (Phoenix, 2013). As those analysing qualitative research emphasise, the interview is a collaborative venture. It is collaborative in the negotiation between interviewer and interviewee and, in team research, in the process of analysis.

In the late 1980s, at an international conference on methodology, I met a French researcher, Martine Burgos, who sparked my interest in the conditions that generate narrative. With other conference members we engaged over two days in a line-by-line analysis of a section of an interview transcript that I had brought to the meeting. I was so impressed by Martine's insights, based on the first lines of the text (the method involved being blind to the subsequent extract), that, around 1991, I invited her to come to London to run a workshop for the Resources in Households group (Chapter 2). In this chapter I draw on her published paper (Burgos, 1988) and an unpublished paper written for the London workshop (Burgos, 1991). In the latter Burgos discusses her own experience of soliciting life stories. She describes 'the inaugural request' made by an interviewer to an interviewee to tell a life story, a strategy that beckons the interviewee into the narrative mode and legitimates it. However, in so far as an interviewee makes a decision to respond to the invitation, then it follows that she or he can decide to decline as well as accept. Burgos found that when she sought to elicit life stories from her research participants only a few took up the challenge. Although her informants did not necessarily produce narratives this did not mean, she insists, that they lacked narrative competence.

From Burgos' point of view, the 'provocation' to tell a life story with the markers of a narrative is the experience of rupture or turning point. The theory made a great deal of sense to me in my experience of what seemed to be spontaneous narratives given by some research participants. As Burgos wrote in 1991, following Paul Ricoeur (1985), the narrator – in response to the inaugural request to take the authorial position – seeks to make a coherent entity out of heterogeneous and often conflicting ideological positions, experiences, feelings, and events that create some kind of disjunction in a person's life. In that sense the narrator is seeking to 'transcend' a rupture and to make sense of it (Burgos, 1988, 1991: 5). The event or rupture, while doubtless real, may be interpreted in relation to the circumstances of the rupture, and the relationship between the narrator and the community (family, village, nation and so on).

But how does this insight square with the view that all interviews are collaborative endeavours? Where researchers seek out narratives or stories from their research participants or act as social mediums or catalysts when they offer them, they do so under particular conditions. First, the interviewer has to convince the interviewee that their life is of interest to a potential audience. Second, the interviewer has to give the interviewee some autonomy to 'impose their own problematic' or way of viewing the world (Burgos, 1991: 13). My experience of becoming attentive to narrative therefore made me both sensitive to the part that researchers play in generating and interpreting data, and careful not to lose sight of the agency of the research participant in the interview process.

Making sense of narratives

The methods employed to make sense of life stories and narratives depend upon the researcher as well as the form of the narrative; the ways in which the researcher organises and interprets the material. For example, biographical and narrative methods can equally be used in the analysis of variable-based quantitative data from surveys or cohort studies that record the events and social transitions in people's life course, as they can be applied to qualitative material. As Jane Elliott (2006: 148) observes, statistical stories can be created by thinking 'along cases rather than across them'. Elliott uses the term 'narrative' here to convey the ways in which a researcher constructs a narrative about aggregate change while taking account of change at the individual level.

The researcher's role in interpreting narrative requires, inter alia, paying attention to the narrative form of the data. Fritz Schütze (1983) was credited with developing the 'biographical–interpretative method', an interviewing and analysis method refined by Gabriel Rosenthal (2004), whose contribution was to examine the dialectical interrelation between experience, memory and narration. The method was adapted in the UK by Tom Wengraf (2001) in the form of the biographic-narrative interpretive method (BNIM).

The biographic–narrative interpretive method

The BNIM incorporates both a biographical or life history approach and a narrative approach. In the BNIM an initial question is posed to the interviewee that aims to provoke a life story. The first tenet of the approach is to treat the life story as a gestalt and to consider the genesis of its creation and construction. A second tenet is to identify the events and social transitions in an interviewee's life course in the context of the periods in which she or he lived. A third tenet is to explore separately the perspective of the narrators in relation to different temporalities – their perspectives as they look back at the past from the vantage point of the present, and their recollections of how they felt and viewed events at the time the events occurred. The method involves the codification of a life story into two parts: the 'lived life' and the 'told story' (Wengraf, 2001). These distinctions are reflected in the initial analysis of the interview in which 'lived life' and 'told story' are separately analysed.

The 'lived life' focuses attention on the shape and chronology of the life course – the timing and ordering of life events and social transitions, irrespective of how the individuals interpreted them. It thus enables analysts to open themselves to hypotheses concerning other life-course directions the informants might have followed and the choices they might have made. The researcher is thereby forced to adopt a realistic stance by identifying the biographical data in the interview and also through recourse to documentary and historical material external to the interview. She or he is thereby cautioned against being 'over-persuaded and implicitly seduced by the interviewee and by their story-telling' (Wengraf and Chamberlayne, 2013: 64).

The second step involves analysing the life story and considering it as a narrative. Stories are not histories. They are told with hindsight and recounted from the vantage point of the present and are shaped by and during the interview encounter (Schiff, 2012). The 'told story' is understood as temporally unfolding. Memory-based narratives of experiences and events relate to the past but refer also to the present and the future (Rosenthal, 2004). Bruner's approach to narrative has many similarities in its emphasis on a 'historically-evolving' self. He writes, 'we constantly construct and reconstruct a self to meet the needs of the situations we encounter, and we do so with the guidance of our memories of the past and our hopes and fears of the future ... resulting in the stories we tell about ourselves, our autobiographies' (Bruner, 2003: 210). A defining feature of the narrative-interpretative aspect of the BNIM is the recognition, therefore, that there is no 'objective' past that is accessible through storytelling, an assumption shared by many narrative researchers (Andrews et al, 2013; Bamberg, 2006a; 2006b). As Polkinghorne (1988: 183) comments: 'Research investigating the realm of meaning aims rather for verisimilitude, or results that have the appearance of truth or reality.'

The life histories and life stories of a grandfather and son

In the years 2011 to 2014, I was part of an ESRC programme on methodology under the aegis of the National Centre for Research Methods (Chapter 2). A research 'node' of the centre, known as Novella (Narratives of varied everyday lives and linked approaches) was funded to focus on narrative analysis. It was led by Ann Phoenix and included several researchers and PhD students at TCRU, and also involved collaboration with researchers who were located at the University of East London and elsewhere in the Institute of Education. This project afforded me and other colleagues an opportunity to look at some of our own research material through a narrative lens. The rest of the chapter is devoted to an illustration of some of the insights that this approach offered.

Two cases have been drawn from the Fatherhood across Three Generations study that was funded by the ESRC from 2008 to 2011 (Brannen, 2015) and were narratively analysed in Novella between 2011and 2014. As set out in Chapter 5, the study's aim was to understand changes in fatherhood across family generations, including among men who had experienced migration. In this chapter I focus on the life stories of one Irish migrant grandfather and his adult son. The method we used and adapted was the BNIM. This involved inviting the men to tell their life stories, with the focus of the study in mind (fatherhood), followed by questions giving them the opportunity to elaborate on aspects of their life stories. To this we added a more conventional interview that focused on the study's specific concerns about fatherhood.

First, I will briefly describe the life histories of the two men. These life histories are then compared and situated in their historical contexts. Next, I will analyse the ways in which they narrate their life stories in ways that do not simply illustrate their life histories. I show how the narrative performance of their stories situates the self and constructs the men's identities for their current purposes in ways that are not necessarily intended or self-conscious (Bamberg, 1997). This is not to suggest that what the narrator is saying is consciously hidden but that it needs deciphering in the data analysis (Josselson, 2004). Nor does it mean imposing external interpretations upon a life story. Rather it is necessary to examine the whole interview and the jigsaw of material, paying attention to the shape of the life trajectory, to how the story is performed and to the silences in the account.

Connor's and Murray's life histories

Connor, a grandfather, was born in poverty-stricken Ireland in 1933 in the aftermath of Ireland's fight for independence and its ensuing civil war. The seventh of seven sons, both his parents died shortly after his birth. Connor spent much of his early life in hospital because of suspected tuberculosis and then, following an accident in the hospital, he was transferred to a convalescent home. After a few years, when he was fit enough to be discharged, he was sent to one of Ireland's industrial schools. These institutions were set up in the mid-19th century to care for orphaned, abandoned or neglected boys and were intended to offer practical training for employment. Aged 17 in 1950, Connor went to northern England and worked in a colliery. He soon returned to Ireland where he found work on a building site and went to night school to learn carpentry. When he was 25 he returned to England, this time to London, with several friends. He continued to work in the construction sector, like most Irish men of his generation in the UK, and made his way up to the position of site foreman. Aged 27, he married an Irish woman (many Irish men of his generation did not marry) and the couple eventually moved into a local authority flat. Their three children were born in the 1960s/70s. At some point the family moved from the flat to a council house that subsequently, in the early Thatcher era (1980s), they were able to purchase under the 'right to buy' scheme. Using labour from his firm Connor extended his house. For the rest of his working life he remained in the construction industry and at interview had recently retired.

Connor's son, Murray, led a very different life. Born in London in 1970, he went to the local Roman Catholic primary school and then to the local Catholic secondary school where his mother worked, first as a cleaner and later as its school secretary. Murray failed his GCSEs but retook some subjects a year later. When he was 17 in

1987 he left school and easily found a job in a finance company. Two years later, in 1989, following a tip-off from a friend he obtained a job as a clerk working for futures traders in the City of London. The financial sector was booming. Within a year he was working on the floor of the London Stock Exchange and began moving in the high-living world of City traders. A few years later, when he was 27, he married a 'non-Catholic' and the couple subsequently had three children. By 2000 trading was computerised. Murray was offered a trader job in New York but then 9/11 happened. By the mid-2000s the boom was over and Murray was no longer making money. The family was living off his savings. His wife took a full-time job and a friend of Murray's offered to back him financially to set up his own finance trading business.

Comparing the life histories of father and son, we can see how biographies reflect the times in which they lived, especially in their formative years, and the stark contrasts between them. A key generational change is the upward mobility and affluence of the younger generation. Connor's early life was marked by the harshness of life in Ireland in the first half on the 20th century (a period of economic stagnation). Following his parents' early deaths, Connor spent his childhood and youth in institutions. He lacked educational opportunities and migrated to the UK, a move that typified his generation. His employment prospects in Britain, as they were for most Irish men at that time, were limited to hard manual work in the mining and construction industries. However, once he became a father he had access to council housing that he was then able to purchase during the Thatcher years.

By contrast, Murray enjoyed a family life during the relatively affluent climate of 1980s London. Unlike Connor he was able to attend secondary school and he gained some qualifications. He entered the labour market at a time and place when the financial sector was booming and found work in the City of London. Murray's trajectory into the world of finance therefore represents both a rise and fall: the rise of financial capitalism in the 1990s and its decline following the computerisation of trading and the banking crash. There are similarities between the life course of father and son as well as contrasts that represent many aspects of the hegemonic masculinity of their times. Both were main breadwinners (Murray for the first years of being a father). Both men had three children (a sharp reduction in number compared with the generations before), and both their wives attained white-collar jobs. Both sent their children to Roman Catholic schools and brought them up as Catholics.

Connor's life story

The Irish men of the grandfather generation who we interviewed migrated to Britain in the 1950s and 1960s and looked back over more than 50 years in Britain and at a late point in the life course. Their stories focused less on the 'functional present' (Mead, 1932) and more on memories of the past. Typically the men positioned themselves as survivors and, in some cases, as heroes in their own stories – having struggled more or less successfully to overcome the obstacles in their paths. Their stories demonstrated pride in having managed to stay in work throughout their lives and not depend on the state; pride in having a family of their own, given that many Irish men of their generation did not marry; and satisfaction in owning their homes. Above all, they attributed 'success' to a driving commitment to hard work, a quality, they said, they inherited from their fathers, many of whom had struggled to subsist in Ireland in the troubles of first half of the 20th century there, or had themselves migrated.

Connor is an exemplary raconteur. He assembles the events in his life chronologically into a narrative; as Ricoeur (1985) suggests in his concept of 'emplotment', he tells a dramatic story. The way informants begin their narratives is often significant (Burgos, 1991). As already suggested, a life story is often provoked by the experience of a rupture or turning point. Connor's opening response to the invitation to tell his life story presages what is to follow. He recounts his life as a set of turning points that he neatly condenses. His early life in poverty-stricken 1930s Ireland was one of great misfortune; it is emblematic and heroic, the stuff of Irish literature.

> 'And the dad [his dad] went to America and then came back.... I was the seventh son.... I'm the last of them by the way. But anyway, father and mother died when I was only 2.... And the mother said like you know "I won't be dead a year, and he'll be behind me" like you know. Which he was.... Well anyway ... (pause) I didn't know them like, you know what I mean? So I don't (pause) in fairness to everybody else like – I didn't miss my mum and dad because I didn't know them. So how can you miss your mum and dad, you know? But you know when you're a baby everybody likes to pick you up, don't they? ... Well I'm getting to the story, but everybody likes to pick you up. Well I didn't know this till years and years and years

after that what happened to me was (pause) one of the nurses picked me up and let me fall.... Yeah, let me fall and broke my back.'

In Connor's narrative there are strong elements of performativity in the way Connor addresses his audience and re-enacts moments in his life, often using direct speech. From the beginning Connor foreshadows a sense of inevitability in the misfortune of his father's death, in this quotation of his mother's words: "I won't be dead a year, and he'll be behind me." What is also clear is that Connor is appealing to his audience by suggesting that, despite the apparent enormity of losing both parents so young and being placed in an institution, this misfortune can be overcome: "I didn't miss my mum and dad because I didn't know them. So how can you miss your mum and dad, you know?" He then further downplays the loss of his parents in the rhetorical question "How can you miss your mum and dad?"

Connor continues to build towards a climax in his story which turns on further misfortune. While drawing his audience into the story ("Well, I'm getting to the story") he also sets a scene of seeming normality – "when you're a baby everybody likes to pick you up, don't they?" before coming to the 'crisis': a nurse picked him up and dropped him, breaking his back. This resulted in several years in hospitals before he was sent to an industrial school where he spent his youth. Connor also minimises the effects of the latter experience, stressing that he was not subject to any sexual abuse, despite the recent adverse publicity that shows how abusive the regimes in these institutions were.

Connor employs considerable narrative skill in telling his life story and in the selections he makes in the interview. Furthermore, Connor's positive gloss on his unfortunate early life is suggestive of a 'break' or turning point. In Turner's terms (Turner, 1974) this is a phase of redressive action that follows a state of liminality that contains the germ of future developments in which an individual turns their life around. The upward turn in Connor's life course takes place after his second migration to Britain, when he is eventually offered a promotion to foreman in a large building firm. In the way that Connor describes this event, the goodness of the present is magnified against the misfortune and poverty of the past (McAdams, 1993: 104). Connor's story about how, on his promotion, his employer gave him a company car is also metonymic, symbolising or standing for Connor's pride in his success and enhanced status, both at the time and in the interview. Again, success is made vivid through the re-enactment of the moment as he employs direct speech.

> 'So I said (pause) "well that was a big job for me" and it meant I could get a company car then you see. (Oh) I said "This is great" … it was a big company like. Gs was the name of them … and then I went from them to a proper really big crowd, you know – it was in the '50s. And then I said to [wife], I said "You can have a go at this now" I said "with this car" I said – it was only an Escort you know. Because when you're higher than a general foreman you get a bigger car…. So of course naturally, what did I do? – I got higher. So I run the job then like you know, I was just sitting behind a desk and everybody would come in "Could I see Mr …" you know, whoever it is, and I felt (pause) I felt great…. But anyway, I never looked back, I really never looked back from then on. I carried on and carried on.'

The transformative aspects of Connor's story are also present in the following 'small story' given in response to a question concerning the experience of discrimination when he first came to the UK. While Connor acknowledges the existence of overt discrimination in Britain towards Irish people in the past, he is reluctant to admit to the experience himself, exempting himself on account of his position at work – his power as foreman to hire and fire personnel. He thereby constructs a positive identity by employing strategies of resistance: distancing himself from the experiences of other Irish people whose biographies may be deemed less successful. In referring to his ethnic identification Connor also positions himself in a positive light in relation to his status as a migrant through 'claims-making' (Spector and Kitsuse, 2001): claiming how members of his family had fought for Britain in two world wars. Thus he seeks to present a multifaceted ethnic identity integrating his identifications with both Ireland and Britain. Further, in looking back from the *present* vantage point (a 'successful life'), he insists to the interviewer – "you must remember now, you've got to remember this, what I'm saying *now*" – on the advantages that Britain gave him.

> 'I'm saying, "I'm Irish, but my people were British Army", and I was delighted. I love Britain, to be honest with you I love Britain, and I've never run down Britain – I would

never run down Britain. My second home don't forget –
you know what I mean? I've got nothing against – they gave
me anything I wanted like you know – and that's exactly
I mean. I have no compunctions about any of the, what
the Brits are – you will get the ignorant type that say "Oh
they shouldn't be in this country" – but now they don't,
but at that time they did. At that time they definitely did.
But you must remember now, you've got to remember this,
what I'm saying now – I was in a position on a job that
no one would say anything to me, otherwise I'd get rid of
them – you know what I mean?'

It is therefore clear that what is also important in determining the way
Connor engages with the narrative mode are the current purposes of
telling his story for the teller. Undoubtedly Connor's story has been
rehearsed, refreshed and modified over the years. His stories are a
performance employing direct quotation to re-enact the moment.
The self-conscious manner of this 'presentation of self' is confirmed
at the end of his interview when Connor offers a summation of his
life, calling on the interviewer to affirm that he has, after all, made a
success of it, "I think I've gone from the top to the bottom like you
know. Really and truly, I think I've done well for you today anyway
like. At least you can put something down now can't you?" In short
his narratives demonstrate how identity is constructed and meaning
made in the interview.

Given the focus of the study was on fatherhood, what Connor does
not choose to elaborate on in his life story is significant. In his life story
his focus on the world of work is a 'default account' of fatherhood.
As we have suggested elsewhere, the concepts employed to denote
fatherhood and fathering as practice are themselves subject to change
as well as changes in men's practices and understandings (Brannen
and Nilsen, 2006). That Connor's discourse on fatherhood was not
about emotional care and practical involvement does not mean that
fatherhood was not a central part of his life. Under direct questioning
about his fathering practices when his children were young Connor
exempts himself on account of his exceptionally long working hours,
including Saturdays and Sundays. His role in the family as he saw it was
to "bring in the money" and "make sure there's plenty on the table".
His relatively brief responses to questions about fatherhood are likely
to reflect fathering practices among many men at the time, particularly
with sons – playing football with them and taking them to matches.
However, his reflective response to a question about whether there was

anyone he could think of who was a role model for him as a father says a great deal about his own lack of a family life when he was a child,

> 'I didn't get a chance you see, cos I was in school, I was in hospital, I was in a convalescent – and then I went to [the industrial school]. I didn't get the chance to realise what a dad'd be like you see. That's what it boils down to you know. So I couldn't tell you exactly what I'd like to be – what a dad should be like, you know what I mean.'

Murray's life story

Connor's performativity and narrative skill are reflected in his son's life story. While their stories have few similarities both are presented through the prism of success. The kernel of Murray's story and his identity is about life as a "playground". Murray reflects at some length in his opening narrative on his childhood, "it was just all play, everything was fun. Because you were free, we were just free to do anything." Just as Connor's opening narrative was a portent of what was to come, so Murray's story begins with a similarly arresting beginning that resonated throughout his interview. After a brief mention of the circumstances of his birth, he turns to his childhood – growing up in 1970s London, a time of slum clearance when a new city was beginning to emerge. He conjures up the "bomb site" where he spent his childhood, calling it "an extended playground".

> 'it was a derelict factory.... that was our playground for when I was growing up. It was just a complete (pause) it was like a bomb site ... all the houses in the area were all being (pause) you know the council were taking them to be rebuilt.... Then that became (pause) ... it became an extended playground.... I wouldn't let my kids go near them now.'

Like the gendered life story of his father, Murray's focuses largely on the world of work, with little mention of fatherhood except in response to interview questions. The central motif of Murray's narrative is about having "fun" in the workplace. Murray recounted in detail the pranks he and his colleagues got up to in his first job in an insurance company, described as "one long jolly". For Murray working in the City was about making money *without* the hard work. Murray said he had rejected the strong work ethic that his father had sought to pass on to him. He recognised that he was attracted by the people who worked in the City because they seemed to be having such a "really good time".

> 'I mean dad would never (pause) he would never miss a day's work in his life. You know they all had (pause), well I think that they all had that sort of mentality that … you were lucky to have a job in the first place, and you know because you've got a job you worked for it – and my dad certainly did. Whereas I didn't (pause) well I sort of did and I didn't. I know that … you get what you put into things, but (pause) yeah I just didn't. I don't know what drew me more into [finance and the City]. I think … it was the sort of people who were doing it – although you know they were a little bit educated and that, but they just seemed to be having a really good time and (pause) and of course Wall Street [the film] came out sort of you know about a year or so later. I thought "well I definitely (pause) definitely want to get into that."'

Like his father, Murray draws on metonyms to convey success. Later in his interview he offers a 'small story' to convey what it was like on the trading floor of the Stock Exchange. He returns to the central motif of his interview – life as a playground:

> 'we had like 300 guys, there was very few women down there, so the place was like a playground, you know, it really was. So I'd literally (pause) you know my previous job was just messing around, I'd gone to another playground, you know, but just on a bigger scale. And all it was, was just grown men … you know not the kids … this was grown men who were doing all the silly things … it was a big playground again, and that was where I was at home.'

On the other hand, important aspects of transmission are evident in the stories of father and son. Murray said he strongly identified with his father as the archetypal sociable Irish man. As he said: "I'm nothing without him." He then went on to detail his father's ability to network, a characteristic that Murray inherited and claims to his own advantage,

> 'I am – I do (pause) I meet who I want to meet and I get everyone, and I do pull a lot of people in the same way

that he does. He does it fantastically … (pause) I surround myself with the right people, whereas he tends to surround himself with everyone.'

Murray's presentation of himself as a father is both similar and different from Connor's. Despite the passage of time both recounted life stories that focused on their role as family breadwinners and the world of work. However, unlike his father's motivation to work hard, Murray's own motivation was unequivocally about making money without working hard. As Murray said, "it has to be money. Money for (pause) you know cos I want everything for the family." Their interpretations of what money was "for" are similar. In terms of fathering practices, it was clear from responses to interview questions that they differed. At the time when Murray was no longer working as a City trader he was able to get home from work earlier. He became more involved with his children's lives, taking the children to school and looking after them two evenings a week. He also talked about expressing love for his children. These practices differ from those of his parents when he was a child, "we were sort of (pause) don't know, weren't really central to their social life. Yeah, we could just be fitted in." By contrast, Murray and his wife organised their leisure around their children. On the other hand, while he sees this as a positive development Murray expresses regret that his children lack the freedom that his parents gave him as a child. As a father he would not allow his children to roam free in the neighbourhood as he used to do.

Thus Murray's life story, narratives and responses to direct questions suggest that his identity construction is complex and multifaceted. He sought to reconcile his present and his future self with different aspects of his past – his Irish ancestry and his relationship with his father as well as defending the choices he made in creating his own very different life path in Britain in the late 1990s and first part of the 21st century.

This example of a grandfather and son gives, I hope, some sense of how a life history and narrative approach, when applied to an intergenerational study, can provide a 'thick description' of continuity and change across generations in relation to family life and other social domains. They show the ways in which life paths and subjectivities are made in different eras and contexts – Murray's in 1990s London and Connor's in the mid-20th-century world of Irish migration. The case also points to some of the invisible processes of transmission that take place successfully (or not) across family generations. Connor was unable to transmit the strong work ethic that he had lived by to his son. On the other hand, Murray had taken from his Irish father some of his personal qualities and interpersonal skills. The two men also share some of the same practices of fatherhood in having been main breadwinners, but they differ in their involvement with their children. Later in his life course, when he was no longer working in the City, Murray described becoming more involved in the care of his children. In particular, reflecting the way intimacy has become the central motif of modern family life, Murray talked about the importance of showing affection to his children. The case also shows how parents negotiate with their adult children and manage intergenerational inequalities and differences; in the case described, those that originate in Connor's migration history and the upward mobility of the succeeding generation.

Rejecting the narrative mode

As I have suggested, some potential narrators reject the narrative mode altogether, only barely hinting at a life untold. This next example is from the same study. Eamon, an 84-year-old grandfather, migrated from Ireland at the age of 19 and worked in construction most of his life in Britain. He was in very poor health at the time of the interview and has since died. He gave no narrative in response to the initial question, "Can you just tell me the story of your life? You can start where you want." All he said was "A very different life altogether." My colleague who interviewed him wrote in her field notes:

> He was very quietly spoken and it was difficult to understand him at times. Given … the fact that he found it impossible to respond to the [initial invitation to narrative], I decided that the best thing was to converse with him…. I therefore spoke much more than I usually would and tended to raise my voice though I don't think he had a hearing problem! There was also a lot of repetition of what he said so that I could confirm I had got it right…. His answers were very brief to start with, but as he relaxed he began to expand on his answers.

Some of his life story unfolded as he recounted small stories along the way. For example, in response to a series of questions he gives some clues about life when he was a child in Ireland. It is not a narrative in the sense of a coherent story.

Interviewer: 'Uhuh. (pause) um (pause) and did your dad work long hours, was it hard work?'

Eamon:	'It was (inaudible) (Uhuh, uhuh) that time there there was no work, only on the farm (Yeah yeah) and there was no money. Nine shillings a week you used to get, dole money. (?) To feed seven of us.'
Interviewer:	'Yeah yeah. I've spoken to some grandfathers about your age who have come over (pause) who came over from Ireland and they didn't have electricity in the farm or – '
Eamon:	'No such thing. (No) No such thing as a tap in the house. (Yeah) All they had was turf for the fire. Everything was cooked on the fire.'
Interviewer:	'Everything was cooked on the fire was it? Uhuh.'
Eamon:	'A turf fire.'
Interviewer:	'Was it cold in the bedrooms when – '
Eamon:	'It certainly was (inaudible)'
Interviewer:	'Yeah yeah.'
Eamon:	'They were all thatched roofs. Mostly all (?)'
Interviewer:	'Thatched roofs, yes. And because your dad was working a lot, did he have other jobs or just on the farm?'
Eamon:	'Just on the farm.'
Interviewer:	'Yeah yeah. Did that mean that you didn't see him much? Or were you able to see a bit of him?'
Eamon:	'I was only there until I was 14, going to school. (Yeah) After that I was gone away, working for the postman.'
Interviewer:	'Yeah you worked on this other farm then and you had to leave home.'
Eamon:	'I had to leave home.'

Ricoeur's (1985) notion of identity as a process of 'emplotment' is useful here. It conveys the ways lives are plotted and storied, as part of the process of identity construction. Ricoeur suggests that there is a tension between the self that is re-presented as continuity – often described in terms of attributes which remain the same over time, and the self presented as discontinuous or changing – how we see ourselves as we once were and how we will become. Like many of the first generation of Irish migrants in the study, Eamon answered the question about his ethnic identification in terms of the county where he was born and grew up. Asked what it means to be Irish he also suggested an ascribed status, "it's just that I'm Irish and that's it. But I'm here so long now." His answer is definitive; his identity is given and is not something he has struggled to hang on to or lose. Nothing more is said. The sad music of the remark that followed 'I'm here so long now' leads me to wonder if Eamon was thinking back to something he had mentioned earlier about having once wanted to return to Ireland (his wife did not want to). But he tells us nothing more. Yet despite the lack of material for narrative analysis it was possible to compare the 'facts' of Eamon's life course with those of other Irish migrant men in the study and to conclude that Eamon's life was similar in many key respects.

Conclusion

Life stories may be understood as sequences of biographical events and life-course transitions that are situated in and shaped by historical time. But they are also stories that people tell about their past and current experiences and the meanings they give to their experiences at the time of telling and how they see themselves in the future. Life stories may be generated when people are explicitly invited to tell them, provided that they are given the space to do so, as in the BNIM approach. On the other hand, storytelling and personal stories may occur in other types of interview. Indeed, in interview methods such as the BNIM not all interviewees accept the invitation to take up the narrative mode (Brannen, 2013).

Life story telling is often provoked by 'having a story to tell' – often related to a break or turning point, or rupture of canonical expectations (Riessman, 2008) that the narrator is seeking to 'transcend'. As I have suggested in the case of Connor and Murray, even though the study (and the initial invitation to tell a life story) signalled that the study was about fatherhood, the two men (and many others in the study, especially the oldest generation) only referred to fatherhood in their life stories through reference to family breadwinning and the world of work. However, to conclude that the two men did not see fatherhood as important to them is to conceptualise fatherhood only through contemporary discourses of 'care' (Brannen and Nilsen, 2006). Fatherhood was not absent from their stories; it was present in both men's strong orientations to their work and to breadwinning that kept them (and the generations before them) away from their children and their homes. In Connor's case, fatherhood took on another form of 'absent presence' in his story about growing up without father figures in his life. While such silences on the part of these men in their life stories may signify the lack of centrality of fatherhood to their identities, in the way we think of it today, this does not mean that they did not have relevant things to say when asked specific questions. Biographic-narrative interpretative methods and similar methods need therefore to be supplemented by more conventional forms of interviewing if they are to address a study's objectives and research questions.

The analysis of the cases in the chapter affords insight into the narrative resources of research participants that they pass on to the next generation. These resources are demonstrated in the interviews of Connor and Murray, who largely told stories about childhood and their lives in the world of work. In Connor's narrative he built towards the climax of his childhood misfortunes in a way that intimated that a turning point is to follow bringing repair and redemption. In Murray's case he began with, and returned to, the central trope of his life which is the idea of life as a playground; he began with childhood and returned to the same idea in his employment as a successful City trader. However, despite the differences between the two men, both displayed considerable storytelling skills that were passed down the generations. Both men employed dramatic devices and performativity in the ways that they engaged with their audience in the interviews. This is affirmed particularly in Murray's claim that he inherited his fathers' considerable social networking competencies.

What was missing from the life-story part of their interviews were references to daily practices as fathers – the care of and relationships with their children. Murray was also unforthcoming about his subsequent mundane working life after the financial bubble burst in 2008. Perhaps this was because he had not yet reached the end of 'the story'. The selections that people make from their lives are often telling but so too are those made by researchers in choosing cases and interview extracts for in depth study. As Rosenthal (1998: 4–5) says 'it is by no means coincidental or insignificant when biographers argue about one phase of their lives but narrate another at great length, and then give only a brief report of yet another part of their lives …'.

From their present vantage points, both men's stories are similar in their gendered representations of their lives as 'successful' while their criteria of success differ. For Connor, a young Irish migrant arriving in the UK in the 1950s, success meant never being out of a job, elevation to site foreman and being a 'good breadwinner', while for Murray, a young man entering the job market in the 1990s, it was about making money in the heady days of the London Stock Exchange. While both stories tell us how they experienced, and continue to experience, the past, they also tell us how they see the present and envision the future. Yet Connor's redemptive story – rising above early misfortune through a mix of hard work and luck and Murray's account of his life as a playboy – are more than a positive gloss, they are ways of living.

Memories are not mirrors that reflect the past. As Antze (1996) observes, memories are monuments that we visit but they are also 'ruins' that are subject to restoration. They are refracted through contemporary time frames and lenses that are shaped by a multiplicity of factors to do with subjectivities, the nature of researchers' questions, the particular research method employed, the cultural resources and repertoires of the teller, the structure of the life course and its crises and turning points, the wider historical context, and the societal canons concerning what terms such as 'success' mean. Researchers' interpretations in understanding the meanings that stories have for individuals are also temporal and reflect our own vantage points.

The researcher's task is to engage in what Giddens (1993) terms the 'double hermeneutic'. The BNIM that was applied in the study separates out the events and life-course transitions from the interviewee's interpretations, thereby enabling the researcher to look at the features of an individual's life trajectory in relation to other similar cases and in relation to the societies in which they lived. But the method needs to be supplemented by other methods, including standardised forms of interviewing.

Individuals' life stories need to be placed in context. Sole informant testimony is dangerous: as Paul Atkinson (2009) argues, it is as necessary to problematise the Romantic notion of narrative as it is to adhere to the idea of bearing witness to what actually happened as a simplistic reflection of lived experience. Research participants are not necessarily best placed to define or even adequately know fully the contexts in which they live (Hammersley, 1989). In a discussion of the agency–structure dilemma, Bertaux and Bertaux-Wiame (1997) suggest that the deployment of a resource shapes an individual's trajectory, whether or not it is given emphasis by the person concerned, and can be key to understanding agency:

> the idea that a life trajectory may be determined – or rather, conditioned – much more easily by the supplying of a resource than by the imposition of a constraint lends an entirely new content to the concept of determination: one which includes both the socio-structural dimension and praxis. (1997: 95)

Life-story research that focuses on a small number of cases has much to contribute to the development of ways of bringing methods and data together. In a rapidly changing world, the demand to understand the realities of individual lives is growing alongside the demand for big data and large-scale national and international evidence. Small-scale life-story research involves turning to more than one data source. In the past there have been some important studies in which different types of data have been brought together, including biographical data, for example, in the work of Glen Elder (1999 [1974]). However, researchers who use a mix of methods in biographical research need to be explicit about how the different data are integrated (Nilsen and Brannen, 2011).

The type of approach discussed and illustrated in this chapter suggests the complex interplay between the way people speak about their experiences and the structures against which such talk needs to be understood (McLeod and Thomson, 2009). This requires both the art of re-presentation and rigorous analysis. It requires the researcher to pull together the critical elements of a life in a convincing and rigorous way to make an argument or to offer an explanation; to identify presences and omissions; to develop disciplined systematic analyses of how biographies are produced, shared and transmitted. Only through such endeavours is it possible to produce a rich and multi-layered analysis. This is a difficult feat as Bertaux observes: 'It takes some training to hear, behind the solo of a human voice, the music of society and culture in the background' (1990: 167–8). However, as those writing about the genre of literary biography recognise, there is no one method of doing this (Lee, 2009: 18).

9

In Conclusion

In this book I have considered the ways in which 'social research matters' at particular times and some of the ways in which it is conducted. I have used my own life as a researcher of family life over four decades to show how research problems reflect specific historical and contemporary contexts, how they are selected at particular moments in time and positioned in relation to a number of social domains. I have also discussed how the funding and organisational environments for social science research affect how research is done. A further aim has been to consider how the specific and broader research context influences which conceptual and methodological developments come to the fore at particular times and become 'acceptable', and how they shape the creation of knowledge and understanding. In this concluding chapter, I want to draw out a few specific points relating to these themes and my own 'take' on where research in my field might develop.

Contexts for the construction of knowledge

The beginning of the book gave a brief account of my own positioning: how I came to follow a career in research and my subsequent pathway in terms of the fields pursued, the particular topics studied and where I have worked. The book went on to consider the organisational contexts in which research is done and discussed different organisational models. My own workplace, although it was located in a university, was one that was devoted primarily to the conduct of social science research. The research organisation depended largely on its own efforts and those of its members to raise funding for salaries and services. The staff had a common stake in the success of the organisation and its research output. This model was contrasted with that of the 'academic entrepreneur', one that has been historically more common in universities, in which tenured academics

179

are employed by the university principally to teach. However, in order to develop their own knowledge and reputations in academia, they are required to procure research funding and, in the last decade or more, preferably large grants that cover some of their own salaries as well as those of 'hired hands' who do much of the research. Today the model that celebrates the work of the research 'leader' is in the ascendant in the context of changes in the role of universities and how they see themselves in the world. The emphasis on entrepreneurial spirit and leadership is exemplified in funding schemes that allocate grants on the basis of individual performance and outstanding personal scholarship. The outputs from many such grants are evaluated largely as the work of the grant holder and not the collective contributions of the research team. Indeed, my own institution promotes 'the stellar researcher' model to inspire academics and research staff as well as to augment institutional prestige and research funding.

In science the tension between these two models of research is epitomised in the recent criticism that has been mounted of the Nobel Prize science committees. The Nobel committees force a category error: they insist on awarding the prize to a few individuals while, in reality, the nature of the scientific enterprise has changed. Teams now perform the bulk of the highest-impact work. Whereas a century ago a patent clerk famously divined the theory of relativity in his spare time, the discovery of the Higgs Bosum requires decades of planning and the efforts of 6,000 researchers. No one person – no troika, even – can claim all the credit.[1] While social science can never match the scale of such endeavours as CERN, the general point about the significance of research teams to the success of projects is, I believe, no less pertinent and research teams should receive their due recognition. The 'hired hand' approach to research needs transformation.

My argument is also that research is a craft learned through the practice of research, a theme that I developed (Chapter 2) in discussing the research environment I have worked in and the teams I have worked with. This model underpinned the ESRC's National Centre for Research Methods (NCRM) in which a large amount of funding was invested over 15 years (2004–19) in the development of research capacity. Through its 'hub and node' model, in particular, NCRM aimed to develop particular methodologies. This model encouraged cross-institutional working and cascaded training that flowed from the research to the wider research community. It is unfortunate, in my view, that in its proposed downsized and reconstituted form, the Research Methods Training Centre appears to be focussing only on training which will mean the Centre will be divorced from the practice of research. This may not be the best decision at a time when research funding has become particularly tough to secure. My hope is that the craft model of doing research will not disappear. It is perhaps worth noting that some of pioneers of social research downplayed the importance of practice, doffing their caps to the then to be written rules of methodological texts and training (Thompson, in press).

Research ideas are not generated in a void; that is, the topics we study have histories that relate both to developments in social science and the body politic. One aim in writing this book was to examine how particular topics of inquiry, that have been addressed by the research teams that I have been part of, came about at particular moments and relate to societal issues as they have developed over time. At the start of writing this book my hope has been to give some sense of what drove the research: how researcher interest in a topic arose and the concerns of different parties involved, including policy makers, funders, disciplines and institutional settings in which the research was carried out. This is a difficult task and I am aware I have only scratched the surface. And, as noted at the start of the book, I have of necessity had to be selective in the work drawn upon. Data from early studies I was involved with were not fully transcribed or they were not digitised and archived.

A key influence on whether a topic becomes a focus of interest within political and research arenas lies in timing and the convergence of the topic with external 'events'. Some of the topics that I have worked on were not firmly established on the social science agenda. When such opportunities arise they afford researchers considerable freedom, unconstrained as they are by existing substantive research. Such situations therefore make the work particularly exciting. The stimulus to conduct research on particular themes takes place within the political, policy or popular climate at the time. In some cases research may chime with the concerns of the moment. More often, however, and many social scientists would take this position, social science adopts a critical stance towards received wisdoms and public discourses. In the early 1980s, opening the 'black box of the household' (Chapter 4) was a matter that spoke to the politics of gender that, by then, had permeated and transformed the sociology of family life. It also had relevance for specific public policy debates of the moment, for example, mothers' access to direct payment of family allowances. International events can also change the climate in which a topic becomes 'researchable'. In the 1990s following the UK's ratification of the UN Convention on the Rights of the Child in 1991, the study of children and childhood grew rapidly in British social science. In studying the domains of family life, early childhood, and other settings some social scientists began to foreground children's perspectives and children's interests in their work (Chapter 6).

Research funding opportunities are key determinants of how much research is done and the kinds of topics studied. The 1990s ushered in significant amounts of funding for social science through the EU's Framework programmes. As I have earlier described, a particular policy interest of the EU concerned the 'reconciliation of work and family life', a focus that at the time was not given priority in policy or research funding in the UK. The EU's policy concerns and funding opportunities provided an opportunity which we, as UK researchers, were able to take advantage of. Through collaboration between two British universities funding was secured from the European Commission's Employment and Social Affairs Directorate and, with colleagues in other European countries, a cross-national team was assembled. The project's objective was to examine young Europeans' views of their futures in relation to work and family (the project is not discussed in the book). The report, *Futures on hold* (Lewis et al, 1998), was published in the UK and Portugal and attracted considerable attention in the context of a growing awareness of the rapid growth in insecure employment among young people and its consequences (see also Brannen et al, 1992). On the back of this, in the early 2000s, a much larger project on working parents in Europe was funded under the EU's Framework 5 programme (Chapter 3). A decade later, another topic for research that was fortuitous in its timing was food in families. An investigation into the food practices of young children began at a time when, because of the continued growth of maternal employment, children were eating in a range of settings (Chapter 7). European funding was next sought for a study of families and food poverty as the effects of austerity policies following the 2008 financial crisis took hold (Chapter 6).

The foci of research interests, in some instances, can be in advance of both social trends and the evidence base. For example, when we set out to research mothers' return to work following childbirth in the early 1980s the study was unusual because relatively few mothers were in the labour market when their children were under school age (Chapter 3). The 'working mothers debate' had yet to feature in the popular media and was not a social policy concern in the UK. By the end of the (longitudinal) project the numbers of mothers returning to work after childbirth had escalated.

Opportunities for research can present themselves in different ways. As the new millennium approached, there was considerable social science interest in the changing world of work. The Future of Work programme was funded by ESRC in the late 1990s. This was an opportunity to look back as well as forward and we were fortunate in gaining a grant to examine how work, in the broad meaning of the term – family care work as well as paid work, had changed over the 20th century. This opportunity led on to an interest in generational relations in families that, at the time, was of marginal interest in UK social science but a focus of policy in many other countries concerned with falling birth rates, changing family forms, increased mobility, labour market change and diminished welfare benefits (Bennett et al, 2019).

Methodological development

One aim in revisiting the projects on which I have worked was to give some sense of how research is done. In the book I have limited the amount of detail concerning research designs and methods. These tend, in any case, to be rather dry subjects. Instead I have preferred to discuss particular aspects of methodology and to give space to particular examples of data analysis. So, in this final chapter, I want to point to some developments and continuities in my own research practice. An enduring methodological strategy has been a preference for mixed-methods and multi-methods approaches, where appropriate to the research questions, matters which I have discussed extensively elsewhere (see Appendix). I have not thought it useful here to go back over this ground with the exception of Chapter 3 that discusses how data collected via one research instrument were analysed both quantitatively and qualitatively (a mixed-methods approach). In other studies we used quantitative (survey) data alongside qualitative methods in a range of ways: to provide extensive data on the populations in which we were interested in order to set intensive studies of small groups into context. In some studies surveys were employed principally as screening methods to select particular samples. Questionnaire surveys were also used for collecting data to compare with data collected via interviews, for example, children's responses to questions about smoking and drugs that we considered might differ according to the method used. In yet other studies a mix of qualitative methods (a multi-methods approach) was used, for example, photographs alongside interviews, as a means of bringing practices and relationships that may be difficult to recall or speak about to the forefront of consciousness. In recent years, as access to existing large-scale datasets became easier, we carried out secondary analysis of these datasets. For example, in cross-national research the rates and characteristics of social phenomena in different countries were compared with a view to situating case material studied by qualitative methods within wider contexts.

Like most qualitative researchers, I have relied a great deal on interviewing as a method. However, the type of interviewing has changed over my research career as, increasingly, I came to value understanding lives in relation to the life course and historical context. In the late 1990s, three of us from TCRU trained in a new interviewing approach in preparation for a study of four-generation families. The method (Biographic-narrative interpretive approach known as BNIM) was intended to retrain experienced interviewers in the process of listening and thereby to assist interviewees in reviewing their lives (Chapters 5 and 8). The interviewing and analytic approach used in this method required attention to narrativity and temporality in relation to the shifting frames of reference of interviewees within the interview. It also required analysis of the historical contexts and intersecting social positionings (class, gender, ethnicity) in which lives unfold, matters that are rarely foregrounded in personal accounts and that need to be made visible by the researcher in analysing the data.

In Chapter 8 I described the way that research participants respond to the interview encounter as a matter of ongoing fascination for me. In analysing data I came to see that the forms of speech used and stories recounted by research participants during interviews required attention. As Plummer writes, the 'turn to narrative' in the social sciences reflects its wider popularity and testifies to the society's major preoccupation with 'identities':

> and what lies at the heart of this enormous outpouring of writing about 'the modern human being' is the idea that a highly individuated, self-conscious and unstable identity is replacing the old, stable, unitary self of traditional communities. The new selves are 'constructed' through shifts and changes in the modern world, and partly create a new sense of permanent identity crisis. The search for 'understanding' and making sense of the self has become a key feature of the modern world. (Plummer, 2001: 83)

As described in Chapter 8, the BNIM approach took account both of the structuring of individual life histories and the form in which interviewees recounted their stories. It afforded insight into practices that are habitual or taken for granted, and into the ways in which interviewees create and maintain their identities. An analytic focus on narrative directed attention to those aspects of individuals' lives they chose to foreground and those they chose not to discuss. Narrative analysis of life stories also afforded insight into research participants' performativity in the interview – a co-construction, but also one that is performed for the self and for the interviewer.

The processes of data analysis that I have engaged in have also shifted in emphasis over time. Later studies on which I have worked employed a case-based approach in preference to thematic analysis that is so commonly used in qualitative research. In a case-based approach, it is necessary to conceptualise cases as cases of 'something', a practice that makes sampling procedures and sampling criteria critical. In case-based research, a holistic approach is needed which requires recourse to both research participants' perspectives and contextual data. As Becker (1970) suggests, by piecing together the mosaic of people's lives we arrive at a bigger picture. A case-based approach in my own research practice was applied when the unit of analysis was not only individuals but countries, organisations, multi-generation families and households of parents and children. Intrinsic to this approach is the process of comparison. Comparing cases requires the careful matching of cases on dimensions that have theoretical significance. It requires rigorous analytic procedures, for example, examining similar items of data in each case and, in writing up the cases, presenting data items in a similar order.

An advantage of case-based analysis, especially when set in different levels of context and types of data, is that it permits the researcher to move from understanding and interpretation towards explanation and generalisation in a non-statistical sense. As in Ragin's (1994) qualitative comparative analysis approach, it offers the opportunity to see 'how different causes combine in complex and sometimes contradictory ways to produce different outcomes' (1994: 138). Thus we may take particular instances of a social phenomenon and examine the conditions under which similar instances take place in a different context. However, this does not mean that what holds for a particular case in a particular context may be generalised, for example, to a country (Brannen, 2005c; 2005d: 2). A multi-level approach in which cases of households are analysed in relation to micro, meso and macro levels offers explanatory sophistication in relating the specific to the diversity of conditions and contingencies (Chapter 6).

Conceptualisation

In the work I have done I have concurred with the view that how we problematise the social world speaks to the realities of the social and material conditions in which people live their lives and not only their meanings, re-presentations and social constructions. A realist ontology that assumes an external reality that is differentiated, structured, contingent and mutable (Sayer, 2001) underpins a methodological orientation towards context, 'caseness' and a comparative approach. Nonetheless, an emphasis on a realist ontology means that, in interpreting our data, the evidence and explanations that we propose must always be judged as fallible and falsifiable (Sayer, 2001). Indeed, comprehensive knowledge is unattainable and impossible.

In my view conceptualisation goes hand in hand with the framing of research questions. In the spirit of Blumer (1954), concepts are 'sensitising' tools that enable researchers to make sense of their data. As Basil Bernstein (2000: 209) suggested, concepts should be 'capacious' enough to encompass research descriptions of social phenomena and to 'lift' the analysis to a meta level. On the other hand, concepts should not be so loose fitting that they explain everything or nothing, as in grand theory. Nor should they be so narrow and specific that they simply reproduce the original material, as in reportage. This 'discursive gap' provides for 're-description' that is necessary to conceptual development.

The different studies discussed in the book from which case material has been selected employ a variety of concepts. I do not propose to offer an exegesis of them all here but will limit myself to a few. One concept that has been important in the study of everyday family life is Berger and Kellner's (1970: 51) thesis that the everyday's 'seemingly objective and taken for granted character' is continually 'mediated and actualised by the individual, so that it can become and remain *his* [sic] world as well'. As Morgan (1985: 203–4) writes, the everyday is occasioned through a 'complex set of interactions between social-structural, the ideological and the historical, on the one hand, and the immediate, the experienced and the day-to-day on the other'. In our study of food the concept of the everyday provided a lens on taken-for-granted practices but also on the 'non-normal', and demonstrated how 'non-normal' situations can be routine daily experiences. In Chapter 7, the case of a mother who described her everyday life provided insight into life on an inner-city social housing estate that was riven with violence and gangs – conditions that most people in this society would consider anything but 'normal'.

The concept of practice has been employed in several studies discussed in the book and has become a key concept in several fields of study. According to Morgan (2011), family practice denotes an emphasis on doing, action and social action; practices are performed on a daily basis in which social actors reproduce habits, relationships, structures and institutions from which they derive meaning. The concept has proved particularly helpful in analysing routinised habits that are not easily reflected upon, for example food, and the emotional aspects of men's relationships with their children (Chapter 5). It affords fluidity so that sets of practices defined in one way may intersect with concepts employed for other purposes, for example, class or gender practices. As Heath et al (2011) argue, citing Strathern (2003), concepts can hold 'different meanings in different social worlds but be imbued with shared meaning to facilitate [their] translation across those worlds; they therefore act as "boundary objects" at the borders of different discourses rather than marking the limits between them' (2011: 46).

The notion of family practice has been important in deconstructing dominant discourses of 'the family' and in conveying the heterogeneity of social relationships and family forms. It decentres 'the family' and disturbs conventions concerning what families 'do', where family life is enacted and what family means. In this deconstruction the term 'family' is disaggregated from the concept of household. Following in the wake of second wave feminism and critiques of male domination in the world of paid work and other public spheres, in the 1980s households were conceptualised, and critiqued, as sites of hierarchical social relationships between men and women in which control of, and access to, resources including money, domestic labour and care giving were inequitably distributed (Chapter 4). In the contemporary British context of austerity policies, the household developed a new currency. Households that struggle most are lone-parent families headed by mothers who suffer from low wages and reduced benefits; some have no income at all because of their lack of legal status. The consequences for household self-provisioning are dire, with mothers unable to take care of and feed their children and themselves to a socially acceptable level (Chapters 4 and 6).

Concepts require linkage, for example, ways of bridging micro and macro levels, and the relation between agency and structure. One concept that bridges materiality and consciousness is ideology. For example, the term 'dominant ideology' had its heyday in the 1970s and the 1980s in explaining how gender inequality was maintained by powerful male interests. Associated with ideology is the concept of false consciousness. As described in Chapter 3, in the post-war period, mothers with young children were encouraged to believe in the status quo, and came to assume that being a full-time mother was 'best'. The same chapter showed how ideologies changed in relation to historical events and new ideas. From the 1980s the ideas known as neoliberalism 'responsibilised' individuals to make their own 'choices'. So, in recent years, discourses about mothers' positionings in the home and the workplace became less overtly gendered in policy framing: 'parents' were expected to make their own decisions about the division between their employment and family time when their children are young and to negotiate individually with employers about their working time (Chapter 3). The workings of labour markets and employers that undermine these so-called choices are thereby concealed by the discursive power of the concept of 'individual freedom'.

Neoliberal ideologies and the trope of the 'market' are central to contemporary capitalism in the context of increased globalisation. They are evident in workplaces that are underpinned by practices concerning 'efficiency', work intensification, individual performance targets and shareholder profit. These practices and ideologies are designed to transform subjectivities of workers and those in receipt of services ('customers'). As demonstrated in the case of a female call centre worker in Chapter 3, while new workplace practices gave her a sense of autonomy they destroyed the boundaries between employment time, family time, and personal time. They are evidenced too in the ways in which parents embrace, or have no alternative but to accept, the extension of responsibility for every aspect of their children's well-being in contexts in which 'parenting stakes' have been raised to levels against which parents who lack the necessary resources are evaluated (Chapters 4, 7).

While family ties are central to understanding family life, the book has drawn out the salience of the concept of family generation. As Carol Smart (2007) argues, families exist in our imaginings and memories as well as in the structure and negotiation of everyday life; they are central to our identities as human beings and who we are in the world. A focus on several family generations permits an understanding of both continuity and change: how family members transmit material, cultural, social, emotional and other resources across generations, and how the next generations act on transmissions from those above them in the context of the opportunities and constraints of their times and social locations. The concept of transmission demonstrates dynamism, creativity and openness in what is passed between family generations, and tensions and ambivalences as well as solidarities. What is transmitted may be rejected or it may be transformed into different resources. Chapters 5 and 8 showed how men across the generations pass on a strong work ethic, and how, in the context of societal and discursive changes in the so-called crisis of masculinity, gender identifications and feelings between fathers and their sons can be transformed or, in the cases discussed (Chapter 5), be reproduced. The cases also showed how an analytic focus on life stories directed attention to the manner in which men narrated their lives and how their lives related to historical context. The analysis of life stories also afforded insight into research participants' performance within an interview as well as how they constructed their identities in family life and other social domains.

Future directions

As I write my own research career is drawing to a close. Inevitably, I wonder what, if I was to go on doing research for the next 20 years, I would like to do next and which research topics and ideas I might want to develop, especially at a time when Britain's future seems so uncertain. I would certainly like to continue to be part of a research team with the sort of comradely and creative colleagues I have found so much pleasure and satisfaction working with, both in the UK and mainland Europe. Perhaps more of a challenge would be developing something along the lines of what I believe is now known as 'the sandpit' model, in which a large group of researchers from a wide variety of traditions come together to design a project around a theme of theoretical and societal significance. Such models demand inter-disciplinary collaboration and a creative application of methods across and beyond traditional quantitative and qualitative methods, including, where appropriate, the re-use of archived data, digital and visual methods and transactional data.

As I look around me there is no shortage of ideas for new research, although undoubtedly some of these ideas will have already been taken up by the time this book is published. I set out a few overleaf by way of illustration. A key concern at the time of writing these paragraphs (early 2019) concerns belonging – 'who is allowed to belong' as well as what it means to belong – as more people are forced to migrate and Britain moves towards exiting the EU. Researchers have written extensively on this multi-layered concept (Mason, 2018). Even so, within this theme, there remain important issues to be explored, in particular that concern migrants with families in the UK who are left in legal limbo and without recourse to public funds because of harsh immigration and welfare policies. These groups have not received the attention they urgently deserve because of the segmentation of researchers into the separate fields of migration and social policy research. Further, attention needs to be paid to notions of attachment to place and country among families who have no recent migration history, both across generations and in different parts of the UK and beyond.

Another issue that requires the attention of those in family studies and with an interest in action research concerns the linkage between families and civil society and civic engagement. The degradation of Britain's material infrastructure is changing the landscape of its towns and cities with deleterious consequences for the social infrastructure. Public places and democratic spaces such as libraries, swimming pools, youth clubs, school playing fields are important 'third spaces' – places beyond home and work that create opportunities to relax, to engage in community life and social interaction (Oldenburg, 1989; Klinenberg, 2018). They are spaces that may particularly benefit those confined by geographical place, such as parents at home with young children, teenagers and elderly people. For example, a library or community garden has the potential to create social ties or extend social networks, enhance well-being and bridge class and generational divisions.

A parallel feature of contemporary Britain is the changing nature and delocalisation of its high streets through the activities of large national and international retail chains and property development companies, and the promotion of online shopping. As independent shops, pubs, post offices and banking facilities have closed, so they are being bought up by property companies that have no interest, other than profit maximisation, in local communities. High streets are increasingly the province of charity shops and cafés with short-term leases, betting shops, fast food outlets and food deserts. New research is needed to map the historical change that is taking place, with special attention to Britain's small towns that are also suffering from the loss of young people. Such change both reflects but also influences family practices and it is likely to do so depending upon a family's socioeconomic status. Studies could compare high streets in areas being subjected to gentrification, corporate investment and 'alternative' social investment, such as community-run initiatives with those in parts of the country marred by underemployment, deindustrialisation and lack of corporate and social investment. They could examine how the changing geography of the high street in Britain's towns and cities is affecting daily life, in particular civic participation and matters such as food provisioning of the least advantaged, in particular low-income families, children, the elderly, those with disabilities, the homeless. It could study social change as it takes place: the decision-making processes and the parties involved in the construction of what comes after – local authorities, national government, property companies, private sector investors and contractors, and local communities.

Finally, in these brief illustrations I feel that housing, including public housing and especially that for young people, is another topic that is ripe for more research. Housing should not be studied separately from the provision of services and from material, cultural and social infrastructures. In recent years the acquisition and transmission of wealth has been widely discussed in popular as well as social science discourse. A recent report from the Resolution Foundation (2018) set the issue in the context of flattened incomes, the escalation in housing costs and an insufficient housing supply, with stark problems especially for low-income parents seeking to help their children on to the housing ladder. What is missing from these debates is a questioning of the assumption that home ownership is the only possible option to which millennials aspire. In many other western countries home ownership is not the norm or a key cultural value. There has also been an absence of public debate about the decline in social housing.

These illustrations are all topics that should be matters of priority for social science and those who study family life. Together they focus on issues that constitute a 'collective good' that is passed on to, and that has consequences for, our children and children's children. These and many other questions about what kind of society we want for future generations, particularly in the context of environment and climate change, demand the attention of researchers, as they do of politicians and policy makers. They require interdisciplinary collaborative research, a historical approach and a visionary perspective that takes seriously what families and civil society bequeath to the generations to follow. Most importantly, in an age of diversity, social inequality and political division, they require us to think about the 'public good' and the kind of society we desire for children to come. 'The world', as Eric Hobsbawm (2003: 418) has written, 'will not get better on its own.'

Appendix

(These are publications of which Julia Brannen is
the first author referred to in the book)

Brannen, J. (1992a) British parents in the wake of the new right: Contradictions and change. In U. Bjornberg (ed.) *European parents in the 1990s: Contradictions and change*, New Brunswick, NJ: Transaction.

Brannen, J. (ed.) (1992b) *Mixing methods: Qualitative and quantitative research*, London: Gower.

Brannen, J. (1995) 'Young people and household work', *Sociology*, 2: 317–38.

Brannen, J. (2002a) 'The use of video in research dissemination: Children as experts on their own family lives', *International Journal of Social Research Methodology: Theory and Practice*, 5(2): 173–81.

Brannen, J. (2002b) 'Lives and time: A sociological journey', Professorial lecture, London: Institute of Education.

Brannen, J. (2004) 'Working qualitatively and quantitatively', in C. Seale, G. Gobo, J. Gubrium and D. Silverman (eds) *Qualitative research practice*, London: Sage.

Brannen, J. (2005a) 'Time and the negotiation of work–family boundaries: Autonomy or illusion?', *Time and Society*, 14(1): 113–31.

Brannen, J. (2005b) 'Introduction: Cross-national seminar on biographical methods', Workshop on comparative biographical research, Thomas Coram Research Unit, Institute of Education, University of London, 24–25 November.

Brannen, J. (2005c) 'Mixing methods: The entry of qualitative and quantitative approaches into the research process', *International Journal of Social Research Methodology*, Special Issue, 8(3): 173–85.

Brannen, J. (2005d) *Mixed methods research: A discussion paper*, NCRM methods review papers, NCRM/005, http://eprints.ncrm.ac.uk

Brannen, J. (2006) 'Cultures of intergenerational transmission in four-generation families', *Sociological Review*, 54(1): 133–54.

Brannen, J. (2008) 'The practice of a mixed methods research strategy: Personal, professional and project considerations', in M. Bergman (ed.) *Advances in mixed methods research: Theories and applications*, London: Sage.

Brannen, J. (2013) 'Life story talk: Some reflections on narrative in qualitative interviews', *Sociological Research Online*, 18(2): 15, http://www.socresonline.org.uk/18/2/15.html

Brannen, J. (2015) *Fathers and sons: Generations, families and migration*, Basingstoke: Palgrave Macmillan.

Brannen, J. (2017) 'Approaches to the study of family life: Practices, context and narrative', in V. Cesnuityte, D. Luck and E. Widner (eds) *Family continuity and change: Contemporary European perspectives*, Basingstoke: Palgrave.

Brannen, J. (forthcoming) *Migrant families in poverty in the UK, Portugal and Norway: A multi-level approach.*

Brannen, J. and Collard, J. (1982) *Marriages in trouble: The process of seeking help.* London: Tavistock.

Brannen, J. and Wilson, G. (eds) (1987) *Give and take in families: Studies in resource distribution.* London: Unwin Hyman.

Brannen, J. and Moss, P. (1988) *New mothers at work: Employment and childcare*, London: Unwin Hyman.

Brannen, J. and Moss, P. (1991) *Managing mothers: Dual earner households after maternity leave*, London: Unwin Hyman.

Brannen, J. and O'Brien, M. (eds) (1995a) *Parenthood and childhood: Proceedings of the ISA Committee for Family Research international conference Children and Families*, London: Institute of Education.

Brannen, J. and O'Brien, M. (1995b) 'Childhood under the sociological gaze: Paradigms and paradoxes', *Sociology*, 29(4): 729–37.

Brannen, J. and O'Brien, M. (eds) (1996) *Children in families: Research and policy*, London: Falmer Press.

Brannen, J, and Storey, P. (1996) *Child Health in Social Context: Parental Employment and the Transition to Secondary School.* London: Health Education Authority.

Brannen, J. and Moss, P. (1998) 'The polarisation and intensification of parental employment: Consequences for children, families and the community', *Work, Family and Community*, 1(3): 229–47.

Brannen, J. and Storey, P. (1998) 'School meals and the start of secondary school – children's food practices at secondary school: the discourse of choice', *Health Education Research*, 13(1): 73–86.

Brannen, J. and Nilsen, A. (2005) 'Individualisation, choice and structure: A discussion of current trends in sociological analysis', *Sociological Review*, 53: 412–28.

Brannen, J. and Nilsen, A. (2006) 'From fatherhood to fathering: Transmission and change in four-generation families', *Sociology*, 40(2): 335–53.

Brannen, J. and Nilsen, A. (2011) 'Comparative biographies in case-based cross-national research: Methodological considerations', *Sociology*, 4: 603–19.

Brannen, J. and O'Connell, R. (2015) 'Data analysis 1: Overview of data analysis strategies', in S. Hesse-Biber and B. Johnson (eds) *Oxford handbook of mixed and multimethod research*, Oxford: Oxford University Press.

Brannen, J. and O'Connell, R. (2017) 'Food practices, intergenerational transmission and memory', *Psychosocial Studies*, Special Issue, 10(2): 44–58.

Brannen, J., Dodd, K., Oakley, A. and Storey, P. (1994) *Young people, health and family life*, Buckingham: Open University Press.

Brannen, J., Heptinstall, E. and Bhopal, K. (2000) *Connecting children: Care and family life in later childhood*, London: Falmer.

Brannen, J., Lewis, S. and Moss, P. (2001) *Workplace change and family life: Report of two case studies*, Report to the Tedworth Trust. London: Thomas Coram Research Unit, Institute of Education.

Brannen, J., Nilsen, A., Lewis, S. and Smithson, J. (2002) *Young Europeans, work and family life: Futures in transition*, London: Routledge.

Brannen, J., Moss, P. and Mooney, A. (2004) *Working and caring over the twentieth century: Change and continuity in four-generation families*, ESRC Future of Work Series, Basingstoke: Palgrave Macmillan.

Brannen, J., Wigfall, V. and Mooney, A. (2012) 'Sons' perspectives on time with dads', *Diskurs Kindheits- und Jugendforschung* Heft 1-2012: 25–41.

Notes

Chapter 1

[1]   All references with Brannen as sole or first author are to be found in the Appendix rather than the References section.

[2]   'Cabbies' was the invention of Irish children in a village in Cork whose terrace backed on to a quarry in which stones and other debris were used to create tiers of cabins on the quarry's sides.

[3]   See: www.educationengland.org.uk/documents/robbins/robbins1963.html

[4]   See: House of Commons Library, www.parliament.uk/documents/commons/lib/research

[5]   Anthony Crosland was the Secretary of State in a new Labour government, when parliamentary approval for the SSRC was given. This took place some twenty years or more after Clement Attlee, Deputy Prime Minister asked Sir John Clapham, a Cambridge economic historian, to chair a committee to consider whether 'additional provision was necessary for research into social and economic questions' (Gaber and Gaber, 2005).

[6]   Scepticism by the 1979 Conservative government about the value of social science research manifested itself in 1981; the then Secretary of State for Education and Science, Sir Keith Joseph, announced that he had asked Lord Rothschild to conduct an independent review into the scale and character of the work of the SSRC (Gaber and Gaber, 2005: 14–15). Rothschild concluded that 'It would be an act of intellectual vandalism to destroy the Council.' However, he did recommend a stronger focus on empirical research and on research considered of 'public concern'. Symbolically the council was renamed the Economic and Social Research Council, losing the crucial word 'science'. See also the account given by John Eldridge (2011), a former chair of the British Sociological Association, concerning the BSA's refutation of the critique made in that period of sociologists as a 'collection of Marxists and radicals'.

[7]   Dr Jack Dominian was a British psychiatrist who founded the Marriage Research Centre that went on to become OneplusOne, a centre for marriage advice. Jack was also a Roman Catholic theologian who argued for a rethink on Christian sexual ethics while simultaneously fighting to uphold the institution of marriage.

[8]   See: www.esrc.ac.uk/research/impact-toolkit/what-is-impact/

Chapter 2

[1]   In 1971 Lord Rothschild reported to government how it could become a customer for the research contracted from the research councils and other sources (HMSO, 1971).

2   For example, see ESRC's definition of research impact as 'the demonstrable contribution that excellent research makes to society and the economy', http://www.esrc.ac.uk/research/impact-toolkit/what-is-impact/
3   For example, an email to members of UCL's Academic Board (27 October 2017) refers to a blog 'On the common saying (among managers) that "Teaching pays and research costs"'. See: www.saveuclagain.wordpress.com

Chapter 3

1   We recruited 255 first time mothers in London via maternity wards, large employers and nurseries, and carried out field methods when their children were four months old (before the mother might return to work). (The total number of referrals followed up was 4,100). The 255 mothers were studied until the children were aged three, when the response rate fell to 243 mothers.
2   We tried to find employees who had joined the bank before and after the organisational changes to see whether responses to change differed depending upon their experience of the workplace. However it was difficult to find new employees with caring responsibilities; for example, many were graduates marking time in the search for better work.
3   I am grateful to Graham Crow for pointing this out to me.

Chapter 4

1   See: www.foodinhardtimes.org

Chapter 6

1   See: www.foodinhardtimes.org
2   The questionnaire is used in different countries as part of the World Health Organization's collaborative cross-national survey.

Chapter 7

1   Manchester was the first city to provide school meals for poor and badly nourished children in 1879.
2   The second wave was funded by the ESRC and the Department of Health.
3   ONS data reported in the *Guardian* (19 February 2018): www.theguardian.com/commentisfree/2018/feb/19/uk-fatter-eating-more-realise-under-report-calories
4   Researchers find it hard to study food systematically because of the challenge of covering the varied and increasing number of contexts in which food is consumed. A further reason is that food practices are transmitted unwittingly through the influences of childhood, parenting and peers. To bring food practices to the surface of reflective consciousness requires creativity in the choice and development of methods but may also demand a range of different approaches.
5   An explicit interview question that asked for the interviewee's life story came as a second step in the development of modern-day biographic research.

Chapter 9

1   See: https://www.scientificamerican.com/article/expand-nobel-prize-award-teams-not-just-individuals/

References

Ainsworth, M.D.S. (1979) 'Infant–mother attachment', *American Psychologist*, 34(10): 932–7.

Ainsworth, M.D.S. (1989) 'Attachments beyond infancy', *American Psychologist*, 44(4): 709–16.

Alanen, L. (1992) *Modern childhood? Exploring the 'child question' in sociology*, Research report 50, Jyvaskyla: University of Jyvaskyla.

Alanen, L. (2003) 'Childhoods: The generational ordering of social relations', in B. Mayall and H. Zeiher (eds) *Childhood in generational perspective*, London: Institute of Education, pp 27–46.

Albertini, M. and Kohli, M. (2013) 'The generational contract in the family: An analysis of transfer regimes in Europe', *European Sociological Review*, 29(4): 828–40.

Alderson, P. (2001) 'Research by children', *International Journal of Social Research Methodology*, 42(2): 139–55.

Alderson, P. and Morrow, V. (2011) *The ethics of research with children and young people: A practical handbook*, London: Sage.

Andrews, M. (2013) 'Never the last word', in M. Andrews, C. Squire and M. Tamboukou (eds) *Doing narrative research*, London: Sage, pp 86–101.

Andrews, M., Squire, C. and Tamboukou, M. (eds) (2013) *Doing narrative research*, London: Sage.

Antze, P (1996) 'Telling stories, making selves: Memory and identity in multiple personality disorder', in P. Antze and M. Lambek (eds) *Tense past: Cultural essays in trauma and memory*, New York: Routledge, pp 2–23.

Arber, S. (1993) 'Inequalities in the household', in D. Morgan and L. Stanley (eds) *Debates in sociology*, Manchester: Manchester University Press, pp 118–40.

Atkinson, P. (2009) 'Knowing selves: Biographical research and the European traditions', Invited plenary paper, European Sociological Association, Lisbon.

Attias-Donfut, C. and Arber, S. (2002) 'Equity and solidarity across the generations', in C. Attias-Donfut and S. Arber (eds) *The myth of generational conflict: The family and state in ageing societies*, London: Routledge, pp 1–22.

Bamberg, M. (1997) 'Positioning between structure and performance', *Journal of Narrative and Life History*, 7(1–4): 335–42.

Bamberg, M. (2006a) 'Stories: Big or small. Why do we care?', *Narrative Inquiry*, 16(1): 139–47.

Bamberg, M. (2006b) 'Biographic-narrative research, quo vadis? A critical review of "big stories" from the perspective of "small stories"', in *Narrative, memory and knowledge: Representations, aesthetics, contexts*, Huddersfield: University of Huddersfield, pp 63–79.

Bamberg, M. and Georgakopoulou, A. (2008) 'Small stories as a new perspective in narrative and identity analysis', *Text and Talk*, 28(3).

Barrett, M. and McIntosh, M. (1982) *The anti-social family*, London: Verso.

Bauman, Z. (1998) *Work, consumerism and the new poor*, Buckingham: Open University Press.

Becker, H. (1967) 'Whose side are we on?', *Problems*, 14: 239–47.

Becker, H. (1970) 'The relevance of life histories', in N.K. Denzin (ed.) *Sociological methods: A source book*, New York: McGraw-Hill.

Becker, H. and Horowitz, I. (1972) 'Radical politics and sociological research: Observations on methodology and ideology', *American Journal of Sociology*, 78(1): 48–66.

Bengtson, V.L., Biblarz, T.J. and Roberts, R.E.L. (2002) *How families still matter: A longitudinal study of youth in two generations*, Cambridge: Cambridge University Press.

Benjamin, O. (1998) 'Therapeutic discourse, power and change: Emotion and negotiation in marital conversations', *Sociology*, 32(4): 771–795.

Bennett, F., Brannen, J. and Hantrais, L. (2019) 'Family change, intergenerational relations and policy implications', *Contemporary Social Science*. https://www.tandfonline.com/doi/full/10.1080/21582041.2018.1519195

Berger, P. and Kellner, H. (1970) 'Marriage and the construction of reality: An exercise in the microsociology of knowledge', in H. Dreitzel (ed.) *Recent sociology no. 2: Patterns of communicative behaviour*, New York: Macmillan, pp 49–73.

Berger, P. and Luckmann, T. (1971) *The social construction of reality: A treatise in the sociology of knowledge*, London: Penguin.

Bernstein, B. (1996) *Pedagogy, symbolic control and identity: Theory, research, critique*, London: Taylor & Francis.

Bernstein, B. (2000) *Pedagogy, symbolic control and identity: Theory, research, critique*, Lanham, MD: Rowman & Littlefield.

Bertaux, D. (1990) 'Oral history approaches to an international social movement', in E. Øyen (ed.) *Comparative methodology*, London: Sage, pp 158–70.

Bertaux, D. and Bertaux-Wiame, I. (1997) 'Heritage and its lineage: A case history of transmission and social mobility over five generations', in D. Bertaux and P. Thompson (eds) *Pathways to social class: A qualitative approach to social mobility*, Oxford: Oxford University Press, pp 62–97.

Bertaux, D and Thompson, P (1997) (eds) *Pathways to social class: A qualitative approach to social mobility*, Oxford: Oxford University Press.

Bertaux-Wiame, I. (2005 [1993]) 'The pull of family ties: Intergenerational relationships and life paths', in D. Bertaux and P. Thompson (eds) *Between generations: Family models, myths and memories* (2nd edn), Oxford: Oxford University Press, pp 39–50.

Bew, J. (2016) *Citizen Clem: A biography of Attlee*, London: Quercus.

Blumer, H. (1954) 'What is wrong with social theory?', *American Sociological Review*, 18: 3–10.

Bourdieu, P. (1973) Cultural reproduction and social reproduction. In R. Brown (ed.) *Knowledge, education and cultural change: Papers in the sociology of education*. London: Tavistock.

Bourdieu, P. (1977) *Outline of a theory of practice*, Cambridge: Cambridge University Press.

Bourdieu, P. (1990) *The logic of practice*, Cambridge: Polity Press.

Bourdieu, P. (1993) *Sociology in question*, London: Sage.

Brannen, P. (1983) *Authority and participation in industry*, London: Batsford Academic.

Brannen, P., Batstone, E., Fatchett, D. and White, P. (1975) *The worker directors*, London: Hutchinson.

Brockmeier, J. (2000) 'Autobiographical time', *Narrative Inquiry*, 10(1): 51–73.

Bruner, J. (2003) 'Self-making narratives', in R. Fivush and C.A. Haden (eds) *Autobiographical memory and the construction of a narrative self*, Mahwah, NJ: Erlbaum, pp 209–25.

Bryman, A. (2001) *Social research methods*, Oxford: Oxford University Press.

Burgos, M. (1988) *Life stories, narrativity and the search for the self.* Publication of the Research Unit for Contemporary Culture, 9, University of Jyvaskyla.

Burgos, M. (1991) 'Some remarks on textual analysis of life stories: Prolegoma to a collective hermeneutic approach', unpublished paper, University of Paris.

Butler, P. (2018) 'Universal credit savaged by public spending watchdog', *The Guardian*, 15 June.

Chalfen, R (1998) 'Interpreting family photography as pictorial communication', in J. Prosser (ed.) *Image-based research: A sourcebook for qualitative researchers*, London: Falmer Press, pp 214–35.

Charles, N. and Kerr, M. (1987) 'Just the way it is: Gender and age differences in family food consumption', in J. Brannen and G. Wilson (eds) *Give and take in families: Studies in resource distribution*. London: Unwin Hyman, pp 155–75.

Christensen, P. and James, A. (2008) *Research with children: Perspectives and practices* (2nd edn), London: Routledge.

Connell, R. (2000) 'Boys on the road: Masculinities, car culture and road safety education', *Journal of Men's Studies*, 8(2): 153–69.

Corsaro, W. (2005) *The sociology of childhood*, Thousand Oaks, CA: Pine Forge Press.

Crawley, H., Hemmings, J. and Price, N. (2011) *Coping with destitution: Survival and livelihood strategies of refused asylum seekers living in the UK*, Swansea: Centre for Migration Policy Research (CMPR), Swansea University.

Crittenden, K. and Hill, R. (1971) 'Coding reliability and validity of interview data', *American Sociological Review*, 36: 1073–80.

Crompton, R. (1999) *The restructuring gender relationships and employment: The decline of the male breadwinner*, Oxford: Oxford University Press.

Daly, J.K. (1996) *Families and time: Keeping pace in a hurried culture*, London: Sage.

Daly, M. (2017) 'Money-related meanings and practices in low-income and poor families', *Sociology*, 51(2): 450–65.

Danieli, A. and Woodhams, C. (2005) 'Emancipatory research methodology and disability: A critique', *International Journal of Social Research*, 6(4): 281–96.

Davis, A., Hirsch, D., Smith, N., Beckhelling, J. and Padley, M. (2012) *A minimum income standard for the UK in 2012: Keeping up in hard times*, York: Joseph Rowntree Foundation.

Dennis, N., Henriquez, F. and Slaughter, C. (1956) *Coal is our life: An analysis of a Yorkshire mining community*, London: Eyre & Spottiswoode.

Denzin N. (1989) *Interpretive biography*, Qualitative research methods series 17, Beverley Hills, CA: Sage.

Denzin, N. (1997) *Interpretive ethnography: Ethnographic practices for the 21st century*, London: Sage.

Department of Employment (1988) *Employment for the 1990s*, London: HMSO.

Dermott, E. (2008) *Intimate fatherhood: A sociological analysis*, London: Routledge.

Dermott, E and Pomati, M (2016) ' "Good" parenting practices: How important are poverty, education and time pressure?', *Sociology*, 50(1): 125–42.

DeVault, M. (1991) *Feeding the family: The social organization of caring as gendered work*, Chicago: University of Chicago Press.

Dexter, Z., Capron, L. and Gregg, L. (2016) Making Life Impossible: How the needs of destitute migrant children are going unmet. The Children's Society. http://www.childrenssociety.org.uk/sites/default/files/making-life-impossible.pdf

Donzelot, J. (1997 [1977]) *The policing of families*, Baltimore, MD: Johns Hopkins University Press.

Douglas, M. (1981) 'Food and culture: Measuring the intricacy of rule systems', *Social Science Information*, 20(1): 1–35.

Dowler, E., Turner, S. and Dobson, B. (2001) *Poverty bites: Food, health and poor families*, London: Child Poverty Action Group.

Duncan, S. and Edwards, R. (1999) *Lone mothers, paid work and gendered moral rationalities*, Basingstoke: Macmillan.

Eaton, G. (2018) 'Boomers vs Millennials', *New Statesman*, 5–11 January.

Edwards, R. and Gilles, V. (2011) 'Clients or consumers, commonplace or pioneers? Navigating the contemporary class politics of family, parenting skills and education', *Ethics and Education*, 6(2): 141–54.

Elder, G. (1999 [1974]) *Children of the Great Depression: Social change in life experience*, Oxford: Westview Press.

Elder, G., Johnson, M. and Crosnoe, R. (2006) 'The emergence and development of life course research', in J. Mortimer and M. Shanahan (eds) *Handbook of the life course*, New York: Springer, pp 3–22.

Eldridge, J. (2011) 'Half-remembrance of things past: Critics and cuts of old', *Sociological Research Online*, 16(3): www.socresonline.org.uk/16/3/20.html

Elliott, J. (2006) *Using narrative in social research*, London: Sage.

Esping-Andersen, G., Gallie, D., Hemerijck, A. and Myles, J. (2002) *Why we need a new welfare state*, Oxford: Oxford University Press.

Estevao, P., Calado, A. and Capucha, L. (2017) 'Resilience: Moving from a "heroic" notion to a sociological concept', *Sociologia*, 85(Sept./ Dec.).

Evans, C.E.L. and Harper, C.E. (2009) 'A history and review of school meal standards', *Journal of Human Nutrition and Diet*, 22: 89–99.

Festinger, L. (1954) 'A theory of social comparison process', *Human Relations*, 7(2): 117–40.

Fielding, M. and Moss, P. (2012) 'Radical democratic education', Paper presented at the American Sociological Association, Denver, CO, 17–20 August.

Finch, J. (1989) *Family obligations and social change*, Cambridge: Polity Press.

Finch, J. and Mason, J. (1993) *Negotiating family responsibilities*, London: Routledge.

Fischler, C. (1988) 'Food, self and identity', *Social Science Information*, 27(2): 275–92.

Fong, V.L. (2004) *Only hope: Coming of age under China's one-child policy.* Stanford, CA: Stanford University Press.

Frankenberg, R. (1957) *Village on the border*, London: Chapman.

Franzosi, R. (1998) 'Narrative analysis: Or why sociologists should be interested in narrative', *Annual Review of Sociology*, 24: 517–54.

Freire, P. *Pedagogy of the oppressed*, New York: Continuum.

Frosh, S. (1997) 'Fathers' ambivalence', in W. Hollway and B. Featherstone (eds) *Mothering and ambivalence*, London: Routledge, pp 37–54.

Gaber, A. and Gaber, I. (2005) *SSRC/ ESRC: The first forty years*, Swindon: Economic and Social Research Council.

Gavron, H. (1966) *The captive wife: Conflicts of housebound mothers.* London: Routledge & Kegan Paul.

Geertz, C. (1973) *The interpretation of culture*, London: Hutchinson.

Giddens, A. (1993) *New rules of sociological method*, Stanford, CA: Stanford University Press.

Gillard, D. (2003) 'Food for thought: Child nutrition, the school dinner and the food industry', www.educationengland.org.uk/ articles/22food.html

Gilles, J (1996) *A world of their own making: Myth, ritual and the quest for family values*, Cambridge, MA: Harvard University Press.

Glennerster, H., Hills, J., Piachaud, D. and Webb, J. (2004) *One hundred years of poverty and policy*, York: Joseph Rowntree Foundation.

Goffman, I. (1970) *Stigma: Notes on the management of spoiled identity*, London: Penguin.

Goodnow, J. (1991) 'The nature of children's responsibility: Children's understanding of "your job"', *Child Development*, 62: 156–65.

Goodnow, J. and Delaney, S. (1989) 'Children's household work: Differentiating types of work and styles of assignment', *Journal of Applied Developmental Psychology*, 10: 209–26.

Gordon, D., Mack, J., Lansley, S., Main, G., Nandy, S., Patsios, D. et al (2013) '*The impoverishment of the UK' PSE UK first results: Living standards*, www.poverty.ac.uk/pse-research/pse-uk-reports

Gouldner, A. (1960) 'The norm of reciprocity: A preliminary statement', *American Sociological Review*, 25: 161–78.

Graham, H. (1987) 'Being poor: Perceptions and coping strategies of lone mothers', in J. Brannen and G. Wilson (eds) *Give and take in families: Studies in resource distribution*, London: Unwin Hyman, pp 56–75.

Grundy, E., Murphy, M. and Shelton, N. (1999) 'Looking beyond the household: Intergenerational perspectives on living kin and contacts with kin in Great Britain', *Population Trends*, 97: 19–27.

Gustafsson, U. (2002) 'School meals policy: The problem with governing children', *Social Policy & Administration*, 36(6): 685–97.

Halsey, A.H. (2004) *A history of sociology in Britain*, Oxford: Oxford University Press.

Hammersley, M. (1989) *The dilemma of qualitative method: Herbert Blumer and the Chicago tradition*, London: Routledge.

Hammersley, M. (2000a) 'Varieties of social research: A typology', *International Journal of Social Research Methodology*, 3(3): 221–31.

Hammersley, M. (2000b) *Taking sides in social research: Essays on partisanship and bias*, London: Routledge.

Hammersley, M. (2017) 'Childhood studies: A sustainable paradigm?', *Childhood*, 24(1): 113–27.

Hammersley, M., Foster, P. and Gomm, R. (2000) 'Case study and generalisation', in R. Gomm, M. Hammersley and P. Foster (eds) *Case study method: Key issues, key texts*, London: Sage, pp 98–115.

Hantrais, L. (2004) *Family policy matters: Responding to family change in Europe*, Bristol: Policy Press.

Harding, S. (1990) 'Starting thought from women's lives: Eight resources for maximizing objectivity', *Journal of Social Philosophy*, 21(2/3): 140–9.

Harper, D. (2002) 'Talking about pictures: A case of photo elicitation', *Visual Studies*, 17(1): 13–26.

Hays, S. (1996) *The cultural contradictions of motherhood*, New Haven, CT: Yale University Press.

Heath, S., MGhee, D. and Trevena, P. (2011) 'Lost in transnationalism: Unravelling the conceptualisation of families and personal life through a transnational gaze', *Sociological Research Online*, 16(4): 1–9.

Hills, J. (2014) 'Benefit or burden: Coming to terms with ageing Britain', Lecture series, British Academy, 26 February.

HMSO (1971) *A framework for government research and development*, Rothschild Report. Cmnd 4814, London: HMSO.

HMSO (1982) *An enquiry into the Social Science Research Council, by Baron Rothschild*, London: HMSO.

Hobsbawm, E. (1994) *Age of extremes: The short 20th century*, London: Michael Joseph.

Hobsbawm, E. (2003) *Interesting times: A twentieth-century life*, London: Abacus.

Hochschild, A. (1997a) *The time bind: When work becomes home and home becomes work*. New York: Metropolitan Books.

Hochschild., A (1997b) *The second shift: Working parents and the revolution at home*, New York: Viking Penguin.

House of Commons Health Committee (2018) *Childhood obesity: Time for action*, Eighth Report of Session 2017–19, https://publications.parliament.uk/pa/cm201719/cmselect/cmhealth/882/88202.htm

House of Commons Library (2012) *Olympic Britain: Social and economic change since the 1908 and 1948 London Games*, www.parliament.uk/documents/commons/lib/research

Hu, HY. and Shi, X. (2019) 'The one-child policy and intergenerational gender equality in China', *Contemporary Social Science*, themed issue on 'Family change, intergenerational relations and policy responses', guest editors: F. Bennett, J. Brannen and L. Hantrais.

Hunt, A. (1968) *A survey of women's employment*, London: HMSO.

James, A. (2007) 'Giving voice to children's voices: Practices and problems, pitfalls and potentials', *American Anthropologist*, 109(2): 261–72.

James, A. and James, A.L. (2004) *Constructing childhood: Theory, policy and social practice*, New York: Palgrave Macmillan.

James, A. and Prout, A. (eds) (1990) *Constructing and reconstructing childhood: Contemporary issues in the sociological study of childhood*, London: Falmer Press.

Jamieson, L. (1998) *Intimacy: Personal relationships in modern cities*, Cambridge: Polity Press.

Jamieson, L. (2011) 'Intimacy as a concept: Explaining social change in the context of globalisation or another form of ethnocentrism', *Sociological Research Online*, 16(4): 1–13.

Jephcott, P. (1962) *Married women working*, London: Allen & Unwin.

Josselson, R. (2004) 'The hermeneutics of faith and suspicion', *Narrative Inquiry*, 14(1): 1–28.

JRF (2017) *UK Poverty Report 2017*, York: Joseph Rowntree Foundation, www.jrf.org.uk/report/uk-poverty-2017

Kaplan, A. (1964) *The conduct of enquiry: Methodology for the behavioral science*, San Francisco: Chandler.

Kellett, M. (2005) 'Children as active researchers: A new paradigm for the 21st century?', http://eprints.ncrm.ac.uk/87/1/Methods ReviewPaperNCRM-003.pdf

Kirkpatrick, S.I., McIntyre, L. and Potestio, M.L. (2010) 'Child hunger and long-term adverse consequences for health', *Archives of Pediatrics and Adolescent Medicine*, 164(8): 754–62.

Klinenberg, E. (2018) *Palaces for the people: How social infrastructure can fight inequality, polarisation and the decline of civic life*, New York: Penguin Random House.

Knight, A., O'Connell, R. and Brannen, J. (2014) 'The temporality of food practices: Intergenerational relations, childhood memories and mothers' food practices in working families with young children', *Families, Relationships and Societies*, 3(2): 303–18.

Knight, A., O'Connell, R. and Brannen, J. (2018) 'Eating with friends, family or not at all: Young people's experiences of food poverty in the UK', *Children & Society*, 32(3): 185–94.

Kohli, M. and Künemunde, H. (2003) 'Intergenerational transfers in the family: What motivates giving?', in V. Bengtson and A. Lowenstein (eds) *Global aging and challenges to families*, New York: Aldine de Gruyter, pp 123–42.

Kohn, M. (1987) 'Cross-national research as an analytic strategy', American Sociological Association Presidential Address, *American Sociological Review*, 52(6): 713–31.

Kohn, M. (ed.) (1989) *Cross-national research in sociology*, London: Sage.

Kovacheva S (2009) 'Organisational social capital and its role in the support of working parents: The case of a public social assistance agency in Bulgaria', in S. Lewis, J. Brannen and A. Nilsen (eds) *Work, family and organisations in transition: European perspectives*, Bristol: Policy Press, pp 63–81.

Kynaston, D. (2007) *A world to build*, London: Bloomsbury.

Kynaston, D. (2017) *New Statesman*, 28 July, p 38.

Lambie-Mumford, H. (2017) *Hungry Britain: The rise of food charity*, Bristol: Policy Press.

Landry, S., Smith, K., Swank, P. and Guttentag, C. (2008) 'A responsive parenting intervention: The optimal timing across early childhood for impacting maternal behaviors and child outcomes', *Developmental Psychology*, 44(5): 1335–53.

Lansley, S. and Mack, J. (2015) *Breadline Britain: The rise of mass poverty*, London: Oneworld.

Lareau, A. (2002) 'Invisible inequality: Social class and childrearing in black and white families', *American Sociological Review*, 67: 747–76.

Lareau, A. (2011) *Unequal childhoods: Class, race and family life*, Berkeley: University of California Press.

Lawlor, D.A. (2013) 'The Vienna Declaration on nutrition and noncommunicable diseases', *British Medical Journal*, 347: f4417.

Lee, E., Macvarish, J. and Bristow, J. (2010) 'Editorial: Risk, health and parenting culture', *Health Risk and Society*, 12(4): 293–300.

Lee, H. (2009) *Biography: A very short introduction*, Oxford: Oxford University Press.

Lévi-Strauss, C. (1969) *The raw and the cooked: Mythologies Volume 1*, Chicago: University of Chicago Press.

Lewis, J. (2002) 'Individualisation, assumptions about the existence of an adult worker model and the shift towards contractualism', in A. Carling, S. Duncan and R. Edwards (eds) *Analysing families: Morality and rationality in policy and practice*, London: Routledge, pp 51–7.

Lewis, S. and Brannen, J. (2011) 'Reflections in working in cross-national research teams', in I. Hojer and S. Hojer (eds) *Familj, vardagsliv och modernitet*, Goteborg: Goteborgs Universitet, pp 275–87.

Lewis, S., Smithson, J., Brannen, J., das Dores Guerreiro, M., Kugelberg, C., Nilsen, A. et al (1998) *Futures on hold: Young Europeans talk about work and family*, Manchester: IOD Research Group.

Lewis, S., Brannen, J. and Nilsen, A. (eds) (2009) *Work, family and organisations in transition: European perspectives*, Bristol: Policy Press.

Lincoln, Y. and Guba, E. (1985) *Naturalistic inquiry*. Beverly Hills, CA: Sage.

Lindesmith, A.R. (1947) *Opiate addiction*, Bloomington, IN: Principia Press.

Lister, R. (2004) *Poverty*, Cambridge: Polity Press.

Lockyer, B. (2013) 'An irregular period? Participation in the Bradford women's liberation movement', *Women's History Review*, http://dx.doi.org/10.1080/09612025.2012.751772

Loopstra, R. and Lalor, D. (2017) *Financial insecurity, food insecurity, and disability: The profile of people receiving emergency food assistance from the Trussell Trust Foodbank Network in Britain*, London: Trussell Trust.

Lopes, C., Oliveira, A., Santos, A., Ramos, E., Severo, M. and Barros, H. (2006) 'Consumo alimentar no Porto', Faculdade de Medicina da Universidade do Porto, https://higiene.med.up.pt/consumoalimentarporto/download/rel-sum_21062006.pdf

Lupton, D. (1994) 'Food, memory and meaning: The symbolic and social nature of food events', *Sociological Review*, 42(4): 664–85.

Lüscher, K, (2005) 'Looking at ambivalences: The contribution of a "new-old" view of inter-generational relations to the study of the life course', *Advances in Life Course Research*, 10: 93–128.

Lüscher, K. and Hoff, A. (2013) 'Intergenerational ambivalence: Beyond solidarity and conflict', in I. Albert and D. Ferring (eds) *Intergenerational relations: European perspectives on family and society*, Bristol: Policy Press, pp 39–63.

Mannheim, K. (1952 [1928]) 'The problem of generations', in *Essays on the Sociology of Knowledge*, London: Routledge & Kegan Paul, pp 276–322.

Martin, J. and Roberts, C. (1984) *The Women and Employment Survey: A lifetime perspective*, London: HMSO.

Mason, J. (2018) *Affinities: Potent connections in personal life*, Cambridge: Polity Press.

Matsaganis, D. and Levanti, C. (2014) 'The distributional effect of austerity and the recession in Southern Europe', *Southern European Society and Politics*, 19(3): 393–412.

Mayall, B. (1994) 'Introduction', in B. Mayall (ed.) *Children's childhoods observed and experienced*, London: Falmer Press.

Mayall, B. (2013) *A history of the sociology of childhood*, London: IOE Press.

Mayall, B. (2017) *Visionary women and visible children, England 1900–1920*, London: Palgrave Macmillan.

Mayall, B. and Zeiher, H. (2003) *Childhood in generational perspective*, London: Institute of Education.

McAdams, D. (1993) *The stories we live by: Personal myths and the making of the self*, New York: The Guilford Press.

McCarthy, H. (2017) 'Women, marriage and paid work in post-war Britain', *Women's History Review*, 26(1): 46–61.

McLeod, J. and Thomson, R. (2009) *Researching social change*, London: Sage.

Mead, G.H. (1932) *The philosophy of the present*, Chicago: University of Chicago Press.

Miewald, C. and McCann, E. (2003) 'Foodscapes and the geographies of poverty: Sustenance, strategy, and politics in an urban neighborhood', *Antipode: A Radical Journal of Geography*, 46(2): 537–56.

Mills, C.W. (1980 [1959]) *The sociological imagination*, London: Penguin.

Mills, D. (2008) *Difficult folk? A political history of social anthropology*, Oxford: Berghahn.

Mills, M., Jepson, A., Coxon, A., Easterby-Smith, P., Hawkins, M. and, Spencer, J. (2006) *ESRC's demographic review of the social sciences*, Swindon: ESRC.

Ministry of Health circular 221/1945

Ministry of Health 37/68

Morgan, D.H.J. (1985) *The family: Social theory*, London: Routledge & Kegan Paul.

Morgan, D.H.J. (1996) *Family connections: An introduction to family studies*, Cambridge: Polity Press.

Morgan, D.H.J. (2011) *Rethinking family practices*, London: Palgrave Macmillan.

Myrdal, A. and Klein, M. (1965) *Women's two roles*, London: Routledge & Kegan Paul.

Najman, J. and Davey Smith, G. (2000) 'The embodiment of class-related and health inequalities: Australian policies', *Australian and New Zealand Journal of Public Health*, 24(1): 3–4.

Naroll, R. (1965) 'Galton's problem the logic of cross-cultural analysis', *Social Research*, 32: 428–51.

Narvaez, R. (2006) 'Embodiment, collective memory and time', *Body and Society,* 12(3), 51–73.

Nielsen, H.B. (2017) *Feeling gender: A generational and psychosocial approach*, London: Palgrave, Open Access Ebook

Nilsen, A. (1996) 'Stories of life, stories of living: Women's narrative and feminist biography', *NORA Nordic Journal of Women's Studies* 1: 16–30.

Nilsen, A. and Brannen, J. (2011) 'The use of mixed methods in biographical research', in A. Tashakorri and C. Teddlie (eds) *The handbook of mixed methods research*, London: Sage, pp 677–96.

Nilsen, A., Brannen, J. and Lewis, S. (2012) *Transitions to parenthood in Europe: A comparative life course perspective*, Bristol: Policy Press.

Nind, M. (2011) 'Participatory data analysis: A step too far', *Qualitative Research*, 11(4): 349–63.

Nind, M. (2014) *What is inclusive research?* London: Bloomsbury Academic.

Nowotny, H. (1994) *Time: The modern and postmodern experience*, Cambridge: Polity Press.

Oakley, A. (1974) *Housewife*, London: Allen Lane.

O'Brien, M. and Shemilt, I. (2003) *Working fathers: Earning and caring*, Research discussion series, Manchester: Equal Opportunities Commission.

O'Connell, R. (forthcoming 2020) *Families and food in hard times*, London: UCL Press.

O'Connell, R. and Brannen, J. (2016) *Food, families and work*, London: Bloomsbury.

O'Connell, R. and Brannen, J. (2019) 'Food poverty and the families the state has turned its back on: The case of the UK', in H. Gaisbauer, G. Schweiger and C. Sedmak (eds) *Absolute poverty in Europe: Interdisciplinary perspectives on a hidden phenomenon*, Bristol: Policy Press.

O'Connell, R., Owen, C., Padley, M., Simon, A. and Brannen, J. (2018) 'Which types of family are at risk of food poverty in the UK? A relative deprivation approach', *Social Policy and Society* 18(1): 1–18.

O'Connell, R., Knight, A. and Brannen, J. (2019) *Living hand to mouth: Children and food in low income families*, London: Child Poverty Action Group.

O'Connor, P. (2013) 'A standard academic career?', in B. Bagilhole and K. White (eds) *Generation and gender in academia*, Basingstoke: Palgrave Macmillan, pp 23–45.

O'Connor, P. (forthcoming) 'Mentoring and sponsorship in higher education: Men's invisible advantage in STEM?', *Higher Education Research and Development*.

Oldenburg, R. (1989) *The great good place: Cafes, coffee shops, community centers, beauty parlors, general stores, bars, hangouts, and how they get you through the day*, New York: Paragon House.

OPCS (Office of Population and Censuses and Surveys) (1989) General Household Survey, Table 9.11, London: HMSO.

Parreñas, R. (2014) 'The intimate labour of transnational communication', *Families, Relationships and Societies*, 3(3): 425–42.

Pawson, R. (1995) 'Quality and quantity, agency and structure, mechanism and context: Dons and cons', *Bulletin de Methodologies Sociologique*, 47(1): 5–48.

Pember Reeves, M. (1988 [1913]) *Round about a pound a week*, London: Virago.

Perry-Jenkins, M., Repetti, R.L. and Crouter, A.C. (2000) 'Work and family in the 1990s', *Journal of Marriage and Family*, 62(4): 981–98.

Phoenix, A. (2013) 'Analysing narrative contexts', in M. Andrews, C. Squire and M. Tamboukou (eds) *Doing narrative research*, London: Sage, pp 72–88.

Phoenix, A. (2014) 'Reframing relevance: Narratives of temporality and methodological turning points on research on families and gender', *International Journal of Social Research Methodology*, 17(2): 105–19.

Phoenix, A. (2019) 'Childhood, wellbeing and transnational migrant families: Conceptual and methodological issues', in M. Tiilikainen, M. Al-Sharmani, and S. Mustasaari (eds) *Wellbeing of transnational Muslim families: Marriage, law and gender* (Studies in Migration and Diaspora), London: Routledge.

Pilcher, J. (1994) 'Mannheim's sociology of generations: An undervalued legacy', *British Journal of Sociology*, 45(3): 481–95.

Plantin, L. and Back-Wiklund, M. (2009) 'Social services as human service: Between loyalties, a Swedish case', in S. Lewis, J. Brannen and A. Nilsen (eds) *Work, family and organisations in transition: European perspectives*, Bristol: Policy Press, pp 49–63.

Platt, J. (1988) 'What can case studies do?', *Studies in Qualitative Methodology*, 1: 1–20.

Plummer, K. (2001) *Documents of life 2: An invitation to a critical humanism*, London: Sage.

Polkinghorne, D.E. (1988) *Narrative knowing and the human sciences*, New York: SUNY Press.

Punch, S., McIntosh, I. and Edmond, R. (2010) 'Children's food practices in families and institutions', *Children's Geographies*, 8: 227–32.

Qvortrup, J. (2000) 'Macroanalysis of childhood', in P. Christensen and A. James (eds) *Research with children: Perspectives and practices*, London: Falmer Press, pp 77–98.

Qvortrup, J., Bardy, M., Sgritta, G. and Wintersberger, H. (eds) (1994) *Childhood matters: Social theory practice and politics*, Aldershot: Gower.

Ragin, C. (1994) *Constructing social research: The utility and diversity of method*, Thousand Oaks, CA: Pine Forge Press.

Ramaekers, S. and Suissa, J. (2011) 'Parents as "educators": Languages of education, pedagogy and "parenting"', *Ethics and Education*, 6(2): 197–212.

Ramaekers, S. and Suissa, J. (2012), *The claims of parenting: Reasons, responsibility and society*, New York: Springer.

Rapoport, R. and Rapoport, R. (1971) *Dual career families*, London: Penguin.

RCPCH and CPAG (2017) *Poverty and child health: Views from the frontline*, London: Royal College of Paediatrics and Child Health and Child Poverty Action Group.

Reckwitz, A (2002) 'Towards a theory of social practice: A development of cultural theorising', *European Journal of Social Theory*, 5(2): 243–63.

Resolution Foundation (2018) *A new generational contract: The final report of the Intergenerational Commission*, London: Resolution Foundation.

Richards, L. (2017) 'Educational divide fuels corrosive populism', Campaign for Social Science, Sage annual lecture, London, 21 November.

Ricoeur, P. (1985) *Oneself as another*, Chicago: University of Chicago Press.

Riessman, C. (1993) *Narrative analysis*, Qualitative Research Methods Series 30, London: Sage.

Riessman, C (2008) *Narrative methods for the human sciences*, Thousand Oaks, CA: Sage.

Riley, D. (1983) *War in the nursery: Theories of the child and mother*, London: Virago.

Rose, N. (1990) *Governing the soul: The shaping of the private self*, London: Routledge.

Rosenthal, G. (2004) 'Biographical research', in C. Seale, G. Gobo, J. Gubrium and D. Silverman (eds) *Qualitative research practice*, London: Sage, pp 48–65.

Roth, J. (1966) 'Hired hand research', *American Sociologist*, 1(4): 190–196.

Rowbotham, S (1997) *A century of women: The history of women in Britain and the United States*, London: Penguin Viking.

Royston, S., Rodrigues, L. and Hounsell, D. (2012) *Fair and square: A policy report on the future of free school meals*, London: The Children's Society.

Rubery, J., Smith. M. and Fagan, C. (1999) *Trends in women's employment in Europe in the 1990s*, London: Routledge.

Sahlins M.D. (1972) *Stone Age economics*, New York: Aldine.

Salmon, P. and Riessman, C. (2013) 'Looking back on narrative research', in M. Andrews, C. Squire and M. Tamboukou (eds) *Doing narrative research*, London: Sage, pp 197–205.

Sayer, A. (2000) *Realism and social science*, London: Sage.

Sayer, A. (2001) 'Reply to Holmwood', *Sociology*, 35(4): 967–84.

Schiff, B. (2012) 'The function of narrative: Towards a narrative psychology of meaning', *Narrative Works: Issues, Investigations and Interventions*, 2(1): 33–47.

Schütze, F. (1983) 'Biographieforschung und narratives interview', *Neue Praxis* 13(3): 283–93.

Scott, J (2017 *Exaggerated claims: The ESRC, 50 years on* (2015) Book review, *Sociology*, 51(2): 500–507.

Seidler, V. (1997) *Man enough: Embodying masculinities*, London: Sage.

Sell, H. (2000) 'Exactness and precision', *International Journal of Social Research Methodology*, 3(2): 135–57.

Sen, A. (1983) 'Poor, relatively speaking', *Oxford Economic Papers*, 35: 153–69.

Sennett, R. (1998) *The corrosion of character: The personal consequences of work in the new capitalism*, London: Norton.

Sevenhuijsen, S. (1999) *Citizenship and the ethics of care: feminist considerations on justice*, London: Routledge.

Shoen, R. and Canudas-Romo, V. (2005) *Population studies 59*, 135–146.

Shove, E, Panzar, M and Watson, M (2012). *The dynamics of social practice: The everyday and how it changes.* London: Sage.

Smart, C (2007) *Personal life: New directions in sociological thinking*, Cambridge: Polity Press.

Smart, C. (2011) 'Families, secrets and memories', *Sociology*, 45(4): 539–43.

Spector, M. and Kitsuse, J.I. (2001) *Constructing social problems*, New York: Taylor and Francis.

Spring Rice, M. (1939) *Working-class wives: Their health and conditions*, London: Penguin.

Strathern, M. (2003) 'Redescribing society', *Minerva*, 41(3): 263–76.

Sutton, D. (2001) *Remembrance of repasts: An anthropology of food and memory*, Oxford: Berg.

Tamboukou, M., Andrews, M. and Squire, C. (2013) 'Introduction: What is narrative research?', in M. Andrews, C. Squire and M. Tamboukou (eds) *Doing narrative research*, London: Sage, pp 1–27.

Taylor, R. (2001) *The future of work–life balance: An ESRC future of work programme seminar series*, Swindon: ESRC.

Thomas, G. (1944) *Women at work: The attitudes of working women towards postwar employment and some related problems*, London: Wartime social survey Reg. 1.3.

Thomas, G. (1948) *Women and industry: An inquiry into the problem of recruiting women for industry, carried out for the Ministries of Labour and National Service*, 104. London: Central Office of Information.

Thompson, E.P. (1967) 'Time, work-discipline and industrial capitalism', *Past & Present*, 38: 56–97.

Thompson, P. (1993) 'Family myth, models and denials in the shaping of individual life paths', in D. Bertaux and P. Thompson (eds) *Between generations: Family models, myths and memories*, Oxford: Oxford University Press, pp 13–38.

Thompson, P., Plummer, K. and Demirova, N. (in press) *Pioneering social research*, Bristol: Policy Press.

Thorne, B. (1987) 'Re-visioning women and social change: Where are the children?', *Gender & Society*, 1(1): 85–109.

Thorne, B. (1993) *Gender play: Girls and boys in school,* New Brunswick, NJ: Rutgers University Press.

Tindall, G. (2010) *The fields beneath: The history of one London village,* London: Eland.

Tizard, B. (1977) *Adoption: A second chance,* London: Free Press.

Tizard, B. (2003) *The Thomas Coram Research Unit, 1973–1990: A memoir,* London: Thomas Coram Research Unit, Institute of Education.

Tizard, B. and Hughes, M. (1984) *Young children learning,* London: John Wiley & Sons.

Townsend, P. (1979) *Poverty in the United Kingdom: a survey of household resources and standards of living,* London: Allen Lane and Penguin Books.

Toynbee, P. (1987) The poverty of a mean society, *The Guardian,* 16 July.

Turner, V. (1974) *Dramas, fields and metaphors: Symbolic action in human society,* Ithaca, NY: Cornell University Press.

Twamley, K., Doidge, M. and Scott, A. (2015) *Sociologists' tales: Contemporary narratives on sociological thought and practice,* Bristol: Policy Press.

Uprichard, E., Nettleton, S. and Chapell, P. (2013) '"Food hates" over the life course: An analysis of food narratives from the UK Mass Observation Archive', *Appetite,* 71: 137–43.

Valagão, M. (2009) 'La sopa y las sopas de plantas silvestres alimentarias en el Alentejo, Portugal', in F.X. Medina, R.A. Palafox and I. de Garine (eds) *Food, imaginaries and cultural frontiers: Essays in honour of Helen Macbeth,* Guadalajara: Universidad de Guadalajara, pp 143–61.

Vincent, C. and Ball, S. (2007) '"Making up" the middle-class child: Families, activities and class dispositions', *Sociology,* 41(6): 1061–77.

Vincent, D. (1991) *Poor citizens: The state and the poor in twentieth-century Britain,* London: Longman.

Wacquant, L. (2006) 'Pierre Bourdieu', in R. Stones (ed.) *Key contemporary thinkers,* London: Macmillan, pp 261–78.

Walby, S. (1999) *New agenda for women,* London: Springer.

Walker, D. (2015) *Exaggerated claims: The ESRC, 50 years on,* London: Sage.

Walker, R. (2014) *The shame of poverty,* Oxford: Oxford University Press.

Warde, A. (1997) *Consumption, food and taste,* London: Sage.

Warde, A. (2005) 'Consumption and theories of practice', *Journal of Consumer Culture,* 5: 131–53.

Wengraf, T. (2001) *Qualitative research interviewing: Biographic narrative and semi-structured methods*, London: Sage.

Wengraf, T. and Chamberlayne, P. (2013) 'Biography-using research (BNIM), Sostris, institutional regimes, and critical psycho-societal realism', in J.D. Turk and A. Mrozowicki (eds), *Realist biography and European policy: An innovative approach to European policy studies*, Leuven: Leuven University Press, pp 63–92.

Wigfall, V, Brannen, J, Mooney, A and Parutis, V. (2013) Finding the right man; Recruiting fathers in inter-generational families across ethnic groups, *Qualitative Research*, 5, 591–607.

Wilson, E. (1980) *Halfway to paradise*, London: Tavistock.

Woolf, V. (1976) *Moments of being: Unpublished autobiographical writings of Virginia Woolf*, Brighton: Sussex University Press.

Wright, K. (2018) *Gender, migration and the intergenerational transfer of well-being*, Basingstoke: Palgrave Macmillan.

Zeiher, H. (2001) 'Dependent, independent and interdependent relations: children as members of the family household in West Berlin', in L Alanen and B Mayall (eds) *Conceptualizing child–adult relations*, London: Routledge, pp 37–54.

Zelizer, V. (1985) *Pricing the priceless child: The changing social value of children*, Chichester: Princeton University Press.

Zweig, F. (1952) *Women's life and labour*, London: Victor Gollancz.

Index

www.ingramcontent.com/pod-product-compliance
Lightning Source LLC
Chambersburg PA
CBHW070924030426
42336CB00014BA/2522